TRADE UNIONS AND IMPERIALISM IN AMERICA
VOLUME II

CANADIAN WORKERS, AMERICAN UNIONS

JACK SCOTT

New Star Books, Vancouver

Copyright © Jack Scott 1978

New Star Books Ltd.
2504 York Avenue
Vancouver, B.C.
V6K 1E3

Canadian Cataloguing in Publication Data

Scott, Jack, 1910-
    Canadian workers, American unions
    (Trade unions and imperialism in America; v. 2)

    Bibliography: p.
    Includes index
    ISBN 0-919888-81-X pa.
    ISBN 0-919888-82-8 bd.

    1. Trade unions—Canada—History. 2.
Trade unions—United States. I. Title.
II. Series.
HD6524.S36   331.88'0971   C79-091001-2

CONTENTS

ABBREVIATIONS*

ACCL: All Canadian Congress of Labour
AMW: Amalgamated Mine Workers
BR&SC: Brotherhood of Railway & Steamship Clerks, Freight Handlers, Express & Station
　　　Employees
CBRT&GW: Canadian Brotherhood of Railway, Transport & General Workers
CCL: Canadian Congress of Labour
CLC: Canadian Labour Congress
CLF: Canadian Labour Federation
CLU: Canadian Labour Union
CLSU: Canadian Lake Seamen's Union
CMA: Canadian Manufacturers Association
CNS: Canadian National Steamships
CNTU: Confederation of National Trade Unions (Quebec)
CPR: Canadian Pacific Railway
CRE: Canadian Railroad Employees
CSU: Canadian Seamen's Union
CUPE: Canadian Union of Public Employees
CIO: Committee for Industrial Organization, afterwards Congress of Industrial Organizations
CCU: Confederation of Canadian Unions
CCF: Cooperative Commonwealth Federation
L&SWU: Lumber and Sawmill Workers' Union
NT&LC: National Trades and Labour Congress
NTU: National Typographical Union
NDP: New Democratic Party
RILU: Red International of Labour Unions
SIU: Seafarers' International Union
SORWUC: Service, Office and Retail Workers' Union of Canada
TLC: Trades and Labour Congress
TUEL: Trade Union Educational League
UAW: United Automobile Workers of America
UBRE: United Brotherhood of Railway Employees
UE: United Electrical, Radio and Machine Workers of America
UTWA: United Textile Workers of America
WCSU: West Coast Seamen's Union
WFM: Western Federation of Miners
WUL: Workers' Unity League

*Additional to those appearing in the first volume.

INTRODUCTION

The United States unions that expanded into Canada in the nineteenth century appropriated to themselves the title "international." The question arises: How appropriate is the term when applied to the American union movement?

The idea of internationalism that is implicit in the term "international union" is a concept which carries considerable weight in the labour movements of most countries, and because of this, an indiscriminate use can be most confusing and misleading. When employed as descriptive of the majority of the union movement in Canada, the term "international" is indeed out of place. The political significance of its usage is that it obscures the actual Americanism of the unions that masquerade as "internationals."

Canada is unique in that it is the only country in the world with unions whose headquarters are located in a foreign country, unions which at the same time are subject to the laws and labour legislation enacted in the country where the headquarters are situated. According to United States unionists (and many of their agents and followers in Canada) this unusual relationship constitutes "internationalism."

When workers in other parts of the world speak about internationalism they are referring to assemblies of working class delegates from many countries who come together to discuss problems of mutual interest on a world level. The national sovereignty of each of the participating delegations is readily acknowledged and strictly observed. Matters that are exclusively domestic in character are left to the jurisdiction of each sovereign national centre. Internationalism on any other basis would most likely be subject to domination by delegates from the largest and most powerful countries. In such a form, true internationalism could not long survive.

7

Canadian-American union relations, as manifested in the form of "international unionism," are notorious for the way in which the American unionists constantly and flagrantly interfere in affairs of purely domestic concern. They have also been know to deliberately obstruct the establishment of proper international connections between the workers of Canada and those of other countries.

It was not the adoption of policies of working class internationalism but rather, as previously noted, the acquisition of branches in Canada that transformed the American organizations from national into "international unions." In fact, the American unions are noted for the absence of acts of international working class solidarity. Within the North American context, an "international union" is simply a United States union with Canadian branches.[1]

A brief glance at the structure of the contemporary Canadian union movement will aid in providing some idea of the dominant role of the so-called internationals in this country.

According to *Labour Organization in Canada*, an annual publication of the Department of Labour, 36.3 per cent of the non-agricultural workers were organized into unions as of 1973. This represents an increase from the 29.7 per cent reported in 1965, an increase due mainly to growth of employment in the public service sector and the expansion of unionism in that area. The publication also reported a decline in the proportion of international union membership, from 72.8 per cent in 1921 to 55.3 per cent in 1973. This change in proportion was, again, largely accounted for by the growth of union membership in government service, and the emergence of a large national union centre in Quebec. However, these statistics can be misleading if other factors are not taken into consideration.

With the exception of the CNTU (Confederation of National Trade Unions) in Quebec, and the still small CCU (Confederation of Canadian Unions), which is largely a western phenomenon, most of the membership in the independent unions is concentrated in the public service and the service industries. The "international" unions on the other hand are entrenched in the industries that comprise the commanding heights of the economy; i.e., the American unions are found almost exclusively in the sectors of the economy where surplus value is created and capitalist profit realized. It is in these same sectors that United States economic domination is most pervasive.

Organizationally, the "internationals" are able to dominate the country's main labour centre—the Canadian Labour Congress (CLC)—and collaboration between American unions and American corporations operating in Canada can play an important part in keeping worrisome independent unions at bay.

Under the 1902 TLC constitution, as amended, the Canadian

independents could gain admission only by submerging their own identity in the particular "international" union provided for them, which would mean abandoning the fight for a Canadian-based movement. Because of this the Canadian independents are prevented from assuming leadership of the struggle for new policies from within Congress ranks.

With the Canadian independent unions thus effectively barred from admission to the Congress, the "internationals" enjoy an effective majority and can dominate Congress affairs, with the Canadian-based unions therein a captive minority subject to the rules and policies made by the American unions. This applies at all levels of Congress organization, through provincial Federations down to local Labour Councils. Thus the labour bodies that get most attention from governments and employers are effectively controlled by the "internationals."

Unfortunately, the independent unions that are compelled to stay outside the Congress are not only relatively weak in numbers, they are too often divided amongst themselves. But more importantly, the really large Canadian-based unions like CUPE (Canadian Union of Public Employees), the CBRT&GW (Canadian Brotherhood of Railway, Transport & General Workers), the hospital workers, the two postal unions, the Public Service Alliance, and others, fail to make a contribution to the fight for independent unions, preferring to remain under American domination in the CLC while making deals concerning jurisdiction and other matters.[2]

It is clear that meaningful autonomy—not to mention independence of action—is impossible in this kind of union structure. The situation is one which bears no real relationship to true internationalism.

The present "international" unions and the American Federation of Labour (AFL) were not the first labour organizations with foreign affiliates to become established in Canada. Others, with more solid international credentials, were on the scene earlier and were subsequently destroyed in the AFL drive for hegemony over labour in North America.

Two British unions—the Amalgamated Society of Engineers and the Amalgamated Society of Carpenters and Joiners—established a number of locals in both Canada and the United States, and in the case of the latter survived well into the period of United States domination. The industrial union movement, the Knights of Labour, spread to England, France, Belgium, New Zealand, and Australia, as well as Canada, before the AFL was founded in 1886. By reason of their more extensive international base, all of these organizations had a more valid claim to international status than the AFL, but none of them ever appropriated the title to their own exclusive use, as the AFL has done. In fact, as will be demonstrated, the AFL did no more than parallel United States economic expansion for the purpose of protecting their own and American imperialist interests.

Simply to illustrate the distortion of genuine international connections between Canada and other countries, and in anticipation of the text, we can cite one clear example. In 1911, the international socialist organization, the Second International, invited the then trade union central of Canada, the Trades and Labour Congress (TLC), to send representatives to an international Congress. Although each national centre had the right to be represented by two delegates, the problem at hand was whether or not Canada could be recognized as a distinct national centre. Officers of the TLC, which was affiliated to the American Federation of Labour, consulted the AFL Executive Council on the matter. The Council refused to release any funds to finance the proposed delegation and objected strongly to the appointment of Canadian delegates under any circumstances. The AFL Council informed the TLC officers: "We insist upon maintaining our position that the delegate from the AFL shall be the delegate representing the American labour movement, of which the Canadian Trades and Labour Congress is a component part."[3]

In fact, as far as the AFL is concerned, Canada is simply equivalent to one of the fifty U.S. State Federations of Labour, and Canadian workers, with respect to their particular trades and industries, come under the jurisdiction of the appropriate American union, now dubbed an "international."

Ironically, in order to qualify as an "international" union in Canada, the organization must have its headquarters in the United States and be in possession of a charter issued under authority of a union affiliated with the AFL, which awards the possessor exclusive jurisdiction over a specific trade or industry.[4] It authorizes the collection of dues and assessments from Canadian workers and, given the appropriate conditions, entitles the chartered affiliate to engage in strikebreaking activities in order to advance "international" unionism.

Some have a more sanguine view of the character of American unions, even while being aware of the pervasive threats to Canadian sovereignty on other fronts. Canadians' criticism of American domination is usually directed at U.S. control of the Canadian economy. U.S. domination of Canadian unions is seldom discussed. The two are viewed mostly as separate and unrelated phenomena, whereas they are in fact complementary aspects of imperialist expansion.

Both the New Democratic Party and the Communist Party of Canada propose to "curb monopoly" rather than seek a way to end the social system that breeds monopoly, and for this purpose they argue that "international" unions are essential in the fight against multinational corporations. This policy, which seeks to perpetuate the limiting of organized labour's activity to the sphere of collective bargaining within the boundaries of the established social order, gives no thought or effort to transforming the movement into a revolutionary fulcrum to change the social system. Secondly, such a policy fails to confront the fact that these are *United States* unions, not internationals, or the fact that they are pledged to uphold the capitalist system and to support American foreign policy objectives—which include the economic domination of Canada.

Sometimes it is suggested that the problem is not American unions, but the bureaucracy with which they are infested. Viewing bureaucracy as the root cause of trade union problems promotes the claim that changing the leadership will change the unions. But it is ideology that is at the root of bureaucracy and class collaborationist policies. To change the unions—and the leadership—one must concentrate on changing the ideological outlook of the working class. From the beginning of trade unionism in this country, Canadian workers were prepared to struggle against manifestations of bureaucracy. They need no particular encouragement in that direction. The fact of the matter is that they were ideologically prepared to accept American union domination while protesting its bureaucratic encrustations. There were no crucial conflicts between Canadian and American unionists over questions of the social system.

The aim of this volume is to examine how the alliance between the United States unions and American imperialism functions in Canadian conditions. In *Yankee Unions, Go Home!* (the first volume of *Trade Unions and Imperialism in America*) the role of "international" unions in Latin America was explored. At first glance it may seem rather absurd to suggest that there is any basis for comparison of Canadian-American trade union relations with the situation that prevails in Latin America. But the considerable difference in tactics employed must not be confused with the basic aims of American imperialism, which in essence are the same in both areas. It would be naive indeed to accept the argument that the United States does not—or does not want to—control Canada at least as effectively as Latin America. The historical record, and existing relations, prove the contrary.

The invasion of Quebec in 1775-76 was the earliest evidence of the imperialist desire of the U.S. to convert the whole of British North America into a single unified state. Efforts at territorial conquest were renewed in the War of 1812, when England was enmeshed in the Napoleonic War. And the Monroe Doctrine a decade later did not exclude Canada from the sweeping claims of American imperial destiny in the western hemisphere.

Once again, after the Civil War, the United States Government tried to use reparations negotiations with England to advance territorial claims that would have cut Canada off from the Pacific, had the claims been conceded in full. And efforts directed toward expansion northward continued through a variety of American financed annexationist movements that were active well into the twentieth century. In the end, however, the United States settled for formal recognition of the political independence of Canada, while simultaneously pressing a policy of economic domination which ensured a large measure of political influence.

The United States union movement in Canada—as in Latin America—plays a crucial role in protecting and advancing American economic and political interests. The precise nature of this role will become clear as the work progresses, but at this point we can say that the specific Canadian situation made the invasion appear far less dramatic than was the case with countries in Latin America.

The United States unionists intervened in the Latin American situation when imperialism there was already in crisis. Deep suspicion of Yankee intentions, fueled by outstanding theorists and writers such as Jose Marti,[5] together with the wide divergences in language, culture, and political and economic aspirations, constituted a hostile environment in which the United States unionists were compelled to operate.

Independent and politically oriented unions began to emerge throughout Latin America in the wake of Spanish decline. Unions that were issuing from the revolutionary struggle were not easy to control, as the AFL quickly discovered. We have seen how a series of efforts to exercise control culminated in the creation of the AIFLD (American Institute for Free Labour Development), which institutionalized class collaboration, cooperated with the imperialist ruling class, and corrupted and coerced local union leaders to do the bidding of the U.S. State Department and advance the foreign interests of the United States in Latin America.

The integration of the Canadian unions into the American imperial network was accomplished in a less spectacular manner, but the end result, if not as brutal, has been no less thorough.

It has been demonstrated in the first volume that part of the motivation for American union intervention in Latin America is directly related to a major concern over depletion of natural resources in the United States, which was hastened by the necessities of war, postwar reconstruction, and Cold War policies. Access to an abundant supply of cheap raw materials is vital to the continued operation and profitability of U.S. capitalism, and no group is more aware of that fact than the leading unionists, who publicly proclaimed it as central to their involvement in Latin America.

If anything, Canada is vastly more important in this respect than any of the countries in Latin America—or even several of them combined. There is little room for doubt, therefore, that American union concern regarding access to Canada's fresh water, energy sources, and varied raw materials is not less than their concern that leads to blatant interference in other parts of the hemisphere. But the absence of real crisis in Canadian-American relations requires forms and methods of intervention that are less flagrant than the tactics employed in other countries. However, it was not always exactly that way.

It will be shown that as early as 1896 the AFL took a direct interest in one depleted resource (pulpwood) and in one element (nickel), the latter having never been discovered in any quantity in the United States. Further, the Federation took steps to protect American interests in these resources when confronted with a potential threat implicit in a conservation campaign launched by the Federation's Canadian representative. And even earlier than that, the American unionists promoted measures to block alleged "cheap labour" from emigrating out of Canada to the United States—and this before the problem became one of large concern in relation to Spanish-American "cheap labour."

Thus it will be seen that the roots of U.S. union policies are basically no different whether applied to Canada or to Latin America. It is only that different conditions—and especially the one related to the absence of crisis in relations—call for the use of a different tactical approach.

This volume will undertake to show how it was possible for Canadian workers to be persuaded that membership in American unions, in which the Canadians would be a minority, might be to their advantage. We will see how, beginning soon after the founding of the AFL, the American unionists used their majority position to arrange affairs in their own interests, and to the detriment of the Canadians.

A significant point that will become clear in the record of events is the fact that the AFL move to take full control of the organized labour movement in Canada originated simultaneously with the beginning of the war against Spain—the period when U.S. imperialism matured.

Whereas the United States national centre was exclusive to craft unions and waged a war on industrial union forms, the Canadian movement, until the turn of the century, accepted in affiliation all unions regardless of organizational form or affiliation. But at the Berlin (Ontario) Convention in 1902 the Americans engineered the splitting of the Canadian centre into two hostile camps, and have dictated a series of divisions ever since.

While some Canadian unionists chose to serve the interests of the AFL, there have been those who fought against domination. This is most evident in periods of crisis when the real objectives of the Americans became most clear. The record will show that the struggle for an independent Canadian movement has been continuous.

A careful reading of this critical examination of Canadian-American union relations will prove conclusively that the United States unionists are determined to continue on a course of domination over the movement in Canada, and that they will be successful in the recruitment of some Canadian unionists to aid them. Taken together with the record of U.S. union activities in Latin America, it will be evident that the policy of domination is pursued in concert with the American corporations, and in the interests of the aims set by U.S. imperialists. By the end of the volume it should become clear that there is a crucial need for resistance to domination, and for the continuation of the struggle for an independent Canadian union movement.

1

INTERNATIONAL UNIONISM:
THE FIRST STAGE

Books and articles on the history of trade unionism in Canada tend to confirm a widely held but mistaken belief that the roots of the Canadian union movement are to be found in the United States. But the truth of the matter is that in both Canada and the United States workers obtained their initial knowledge of organizational methods, and their trades union consciousness, from sources in Britain. The ideological influence of movements located in the industrialized regions of Europe was a powerful factor in the formative period of the North American trade unions.[1]

Trade union organization was a permanent feature of the social scene prior to 1850, but for a time was confined mainly to the typographical trade. The Toronto Typographical Society was established on a permanent basis in 1832.[2] The Toronto society owed its existence to the independent initiative of local tradesmen, and operated locally for several years before making contact with similar societies in other parts of British North America. But while entirely local in terms of organizational initiative, the Toronto unionists were not ignorant of, nor uninfluenced by, the emergence and experience of organizations elsewhere in the world. This is evident from a statement that appears in the earliest records of the Society.

> Owing to the many innovations which have been made upon the long established wages of the professors of the art of printing . . . it was deemed expedient by the Journeymen Printers of York that they should form themselves into a body, similar to societies in other parts of the world.[3]

Difficulty of travel and communication, especially in the Canadas, constituted an insularity from which it was hard to break out. However, a speech given at the Society's annual banquet in 1848 showed further definite knowledge of the existence of other organizations similar in nature when the speaker referred to the "several trade societies throughout the province."[4]   The first international contact occurred when Peter Brown, father of George Brown, who founded the *Globe*, arrived from New York and began publication of the *Banner*, a semi-religious journal that supported the Free Church. The anti-labour Browns challenged the status of the Toronto society with the dismissal of several of its leading members and the open declaration of a non-union shop policy. The society issued a "Plain Statement of Facts" in 250 copies denouncing Brown's anti-labour actions, and the Secretary was instructed to communicate with the society at Buffalo, informing its members of the "actual state of things at the *Banner* office."[5] (It is probable that the close proximity of Buffalo to Toronto made it especially important that the Buffalo tradesmen be kept informed of the Toronto situation.)

The first unions locating in Canada that might be called internationals were British, not American. The Amalgamated Society of Engineers, a British union with a presence already established in the United States, employed the facilities of its New York branch to set up a Toronto local in 1850. During the following several years the society expanded, setting up additional locals at Montreal, Kingston, London, and Stratford.

The Amalgamated Society of Carpenters and Joiners, which, like its British counterpart in the engineering industry, had branches in the United States, arrived in Canada in 1860, and became the first permanent union organization in the Ontario building trades industry. Despite constant international (U.S.) union attempts to destroy it (on the grounds that it was "not an international union") the Amalgamated Carpenters survived in Canada until near the end of the thirties.[6]

Involved in a difficult battle to enforce the nine-hour day in Britain, the Carpenters Society appealed to the Toronto Typographers for financial assistance. The secretary of the Typographical Society was instructed to respond to the appeal with the reply that: ". . . on account of the distance which separates us from those engaged in the contest, and the many claims recently made upon our finances by persons connected with our own profession, we do not consider it expedient to accede to their request."[7]

The National Typographical Union of the United States was founded in 1852, and in 1854 its members adopted a resolution proposing a system whereby membership cards of the two associations would become interchangeable. The records of the Toronto society show that the practice of membership transfer was well established before 1860, and lists of members in good standing were being exchanged with American locals along with information on the condition of the trade in the various communities. Records from 1860 show that twenty-five members of the Toronto society were subscribing to the *Printer*, the official journal of the American union.[8]

Until 1860, the American organization annually discussed the problem of card transfers, at which time it proposed a new plan for a single union covering tradesmen in both countries. Arguing their case for a single continental membership, the American unionists reasoned:

> It will, if we succeed in bringing these unions under our jurisdiction, strengthen both our numbers and our finances; it will do away with the difficulties that now exist in regard to the exchange of cards . . . and it will be the means of strengthening the bonds of fellowship and good feeling that should exist between ourselves and our sister countries.[9]

An agreement was finally worked out between the two national associations in 1865, and the constitution of the National Typographical Society (U.S), which then became the International Typographical Union (ITU), was amended to allow for the affiliation of Canadian locals. The first charter of the "international" in Canada was issued to the St. John, New Brunswick Local No. 85. The second charter to be installed went to Toronto Local No. 91, and others quickly followed.

However, although discussions regarding a common membership started first in the typographical trade, it was not the first of the trades to set up Canadian branches. That dubious honour belongs to the iron molders, with five Canadian locals affiliating between 1861 and 1863.[10] And it was during this decade of the sixties that a veritable torrent of affiliations was completed. Such organizations as the cigar makers, the journeymen coopers, several of the railway brotherhoods, and the Knights of St. Crispin established a presence in Canada. But it must not be inferred that it was United States trades organizations alone that flourished in Canada in this period. Then, as always, distinctively Canadian unions struggled for existence in a hostile climate, and often under the looming shadow of the larger "internationals." Shipbuilding, bakeries, tailoring, and bricklaying were sectors of the trades where Canadian unions retained considerable strength into the 1880s.

Of course, this was the early stage of the penetration of Canada by United States unions, as yet largely—though not entirely—unruffled by the bureaucratic domination that was the main feature of the relationship which was to develop. The "internationals" were still individual unions, mostly concerned with problems internal to their own trade or industry, and not yet united in a federation with a well developed ideology. There was apparently no great desire on the part of the Americans to intervene in purely domestic affairs, or in matters clearly outside immediate concerns of the trade or calling. Class collaboration and ruling class ideology had not become institutionalized to the extent that they would become under the aegis of the American Federation of Labour (AFL). While not entirely free from complications and elements of conflict, there was an easiness in the relationship; such a condition would be eroded in the 1890s as the American drive for empire, supported by the AFL, gained momentum.

There were times in the early stages when Canadian initiative was welcomed by spokesmen for the American unions (in contrast to later years when initiative was suppressed). In 1873, the Toronto Trades Assembly and the Nine-Hour League (the former founded in 1871 and the latter in 1872) combined to call a Convention for the founding of the Canadian Labour Union (CLU), later reorganized as the Trades and Labour Congress (TLC). The Convention call said that the proposed body would

> Take into consideration the various questions that at present directly affect the interests of labour in this country—such, for instance, as the Trade Union Bill, which the present administration of the Dominion have signified their willingness to amend so as to meet the reasonable wishes of trade unionists . . . the creation of a proper Lien Law . . . questions bearing on the relation between employers and workmen that have been so carelessly handled by our legislators of late.[11]

Molders' union spokesmen greeted the Canadian development, and at the same time gave proof that they were conscious of the fact that the two organizations were operating in different countries with different problems. The official journal of the Molders editorialized on the Canadian development:

> In another column we published the call for an Industrial Congress of the trade unions of Canada. We heartily endorse the call, and hope to see our Canadian unions all represented. The objects sought can only be obtained by such an organization. The Industrial Congress of the United States would be valueless to our Canadian brothers, as most of the wrongs sought to be redressed must be redressed by the Canadian Parliament, and a demand from an Industrial Congress composed largely of delegates from the United States would be laughed at by the Parliament; for this reason Canadian Trade Unions were not invited to be represented at Cleveland. The two Congresses can and will act in harmony on all questions in which their combined efforts will be mutually advantageous; but upon such questions as Labour Bureaus, apprentice laws, coolie labour and prison labour, it must be evident that separate action is necessary.[12]

The journal also took note of, and commented on, the holding of the second convention of the CLU: "Like their brothers on this side of the line, they find that to make their power felt, and thus secure by legislation the many rights withheld from them, they must have an organization that will consolidate all the trade unions under one head for general purposes, while each union will retain all its special privileges and do its special work as heretofore, only its powers to do so increased by the general union."[13]

Still inherent in this statement was recognition of the need for a separate organization to handle particular local problems, *but operating within the limits allowed a State Federation of Labour*. The "each union" referred to is a *United States* body controlled abroad, while the "one head" is a *Canadian* body; the contradictions inherent in this association fueled the conflict that was increasingly to plague Canadian-American trade union relations. The founding of the AFL in 1886 and the subsequent affiliation of Canadian unionists to the Federation through their membership in the "internationals" made the status of State Federation a reality.

The full impact of the contradiction would not be felt until the 1890s, when the emerging American business unionism would openly associate with capital in seeking to dominate the hemisphere. But even in those near-halcyon days predating the consolidation of the Federation and the institutionalization of class collaboration, there were incidents that pointed to trouble ahead.

The Toronto Typographical Society had been affiliated to the "international" for little more than a year when there was a threat of withdrawal. The trouble arose over a bureaucratic decision to raise dues without consulting the membership. This dispute was settled to the satisfaction of the Toronto local and secession was headed off.

The typographical dispute was a relatively simple one, mainly involving bureaucratic bungling accentuated by national differences. But already, more serious disputes were germinating. One problem area was the sizeable French presence in Canada, which the "international" leaders either ignored or treated with contempt. One example of this attitude is found in the remarks made by William Sylvis when he toured Canada in 1873 on behalf of the molders' organization. Sylvis called Montreal "Frog Town," and referred to Quebec workers with contempt.[14]

A strike by the Toronto molders in the winter of 1870-1871 produced further cleavage when members of Local 13 in Buffalo scabbed on their Canadian brothers.[15] And the year 1883 saw more divisions as employers took advantage of an economic crisis to institute wage cuts, which international officers recommended the men should accept. In December the international Executive Board of the molders rejected a Toronto request to sanction strike action—in effect, a denial of strike relief. As a result of this dispute, the Toronto molders began a campaign for withdrawal from the international and for the formation of a Canadian union of molders. The secessionists argued that the interests of Canadian foundry workers would be better served if the power to control their own affairs was in their own hands. They said that since the finances were controlled by the international, the locals in Canada were deprived of the resources necessary for strike support, and consequently there remained to them no alternative but to comply with the dictates of the employers. The debate on secession raged unabated throughout most of 1884, but ended with the international still in control of the situation.

Important as they were though, these bouts were but preliminaries to the main battle for control that would come in the 1890s following the consolidation of the AFL and the rising consciousness of imperial destiny in America.

2

BUSINESS UNIONISM AND THE CONTINENTAL LABOUR MARKET

Canadian economic development has followed a similar pattern in both the capital and labour markets. In the first phase of development Britain was the chief source of capital for investment. Similarly, labour in its initial phase of organization, between 1850 and 1874, emerged under British influence as British immigrants contributed the major supply of skilled workers, and British unions played a leading role in the formation of Canadian unions and the shaping of union policy.

As United States direct investment in Canada increased in importance and proportion, it was paralleled by a corresponding rise in the influence of American trade unions and a decline of British influence. Since the American unionists supported United States imperial objectives abroad, it was natural that they should follow the course of American expansion into foreign countries. Canada was convenient and, for the most part, friendly to the economic invaders.

The British unions that expanded into Canada—and the United States—in the mid-nineteenth century had already discarded the old idealism and militancy linked to a primitive and often utopian class outlook. The "new unionism," comprised mainly of skilled workers, had decided to make the best of the established order, to "live with" capitalism. A ready response was found from elements of the ruling class. In 1835 the Compositors of London led the way in rejecting the militant past when they issued their class collaborationist declaration:

> Unfortunately all Trade Unions hitherto formed have relied for success upon extorted oaths and physical force . . . they have stigmatized their employers as grasping taskmasters, but as soon as they (the workmen) were united and powerful, then they became tyrants in their turn, and unreasonably endeavoured to exact more than the nature of their employment demanded . . . Let the

Compositors of London show the artisans of England a brighter and better example.[1]

The Convention of the ironmolders in 1846 brought this new policy of English trades unionism into still clearer focus in a resolution that was critical of, if not hostile to, strike action:

Strikes are prolific . . . they beget others . . . How often have disputes been averted by a few timely words with employers? The system of allowing disputes to be sanctioned by members generally labouring under some excitement . . . is decidedly bad. Our members do not feel the responsibility on these occasions which they ought . . . We have handed over for our future the power of sanctioning disputes to the Executive Committee alone.[2]

These stated policies of the new unionism were based on the concept that labour is a commodity like any other, governed by the law of supply and demand. In order to become dominant in Britain proponents of the new type of trades organization had to bury all of the old traditions of working class militancy.

But new unionism arrived in North America simultaneous with the origins of trades unionism. Of course, employer intransigence, and the temporary presence of a radical, politically oriented union centre made for militancy to improve wages and working conditions against the opposition of employers. But along with the militancy, and overshadowing it, went the desire to gain acceptance in the general community and cooperation from the employers. Throughout, the influence of new unionism was maintained through close contact with the societies in Britain, the actual presence of new unionist locals in North America, and in contact with new unionist immigrants from Britain. These were the factors that did much to prepare the organizational and ideological base for the triumph of business unionism, which matured and consolidated with the founding of the AFL.

Yearley discusses how even liberal elements, such as those around *The Nation*, recommended British style unionism to American workers as the ultimate solution to the problems and contradictions disrupting harmony in union-employer relations. He points out that "it was shown that only 6 per cent of British trade union expenditures went into the support of strikes," and quotes a writer in *The Nation* who claimed that 99 per cent of the funds in Britain's most powerful unions went into benefit programs.

Noting how liberal elements promoted new style unionism Yearley comments: "The emergence of respectable leaders among workingmen was underscored, as well as the fact that disreputable elements had been placed under a ban." He goes on to say it was "held that British unions were led by men of the highest character and judgment." And the New

York *Tribune* (the paper Marx and Engels wrote for) advised U.S. unionists that "when they resorted to strikes and violence they were blindly adopting the abandoned weapons of their English Brethren."

The focus of the debate was on the emphasis that the more successfully unions were organized and able to carry on their work, the more harmonious would be their relations with employers, and less likely would it become that anyone would start hasty, violent, or unlawful action. "Stable unionism," in other words, "was capable of making a real contribution to workingmen and to the community."[3]

It is plain to see from what source American unions obtained their ideas for union organization. Also discussed between the British and American unions was the problem of exchange of union cards, about the same time the question was raised with some unions in Canada. But as a result of a common border, and of considerable mobility of the work force, exchange proposals took the form of the proposition for a single continental union jurisdiction for each of the established craft organizations.

Given the fact that unionized workers in both countries were influenced by the same source (which led to a common view on methods of organization), and seeing that there were no important ideological differences dividing the workers in the two countries, the proposition seemed a logical one, and this, together with all other factors, conspired to render U.S. domination of Canadian unions relatively easy of achievement. Common cultural, linguistic, and social roots (with the important exception of French Canadians), together with geographical proximity, provided the essential ingredients necessary to the success of the scheme. Although a bit exaggerated in its fulsome acclaim for Canadian-American friendship and solidarity, an address by the noted Canadian publisher, editor, and journalist, John W. Dafoe, reveals some of the basic conditions that helped make domination possible:

> Canada is an American country by virtue of a common ancestry with the people of the United States. When one talks of a common ancestry between Canadians and Americans, people say "yes, they had a common ancestry in England." But it is something closer than that. The common ancestry to which I refer occupied the American colonies prior to the Revolution. The English-speaking provinces in Canada were settled by citizens of the English colonies along the Atlantic seaboard. The generations which laid the cultural foundations of Canada and their forebears had lived in those colonies for one hundred and fifty years—four or five generations. They had lived divorced from English influences, thrown very largely upon their own resources, and faced with problems upon which the experience of England threw no light.[4]

From the trade union side these sentiments were echoed by a Labour Day speaker in Toronto—most appropriately, an American speaker, who said:

> The bonds of friendship and understanding which happily exist between our two great countries have been nourished and strengthened by the international trade union movement which so continuously brings Canadian and American wage-earners together for the consideration of the economic and industrial problems which they have in common. Their basic problems are largely identical. Both countries were a wilderness but a few generations ago. Both were settled by a hearty pioneering stock having a common origin. Both have developed their industries in much the same manner.
>
> As time passed and both countries prospered, Canadian capital invested heavily in American industries, and because of the brilliant promise for development in Canada, American investors crossed the boundary line. When corporations with their American methods of production established branch plants in Canada, the employment policy which these corporations carried out in the United States was applied as far as possible in the Canadian plants.
>
> The flow of travel between the two countries, the flow of capital, the establishing of the American branch plants in Canada, the contact between the bankers of the two countries, the introduction of similar methods and processes in agriculture and manufacturing, the similarity in industrial policy, the employing attitude towards labour, have made it more and more necessary that the workmen of both countries, facing similar problems, should strengthen their international trade unions.
>
> In a large measure the financial, commercial, and industrial problems of both countries have a similar character and entail similar results. No major problems affecting the wage-earners of one country can develop without rightly affecting the other.
>
> The prosperity or depression existing in one country immediately reflects itself across the international boundary line. When serious unemployment exists on one side, it is certain to intrude its baleful influence upon the other.[5]

Common to both these addresses, and to statements by Sylvis, AFL President Gompers, and other recognized spokesmen for the American union movement, is the recognition of the cross-border affinity between Anglophone capitalists of both countries, and likewise between Anglophone skilled workers. The immigrants from many other nations, and most especially the French in Quebec, are not part of our "common heritage" in the eyes of these speakers.

One point that comes clear from all the discussion regarding "common ancestry," etc., is the fact that Canada had developed as part of a continental market featured by large-scale movement of capital and labour across the Canadian-American border. The ease of mobility of workers among the centres of employment of Canada and the northern United States became a characteristic of the structure of the continental labour market. By the 1870s there had emerged a self-adjusting labour market on a continental scale, the consequence of almost complete freedom of movement across the international boundary. With little more than personal choice influencing their decision, workers tended to move towards centres of available employment. A Toronto Typographical Society summary of activities covering the year 1865 emphasizes this mobility factor in the printing trades during a recession in Canada when it noted that ". . . a great depression of business prevailed throughout the larger part of the year, necessitating the removal of many members of your Society to the neighbouring States, where, we believe, all of them have been highly successful."[6]

Evidence of movement in the opposite direction is found in the establishment of the local of cigar makers in Montreal in 1865 which, according to Logan, was organized "at the instance of Hungarian workers who had come from the United States in search of work."[7]

This relationship with the more highly developed and more heavily populated United States often posed a serious threat to the security of Canadian workers. The movement of the printers was probably due to the effects of the Civil War, and the molders confronted an even more serious situation than the printers. Contemporary records show that "the Canadian molding industry was experiencing secondary effects from the development of the industry in the United States. The foundries there did not share in the profits of the American munitions industry, and the labour market was crowded with Americans who, with one eye on the draft in the United States, were willing to work for any wages and under any conditions." So many crossed the border that the trade in Toronto, Montreal, Brantford, and Hamilton was "wrecked by molders from the states."[8]

Union locals in the United States, which issued cards in fictitious names to draft dodgers escaping military service by crossing into Canada, compounded the problem. Commenting on the situation in 1864, the journal of the iron molders said that "Canada is again looking up, and only for the skedaddlers from the states would be all right."[9]

In view of the conditions it is not surprising that the first affiliations of Canadian unions to "internationals" developed around the end of the Civil War. The general situation certainly abetted the development of a continental market, and a crucial factor contributing to this path of economic development is touched upon by Mackintosh, who says:

Canadian industrial development was about thirty years behind that of the United States and new Canadian industries drew craftsmen not only from Britain but from the American states. Iron and steel workers were brought to Montreal in 1856 from the United States, the worker there being accustomed to the peculiar tempering of the steel required for our cold climate. After the Civil War there was a heavy immigration from the United States, some of which represented Canadians who had emigrated in the 50's. Cotton operatives came from New England in 1878 and boot and shoe workers early in the 70's while large numbers of mechanics from the United States entered Canada after the panic of 1873.[10]

However, while historical conditions thus successfully conspired in the creation of a continental market dominated by United States capital, there were contradictions left unresolved. Naked aggression, annexationist plots, and economic domination had not resolved the crucial problem of the international boundary. Geographically, and to an extensive degree economically, the continent was a close-knit region, but comprised of two separate nations nevertheless. And to an increasing degree the border came to represent political, cultural, and social differences that could not be erased by methods of economic domination. The relationship contained the seeds of conflict—a conflict from which the relations between Canadian and American trade unions would not and could not be exempt.

3

FOUNDATIONS OF EMPIRE:
TERRITORIAL AND ECONOMIC
EXPANSIONISM

The American economy achieved remarkable results during the decade of the 1890s, overtaking, and in many sectors surpassing, the older established industries of Europe. In this last decade of the nineteenth century United States exports in the field of manufactured goods more than doubled from $158 million to $339 million, and increased yet another $100 million just after the turn of the century.[1] Although these exports represented only a fraction of total production, they were crucial to the American economy. A leading political economist of the time stressed that "this is a war to the death—a struggle no longer against single nations but against a continent. There is not room in the economy of the world for two centres of wealth and empire. One organism, in the end, will destroy the other. The weaker must succumb. Under commercial competition, that society will survive which works cheapest; but to be undersold is often more fatal to a population than to be conquered."[2]

Business journals in the United States began to discuss the economic advantages of expansionism prior to the Spanish-American War.[3] American capitalists, concerned about America's capacity to produce more than the nation could consume, reacted to the European policy of rising tariffs by turning their attention to the business of acquiring colonies and spheres of influence.[4]

When he was engaged in debating the expansionist policies with the so-called anti-imperialists in 1900, ex-Secretary of State John W. Foster wrote, "Whatever difference of opinion may exist among American citizens respecting the policy of territorial expansion, all seem to be agreed upon the desirability of commercial expansion. In fact it has come to be a necessity to find new and enlarged markets for our agricultural and manufactured products. We cannot maintain our present industrial prosperity without them."[5]

Despite some differences on questions of tactics there was general

26

agreement among all sectors of society in the United States—including trade unionists—on the critical necessity for economic expansion in the interests of capitalist stability and prosperity. According to Williams, "Corporation leaders and intellectuals like Brooks Adams quite agreed that the nation's tremendous economic strength would underwrite a tremendous empire. Writing bluntly about America's Economic Supremacy in 1899-1900, Adams concluded that victory in the Spanish-American War was merely a prelude to triumph in the main contest for world predominance."[6]

President Taft drew attention to the fact that an increasing amount of American capital was being invested abroad, and that United States manufactured goods were insistently seeking out foreign markets that held promise of absorbing the nation's surplus products.[7] The New York *Financier* reported that in the space of a few years Canada, Mexico, and some other parts of the world had attracted at least one billion dollars of United States investment.[8] The years of United States industrial expansion were summed up for Canadian trade unionists in a convention report as follows: "The age in which we live is one of organization and consolidation. This does not apply merely to capital, or industrial enterprise, or financial management and controls, but it encompasses practically every phase of human life."[9]

The ruling class of the United States always looked upon Canada as an inseparable part of the continental market, and had several times experimented with attempts to include the British North American colonies in the American union. Direct invasion methods in 1775-1776 proved unsuccessful, and a repeat performance in 1812 almost ended in disaster for the Americans. In the negotiations with Britain on reparations following the Civil War, the American negotiators attempted to reach a settlement that would have effectively cut Canada off from access to the Pacific; this, together with the United States penetration of the Canadian prairie region, would have ended the possibility of building a Canadian nation.

Confederation was as much a response to American threats of annexation as it was a measure to guarantee the debts incurred in railroad construction. The two were inseparable, and in both cases large scale British interests were at stake. It was Britain, in cooperation with the British-oriented Canadian merchants and bankers, that pushed through the Confederation proposal. An American historian says that the idea of continental union of Canada and the United States has represented "perhaps the most serious as well as the most persistent sentiment in the history of American expansionism."[10]

In spite of the openly expressed sentiments in favour of annexation, the early stages of United States economic expansion into Canada seem to have attracted very little official or public attention in either country. But not content with economic domination alone, some American capitalists in 1898 revived the campaign for territorial annexation. The New York *Times* reported a project approved by New York merchants that proposed reciprocal trade and wider economic union with Canada, preliminary to total union of the two countries:

> The Merchants' Association of New York yesterday sent a letter to Chandler P. Anderson, Secretary State Department, Washington, D.C., referring to the invitations for correspondence or suggestions for the consideration of the Joint High Commission between the United States and Canada which will convene at Quebec on August 28. The letter says in part:
>
> "This organization is heartily in favour of the movement and is desirous of having closer and more reciprocal trade between this country and Canada, for since this subject has been under consideration we have been active in pushing it, and want to see everything done that can possibly be done to settle various questions which have been in dispute between the two countries, so that we may be united for wider commercial relations with Canada.
>
> "This organization has very much at heart the expansion of the export trade of the manufactured articles of this country. To that end it has interested itself in the bill now in Congress, providing for a reform of the consular service.
>
> "This subject becomes of great importance just now through the opening up of the West Indies and through the development which has taken place in Africa and South America, as well as in the probability of opening up China in the near future. This nation has developed so rapidly and has so busied itself with its internal affairs that it has not as a nation paid proper attention to pushing its manufactured products, which now, in many instances, are being over-manufactured, and for which a market must be found abroad, unless we want to have our industries glutted.
>
> "The step now being taken in connection with Canada is an important one in this direction, and the object of this letter is simply to impress upon the Commission the desire of the Merchants' Association of New York that everything possible be done to bring about the end desired, and to bring it about as speedily as possible."[11]

In 1904 a founder of the Continental Reciprocity League disclosed information regarding secret discussions on the subject of annexation between Canadian politicians and United States capitalists led by Andrew Carnegie. According to this informant, who was present at the discussions,

Carnegie was prepared to finance the purchase of Canadian annexation if it could be bought:

> Upon the 4th day of November 1893, Wilfrid Laurier held a meeting of his friends in Montreal and that meeting sent a delegation to New York to ask funds of the National Continental Union League for the elections it was supposed would take place in the spring of 1894. Israel J. Tarte, J.E. Robideaux, Louis Joseph Papineau and Mr. Langelier were on the delegation, and Sir Oliver Mowat was represented by John Morrison of Toronto.
>
> $50,000 was asked to buy *Le Monde*, and Morrison asked for $50,000 to start a labour paper in Toronto.
>
> Mr. Carnegie asked Mr. Tarte how much it would require to secure continental union; Mr. Tarte replied $1,000,000. Mr. Carnegie replied that if he was sure that amount would do it he would give it himself.[12]

Some Canadian manufacturers were still discussing the terms of continental union with their American counterparts at the turn of the century. According to a Toronto *Globe* dispatch from Boston, Canadian capitalists were involved in a cordial discussion with their United States colleagues concerning steps towards union:

> The Canadian Manufacturers Association was represented by President John F. Ellis and Secretary T.A. Russell at the annual convention of the National Association of Manufacturers of the United States held in Boston a few days ago. The question of the extension of trade and commerce was thoroughly discussed by the seven hundred delegates present. A most cordial spirit was manifested in the discussion of trade relations with Canada. The manufacturers of the United States were most anxious to find a market for their wares in Canada. As one speaker expressed it at the open meeting of the Association:
>
> "Wherever the English-speaking race is found there we can place our wares on the market and find a ready sale. Consequently the American manufacturers look most anxiously to Canada in order to find an outlet for their stocks."[13]

Within a few months of the adjournment of the convention at Boston, there appeared a new organization—possibly founded by the 700 delegates at the convention—with the declared aim of realizing a "continental union." The New York *Times* reported on the deliberations, which included plans for extension into Canada:

The National Continental Union League has been incorporated and a meeting is to be held at the Astor House on Thursday, June 21, for the election of officers. Andrew H. Green of this city is the nominee for President of the League, and Paul Dana and William Bourke Cockran will be elected vice-presidents. An advisory committee consisting of five members for each state in the union, and five for each province in Canada, will also be elected. The object of the League is set forth in a declaration which has been signed by nearly 700 citizens . . . The declaration of the National Continental Union League in part follows:

"We declare that all peaceful and honourable means should be used to consummate the political union of Canada and the United States.

"In our opinion the time has come when it is desirable that Europe should cease to direct or control the political or domestic affairs of any portion of the continent, and we believe that such cessation will tend to unite all English-speaking communities throughout the world in one common effort to develop, promote, and extend and defend constitutional government, and will be for the best interests of humanity.

"We firmly believe that the extension of the boundaries of the United States from the Gulf of Mexico to the Arctic Sea and from Newfoundland to Vancouver, will promote the happiness and best interests of all the people, materially lessen the per capita cost of government and defense, and be preservative of the peace of both North and South America and of the world.

"A branch of the League will be organized in every State in the United States, and in every Province in the Dominion of Canada."[14]

It is perfectly clear that the American ruling class, as far back as the 1890s, had perfected the general outlines of a plan whereby the United States would achieve world hegemony. To reach this desired goal, two preliminary accomplishments were seen as crucial to the whole plan: 1. Complete domination over the western hemisphere; and 2. The creation of an English-speaking union in which the United States would be the core. Canada was naturally looked upon as a crucial factor in the achievement of both preliminary objectives, and men like Henry Cabot Lodge, who proclaimed the divine right of the United States to be the dominant power in the western hemisphere, presupposed the annexation of Canada as a necessary first step.[15] And the anti-imperialists of 1898 had no qualms about the annexation of territory inhabited by "blood brothers." Champ Clark described Canadians as "people of our blood. They speak our language. Their institutions are much like ours. They are trained in the difficult art of self government." And Richard Olney maintained that "there is a patriotism of race as well as of country."[16] Canada loomed large in the planning of American imperialist strategy.

But while the annexationist movement of the 1890s played an important part in exposing American imperialist designs on Canada, territorial annexation never really got off the ground as a serious policy. The imperative was the need for access to Canadian markets and resources, and it was early realized that enlarged economic intercourse and the goal of domination could be accomplished by means other than annexation, and would probably lead to economic and political union in the long run. In any event, the very large American corporations with the money to invest had established large financial interests in Canada which, among other advantages, allowed them to compete within the empire preferential tariff wall, a wall which even excluded other smaller United States competitors unable to locate in Canada. Canadian hostility towards territorial annexation, especially among the banker and merchant class, might well place in jeopardy the American economic stake in the country, if pushed too far.

Canadian capitalists, it was thought, could be left the freedom to operate within certain spheres of the economy complementary to United States needs. The Canadian bourgeoisie could also be delegated the responsibility of maintaining political stability and of defending investor interests in the country. It was considered to be by far the best choice in the short run. In the long term view, United States economic domination, coupled with Canadian ruling class dependence on the American imperialists, would accomplish the cherished goal of hemispheric domination, and maybe even an English-speaking union through the use of Canadian links. In any event, United States economic penetration of Canada gathered momentum.

The United States Consul-General in Montreal reported that "never in the history of Canada has the industrial outlook been so bright as it is today. The present year promised to be made memorable by the establishment of new and immense enterprises and the extension of many existing ones." He went on to add that most of these enterprises were aided by American capital. And according to the *Monetary Times of Canada* the commercial invasion by United States interests covered a long list of manufactured items, including: asbestos, barrels, blind rollers, buttons, carpet sweepers, corsets, condensed milk, bags, corks, carriages, couches, brass goods, billiard tables, cords, cash registers, disinfectant, fly paper, files, fire extinguishers, fountain pens, gramophones, hardware, pickles, presses, pulleys, razors, rubbers, sealers, shoes, scales, typewriters, watch cases, and tobacco. Americans were also strong in steel making and in the mining of ores. In most of the hardrock mining centres of British Columbia, one-third of the population was American. And as early as 1890, a Royal Commission reported that over one-half of the capital invested in mining operations in Ontario was American.[17]

Throughout the winter of 1902-03, Central Canada experienced some of the disadvantages of the continental market system. Eastern and western regions of the country had ample supplies of coal, but Ontario and Quebec, dependent upon the mines of Pennsylvania, shivered all through the winter because of the effects of a strike in the U.S. anthracite mines. The *Labour Gazette* complained that: "Seldom has a single industrial disturbance in another country affected so closely the homes of the masses of the people of this country, or been the cause of as much widespread anxiety as the present difficulty."[18]

By 1914 American investment in Canada reached the grand total of $618.4 million, representing one-quarter of all United States investment abroad. Most British investment was portfolio while United States funds were in the form of direct investment in the factories and mines of Canada. The reality of direct investment involved the extension into Canada of industrial organization and control based in the U.S., constituting a clear manifestation of the continental market structure.

An example of continental market operation insofar as it affected trade unions was evident in the stove manufacturing industry, especially after the establishment of the National Stove Founders' Association in 1898. The Association enrolled in membership more than 600 firms in both the United States and Canada. A continental agreement was then signed with the union of iron molders for the regulation of wages, working conditions, and labour supply over the whole continent.[19]   The agreement provided for the setting up of a joint board of arbitration to handle all disputes that might arise during the life of the contract. Two Canadian locals of the international failed to reach agreement with their employers and went out on strike. But in spite of this minor defection, the point of emphasis was still that both the union and the association of employers were continental in scope, and the forty-ninth parallel presented no insurmountable difficulty in the path of their effective operation.[20]

Although there had been some loud, but limited, protest against territorial conquest on the part of a few union spokesmen, the AFL experienced no great difficulty in swallowing the policies imposed by commercial expansion. After all, they were fully committed to economic expansion as necessary to the welfare of the American capitalist system. In the wake of armed conquest the Federation officers planned, and carried out, organizational activities in the Philippines, Hawaii, and Puerto Rico.[21] And by 1905 Gompers was in a position to be able to inform convention delegates that the Federation's "limits are no longer from Maine to California, from the lakes to the gulf, but we include the whole of the United States, Canada, Hawaii, Cuba, Puerto Rico, Mexico, the Philippines, and British Columbia."

Just as the organization followed the conquering American army into many lands, the AFL followed invading United States capital into Canada.

Beginning in the 1890s the Federation and the "internationals" relentlessly pursued the goal of domination over the Canadian union movement. To that end, independent unions (all those that did not pay homage to the Federation and its policies) were condemned as "dual unions," and scheduled for destruction. United States capital and United States unions invaded Canada simultaneously. That the events occurred simultaneously was more than just fortuitous.

4

MANAGING A COLONY—
UNION STYLE

The founding of the American Federation of Labour signified a great deal more than a simple advance in organization. The emergence of the Federation was a practical manifestation of the maturing of business unionism and the institutionalization of class collaboration in the organized labour movement in America. And it was not just coincidental that this occurred precisely at the time when the ruling class of the United States was reconnoitering the terrain for new areas of conquest.

But the Federation's first few years were necessarily spent in domestic consolidation, and in the settling of accounts with enemies such as industrial unionism and politically-oriented labour groups. Beyond the U.S. borders the AFL did not seem so fearsome. The Canada Trades Congress, engaged in the founding of a Canadian centre, could not but welcome a similar initiative in the United States—especially since there were no contradictions between them concerning questions of ideology.

In Canada, the prevailing attitude amongst unionists seemed to be one of differentiating between the various "international" unions and the Federation. The seeds of conflict contained in the affiliation of Canadian unions to the AFL through membership in the "internationals" were not apparent to the Canadians. The Federation was generally looked upon as the counterpart of the TLC, uniting all labour organizations—whether trades union, industrial or political—in a single body for the purpose of working together on matters of common concern, such as the securing of legislation in the interests of the working class.

But unlike the TLC, the AFL was an exclusive organization devoted to the skilled trades and determined on the destruction of all and every group that might compete for working class support. Problems of union jurisdiction, which ranked high on the agenda of the AFL, got no attention at all in the TLC. Nor did the TLC think through the fact that the AFL, being pledged to uphold the American social system, would be unable to

34

stand idle where the United States interests in Canada might appear to be threatened.

Efforts conducted through the internationals to have the TLC conform with patterns of union structure, government, and policies advocated by the AFL met with resistance, and bred conflict between the two before the Federation and the Congress were a decade old. An open manifestation of this conflict surfaced when two representatives of a Montreal Assembly of the Knights of Labour introduced a motion at a TLC convention calling for greater concentration on political action:

> It being proven that this Congress has outlived its usefulness through its incapacity to obtain even a fraction of justice from the Federal and Provincial governments; be it resolved that before its adjournment this Congress be reconstructed on a system in accord with the ideas of the age, and which may permit it to grant charters for the organization of workers' societies in no matter what branch of work, to the end that at all times we may be in a position to concentrate our forces for the political battle, being convinced that to petition governments for reforms is a loss of time, and that it is only by independent political action, like that of the Socialist Workers Party, that we will obtain the measure of justice that we have so long sought.[1]

Another resolution, which was a virtual declaration of independence and introduced jointly by a member of the industrial Knights and a member of the trades, called for the formation of a "Canadian association with full powers of organizing, granting charters, levying taxes, and performing any other duties pertaining to a national union."[2]

These resolutions constituted an open challenge to the principles and policies advanced by the international unions and the Federation; and both passed, with the Executive being charged with the responsibility for carrying out the work necessary to make them operative. The issues raised in these resolutions contained sufficient inflammatory material to start a conflagration, which was soon to be fueled by still other controversial issues.

Canadian unions had been induced to affiliate with the internationals, largely on the grounds that it would facilitate an exchange of cards between American and Canadian unions. The natural assumption was that no restrictions would be proposed by either side that would impede border crossing by union members in search of employment. On the other hand, one of the stated reasons for the formation of the Federation was to coordinate action in the interests of tightening the immigration laws so as to halt the flow of "cheap labour" into the country. From the beginning, Federation spokesmen campaigned for a stringent alien labour law and by

1895 it became clear that the desired act was to have Canada as one of its main targets. Gompers solicited and published an article by a United States Immigration Commissioner in which the policy of placing restrictions on immigration from Canada was forcefully stated:

> There is one danger which should be brought forcibly home to the members of labour orgaizations, and it is more real now that the present enforcement of the law has practically stopped the introduction of labourers under contract—that is, the coming to this country of migratory labourers, or "birds of passage," without intention of permanently remaining here; of immigrants from Europe and Canada, and especially from the latter. Not less than 100,000 persons . . . come to the United States from Canada, and at least 50 per cent of these return to their homes after the working season is over, to come again the next year, and repeating the performance an indefinite number of times. As secretary of the Commission referred to above, I had occasion to look into this matter in the cities and towns bordering on the Canadian frontier, notably Detroit and Buffalo, and in Boston . . . and from this investigation I am satisfied that the danger from this class of immigrants is very large—more serious than those from Europe . . . the transient immigrants from the Dominion of Canada . . . have reduced wages in the trades in which they have entered from 25 to 50 per cent, and unless legislation speedily comes, this great injustice and wrong will continue.[3]

If this was not deliberately designed to foster a spirit of anti-Canadianism, then it did an effective job without design. And the article pinpointed the limitations of the continental labour market and the shallowness of the international content of "international" unionism. Since the American unionists consistently refused to have their Canadian brothers exempted from the provisions of the proposed act, it would seem that a contract was broken in a less than honourable fashion.

A perusal of the Federation records will leave one with the impression that injuries inflicted by "undesirable" immigrants were all one-sided. No attention whatever was paid to the flow in the opposite direction which sometimes had tragic consequences, as in the following recorded instance:

> It has been shown on the floor of the House of Commons, that Canadian labourers have been deported from the United States . . . Italians have been brought from Buffalo under contract to work on the Grand Trunk Railway, and during the late strike of the trackmen belonging to that Company many instances could be given of people being brought into Canada under contract. We remember with horror, however, the suicide of Alexander Reder, the cloak maker, in

the city of Toronto. This is a sad commentary on our civilization. He had been imported with others, under contract, by the T. Eaton Co., Limited, to take the places of workers on strike, and upon finding this out, he preferred self destruction to being a scab. On making appeal to Lubelski, Eaton Co.'s agent, for money to pay his fare back to New York, he was refused; the desperate man then said the only alternative was suicide; Lubelski replied, "He did not care what he did, he could hang or drown." Everlasting honour is due the man who would die rather than bring defeat and disaster upon his fellows.[4]

The campaign for the exclusion of Canadians under the proposed alien labour law and the draining of union funds from Canada in the form of dues to international unions, at a time when the TLC was seriously crippled financially, combined to provoke bitter criticism from unionists in Canada. In a letter addressed to the TLC, Gompers tried to defuse the pending conflict, while defending the AFL position:

> I can see the apparent justice of the complaint you made against the operations of the Alien Contract Labour Law of the United States, and its application to our fellow workers and particularly our fellow unionists of Canada. Beyond doubt, there are some cases of hardship and injustice resulting from the application of that law, but I think that you will agree with me when I say that the wage workers of the United States were compelled to adopt some method by which their interests could be protected . . . I recognize the difficulty confronting us today, and the justice of the complaint of members of local unions attached to the international unions, if their cards should not secure them the rights of work and membership everywhere . . .
>
> You say that your Congress is to convene at Quebec on September 15th, when the subject matter will be discussed. I do hope that grave consideration will be given the matter and that no ill-advised action will be taken. Were it not for the fact that I have an important engagement elsewhere at this time, I should make it my business to be in attendance. May I make this suggestion—that your Congress may select a fraternal delegate to the convention of the American Federation of Labour . . . I am sure that the selection of a fraternal delegate would help to the solution of this question.[5]

Gompers' attempted justification of the American position got a cold reception from the assembled TLC delegates. It was most unlikely that the Congress possessed sufficient funds for the financing of a fraternal delegate—and the matter of finances constituted yet another area of grievance resulting from the fact that, while the Congress was staggering along chronically short of funds and unable to finance essential activities, the international unions were paying per capita tax to the Federation on behalf of their Canadian members. There were protests and demands made for the tax to be turned over to the Trades Congress.

Secession was in the air as the list of grievances against the Federation lengthened, and in February 1898 a local of the tailors' international had seceded to become Local No. 1 of the Journeymen Tailors' Union of Canada, calling on other locals across the country to follow their example. The seceding tailors reasoned that too much money was flowing across the border into American coffers, and since the United States alien labour law had eliminated any advantages accruing to Canadian members of international unions, it would be a most appropriate move to establish a Canadian union movement. Printers in Vancouver, replying to a TLC request for funds, proposed that the Congress demand that the per capita tax presently being paid to the AFL by the international on behalf of Canadian unionists be retained in Canada.

In view of the prevailing situation and the conflict with American union policies, the AFL and the internationals could have advised the Canadians to go their separate and independent way, with a pledge of support and international solidarity. But empires are seldom dismantled voluntarily, and the AFL empire builders were no different from any others in this regard. They demonstrated a determination to hold on to their Canadian "colony."

It was at this critical point in Canadian-American union relations, and no doubt influenced by current problems, that the Federation appointed its first paid representative in Canada.

In late 1896 P.J. Loughrin, a Sault Ste. Marie businessman, wrote to the Federation President suggesting that he, Loughrin, had the necessary talents to become an excellent union organizer. Considering the situation in cross-border relations at the time and the Federation's determination to hold on to the Canadian franchise, it is understandable that Gompers would be easily persuaded, and he forthwith appointed Loughrin AFL organizer for all of Canada—a decision he would shortly regret.

In Loughrin's immediate home area there were two resources of increasing importance to America's industrial development. The first was nickel, an element never found in any substantial amount in the United States but in plentiful supply in Ontario, in deposits that were being worked by both United States and British interests before the middle of the nineteenth century. Nickel was important to the manufacture of steel, especially for use in armour plating. Raw ore was being shipped from Canada for refining in the United States, and it was not until the 1920s that even limited processing would be done in the country of origin. The second resource was pulpwood for fine papers and newsprint. It also was plentiful in Ontario and Quebec while sources in the United States and other places were being rapidly depleted.

Before 1909, American industrialists considered Canada to be just a supplier of raw materials. In addition to exporting raw ore for refinement in the U.S., they acquired extensive timber rights in Canada and imported a considerable proportion of their pulpwood requirements. Protected by their own tariff wall, and not being compelled to make any sizeable investment in the Canadian end of the operation, American producers were highly satisfied with their situation. It was not until well into the twentieth century (in British Columbia not until 1913) that legislative action in Canada would force the United States producers to move part of their operation across the border to create jobs for Canadian workers.

It is a foregone conclusion that Gompers and his AFL colleagues, possessing as they did a keen sense of appreciation for United States interests abroad and the dangers threatening them, were fully conscious of the potentially precarious situation concerning continued control of the resources in Canada—especially since any critical shift in policy could threaten thousands of American jobs to the advantage of Canadian workers. And it was on this rock of direct economic interest that Loughrin's union ship foundered.

The fall and winter of 1896-1897, when Loughrin was pursuing his union activities, was a period of severe economic depression that was having a particularly hard effect on the Canadian resources industry. As he travelled about the country Loughrin observed that every city, town, and village had its quota of unemployed workers roaming the streets. At the same time he noted that raw ore and unprocessed pulpwood were being shipped out of the country, and he opined that if these were put through a manufacturing process in Canada thousands of jobs would be created and the ranks of the unemployed correspondingly reduced.

Being a man of action, Loughrin decided to use his position as AFL representative to sponsor a campaign for legislative action to compel American manufacturers to process the available raw materials in Canada. He set out his proposition in some detail, and since it was the central issue causing his dismissal just six months after his appointment, it seems appropriate to cite it at some length, as reported in the *Globe*:

> . . . "I would ask your cooperation and any assistance that you may be enabled to give the labour cause of our common country. It is unnecessary for me to call your attention to the state of trade and labour during the past two years. The scarcity of work has placed the general trade of the country in a state of depression. We extended the hand of good-fellowship to the United States, looking for better terms as to trade relations for the benefit of all, but they have so flatly refused any attempt to approach them on that subject that there is no other course left for us but to protect a few of our industries and raw materials—of which latter we have practically an inexhaustible supply

(especially of pulpwood and nickel)—from the inroads made by the United States upon our forests and mines, and for which the Government of the country and the labouring classes receive no revenue or benefit. There are 600,000 cords of pulpwood exported annually to the United States free of duty, of which our people receive from $2 to $3 per cord, delivered at a railway track. This leaves only about $1.25 for labour, as surely the wood is worth $1.75. This raw material is taken out of our country by American capitalists, who put from $7 to $11 worth of labour on each cord when manufactured into pulp or paper, making an average of $9 per cord on the aforesaid 600,000 cords—thereby depriving our Canadian labourers of about $5,600,000 worth of labour annually on the pulpwood alone, which should certainly be manufactured in Canada out of the raw material of which we have such an abundance from the Gulf of St. Lawrence to the waters of the Hudson Bay. I might say that if a scheme were proposed for building a railway 300 miles long, it would be looked upon in the nature of a boom, and people would rush in that direction for employment. But such a railway would not expend on labour any more than would be expended in one year if the raw material were kept at home and manufactured into pulp and paper here. The pulp industry, once established, would add materially to the income and prosperity of the labouring classes of all grades throughout Canada. What I ask, and justly petition, the Boards of Trade, Municipal Councils and my fellow-citizens generally throughout Canada is that they urge upon our legislators the necessity of protecting our interests and harbouring what justly belongs to us, by putting an export duty on pulpwood and giving us an alien labour law corresponding in all respects with that in force in the United States, and with this end in view, I will endeavour, during my four-weeks tour through the Dominion, to meet and explain the matter personally to as many of the representatives of the labour unions as is possible for me to do.

"In the United States today," said Mr. Loughrin, "there are 914 pulp, paper mills in operation, which are averaging, and this is a low average, twenty tons per day. This is 18,280 tons of pulp per day used, or 5,484,000 tons a year. At $20 per ton this is an outlay of $100,000,000 a year for pulp alone. Calculating the labour employed at 100 hands in each mill, this is 91,400 in all, and at $35 per month for each man employed, wages amounting to $3,199,000 a month are paid, or $38,388,000 a year.

"Now it will be seen at once by any common sense man who will take the trouble to look into this question, and who is not biased by selfish motives, that there is no room here for a political issue, in any sense of the term. It is a matter which claims the attention of any man who has the interests of the country at heart and the well-being of our fellow-citizens and labouring classes generally. I can see no valid reason why we should not reach out and grasp some of this valuable trade, and that, too, without any aim of retaliation in view.

"Again our nickel ore contains the most important element in the manufacture of the sulphite fibre, which is the sulphur, and this valuable element is now being absolutely wasted—passing from the nickel works in the smoke and making the atmosphere in the neighbourhood of the mines disagreeable.

"For a moment let me touch on our nickel resources in the Sudbury district. Our United States neighbours have been mining in that district since 1889. There have, in that time, been 500,000 tons of ore mined and 475,000 tons smelted. That is 940,000,000 pounds which at 4 per cent would be 37,000,000 pounds of marketable nickel produced. At 40 cents per pound this means $14,000,000. The copper in this amount of ore would amount to about 28,200,000 pounds, and at 10 cents per pound this would mean $2,820,000. There would also be sulphur, concentrates, acids, and salts to the value of about $3,000,000 which makes a grand total of $20,860,000 which has been taken out of this district alone in about seven years of operation.

"I have not the slightest inclination in the world of retarding the industry either in nickel or pulpwood, but I can see no argument in favour of allowing the material to go out of our country practically in a raw state. The labour necessary to the refining of them into marketable articles should be expended in and for the benefit of the country where the material is produced. . . .

"It can readily be seen that the pulpwood resources of the United States must, at an early date, succumb to the enormous consumption at the present rate at which they are depleting their own forests, and it is just a matter of a few years till we are able to dictate terms to the world for pulp and paper as well as nickel. Let there be no mistake about this; the export duty will not deter the United States from buying our pulpwood. They must have it. . . .

"I have no other object in view," Mr. Loughrin said, "than to do my utmost to secure labour for the idle men of Canada with whom every town and city in the country is overcrowded. With this end in view, as well as the framing of an alien labour law that will give the same protection to the Canadian as the American enjoys in the labour markets of the world, I have communicated with Mr. Samuel Gompers, the President of the American Federation of Labour, whom I represent in Canada, to use his influence with the United States Congress to have the following clause inserted in the bill now before Congress: Any member of an International or Federal Labour Union affiliated with the American Federation of Labour, holding a travelling card of the said International or Federal Labour Union, shall be exempt from the provisions of this bill.

"I am satisfied that if Mr. Gompers succeeds in securing the insertion of that clause I shall have no trouble in getting an identical clause in the bill now before the House of Commons of Canada. As nearly all unions in Canada are now affiliated with the AFL, this would be glad news to all union labourers."[6]

There were several items peripheral to the central point in the Loughrin-Gompers dispute which should be mentioned: There is no doubt that the Canadian organizer was so uncooperative in plans for a Canada tour by Gompers that the whole idea had to be scrapped. And there seems to be no question of Loughrin using (abusing?) his position as AFL representative to advance the interests of the Liberal Party. The former was both frustrating and embarrassing for Gompers, but could be borne provided that general union business did not suffer. As for the latter, it violated the firm AFL principle of "no partisan politics," but the Federation President had informed Loughrin that he would not object if it could be turned to the advantage of the international unions. These were nuisance items, but not sufficient to warrant precipitate action. But other issues could not be ignored. These were central, and Loughrin, in a 1909 interview published in *Canadian Annual Review*, said that he was dismissed from his post as AFL representative for having advocated a tax on raw material exports.

Gompers' reason for appointing Loughrin was for the purpose of calming troubled waters, and consolidating and extending international unionism in Canada. But Loughrin, in the name of the Federation, pursued other objectives that could well have the effect of disturbing the status quo in Canadian-American economic relations—Canada the supplier of raw materials, and the United States the industrial manufacturer. That was certainly a violation of the fundamental principles defended by the United States union movement—to advance and support America's economic interests abroad. The fact that Loughrin was prepared to allow for the interests of American trade union members, whereas Gompers and his associates were not, carried no weight in the Federation.

Gompers obtained a copy of the Loughrin petition and interview, probably from Loughrin himself, who appears to have been so naive as to expect Federation support. The material was immediately brought to the attention of the AFL Executive Council, where it was entered as conclusive evidence of Loughrin's "treachery." Following discussion of the matter Gompers heatedly informed his appointee that the documents "demonstrate beyond the peradventure of a doubt that you are using the commission issued to you as a general organizer, for purposes other than that for which the labour movement stands. It appears that you are not only using the commission for business purposes but to estrange the workingmen of the Dominion of Canada and the United States."[7]

Loughrin was dismissed from his union post on May 1, 1897, after just six months on the job. The Federation charge that Loughrin was dividing the workers by expressing an opinion on how Canada's natural resources should be managed has the appearance of an obscenity in the light of how the AFL continued their policy of shafting their Canadian brothers. Even as they were preparing the dismissal of Loughrin for "divisive" activities, Federation officers were submitting proposals to the United States Congress for the tightening of immigration laws, with the main thrust of the proposals against Canadian workers, including international union members. The proposals included:

1. A law regulating immigration into the United States from contiguous foreign countries by water or land carriage, which will protect our own workmen from the importation of transient cheap labour across our frontier.

Provision should also be made therein to exclude aliens coming year after year to perform labour in the United States with no intention to settle therein.

2. That all transportation companies engaged in transporting aliens to and from the United States shall by law be required to furnish a list or manifest of all outgoing alien passengers, together with such information as the Secretary of the Treasury may require for statistical purposes and the administration of the immigration laws.

From these lists the authorities will be able to ascertain the exact volume of emigration and to verify the status of returning aliens claiming to be alien residents.

Emphasizing the main centre of attack, Gompers editorialized on the transgressions of Canadian workers, with the French Canadians coming in for special mention, all of which was no doubt done in the spirit of uniting the workers on the continent:

There is one matter now pending before Congress which we can treat of at this time, namely, that of immigration from and via Canada to the United States. Much has been said about the brotherly feeling which should exist between labourers all over the world, but it should not be forgotten that in the interchange of favours between this country and Canada, the United States has received immeasurably the worst of the bargain. The discussion before the last Congress, which is no doubt familiar to all, mostly referred to that class of immigrants coming from Canada and going to Western New York, Ohio, Michigan, and, in fact, all the states on the border. The various conventions of all American Federation of Labour and the various

labour organizations in Buffalo, Detroit, and similar cities have gone
on record concerning the damage which has been done the citizen
labourers of these communities by the transient immigrants coming
from across the border, and the report of the commission, which has
already been referred to, deals extensively with that question.

Another feature of the Canadian question, and one which has been
lightly treated of in the immigration debates, is the immigration from
Quebec and the eastern provinces, New Brunswick, Nova Scotia, and
Newfoundland. The French Canadian has migrated in large numbers
to the manufacturing communities of New England while the natives
of New Brunswick, Nova Scotia, and Newfoundland have flooded the
building trades of the same section . . . It cannot be disputed that they
have succeeded in reducing the market rate of wages wherever this
transient class has come in contact with the native workmen of the
United States.[8]

If there appears to be the semblance of madness or enigma in the AFL
judgment on what constitutes estrangement, the solution will be
discovered in the dark recesses of the imperial mind. American unionists
had linked their fate with American capitalism and its imperialist
manifestation. In the circumstances, United States interests must be
sustained above all, meaning that the nationalist aberrations of a Loughrin
could not be tolerated, and the interests of workers in the economic
colony—even those of "international" union members—must be
considered secondary to those of the workers in the metropolitan area.

As though in a deliberate attempt to compound Gompers' Canadian
problems, proceedings of the 1897 Convention of the Trades and Labour
Congress are evidence of increasing hostility concerning the collection and
disposal of dues in the international union movement which, as previously
noted, fostered strong secessionist sentiments in the Congress ranks. Some
of the union members in Canada who had made a study of the problem
pointed out that while the legislative activities of the Trades Congress were
virtually non-existent due to lack of finances, AFL expenditures, at least
partly financed by Canadian dues and assessments, had risen seven-fold in
the space of a few years. Some Convention delegates raised demands for
the "nationalization" of the union movement in Canada, and a decision
along those lines was narrowly averted by a proposal contained in the
officers' report. It reported on action taken regarding criticisms raised at
the Convention of 1896:

Shortly after the close of last session the correspondence ordered by
your body between your body and President Gompers, of the
American Federation of Labour, was dispatched. The same was laid
before the session of that body in Cincinnati, but so far no reply or

acknowledgement has been received. Before the session Mr. Gompers
was very anxious to have our Congress represented by a fraternal
delegate, but your committee could not see their way clear to send
one. While on the subject of American Federation of Labour, your
Committee believe that your Congress is entitled to some of the
money paid to the Federation by Canadian members of International
Unions. At the present time every International Union in America is a
member of that body, and at the same time every International is
represented in our Congress by one or more of the Canadian Local
Unions. Your Committee would therefore recommend that the
Executive Committee strongly urge on the Local Unions of the
various International bodies to petition their respective organizations
to turn over to this Congress for legislative purposes the amount of the
per capita tax now paid the Federation on their Canadian members.

What is noteworthy about this approach is the calculated effort to
by-pass the AFL and deal with the international unions as separate bodies.
In this there is still a lingering concept of the Congress and the Federation
as co-equal national bodies with separate constituencies and tasks. In the
end, however, the Congress would submit to State Federation of Labour
status, which was the only solution acceptable to the AFL and the
international unions.

A letter from TLC Secretary George Dower advised AFL Convention
delegates of the list of Canadian grievances, and on the motion of P.J.
McGuire, head of the Carpenters' Union and close associate of Gompers,
the Convention named Thomas I. Kidd of the Woodworkers, fraternal
delegate to the Trades Congress Convention scheduled for Winnipeg in
1898. At the same time that it took this supposedly friendly action, the
Federation Convention endorsed the crusade for border restrictions by a
vote of more than five to one.[9]

But the Canadian unionists were not so easily placated and the
Federation Executive Council met in April 1898, as a wave of secessionist
sentiment swept the Canadian movement. The immediate problem was
how to stall off disaster and hope that Kidd could effect a permanent
settlement at the September Convention. Gompers belatedly informed the
Council that Dower's letter suggested that a grant of $100.00 for legislative
work would appease the Canadian unionists. The Executive Council
unanimously approved the required expenditure, which represented an
average of less than one cent for each of the ten thousand international
union members in Canada. As to the future of Canadian-American trade
union relations, Federation hopes rested squarely on the ability of
fraternal delegate Kidd to placate the unruly Canadians who were
unreasonably suggesting that independence might be a better way.

5

1898:

YEAR OF DECISION

The Trades Congress Convention of 1898 was a watershed, a turning point, in the history of the organized labour movement in Canada. The amendments to the constitution that would transform the Canada Congress into a State Federation of Labour would be formally adopted four and five years later. But the path of development was clearly delineated, and most of the personnel set in place, in 1898.

Congress officers had made an effort—though far from valiant—to maintain the integrity and declining independence of the Congress when they asserted their *right* to be assigned a portion of the dues collected by the international unions in Canada. In the end they settled for a *grant* from the Federation, thereby accepting a policy that sealed their fate as a dependent national body.

The practice of secret meetings instituted at the Winnipeg Convention deprives us of any easy way in which to understand exactly what happened at that fateful gathering. Even the address of the first ever fraternal delegate to attend a Congress Convention is not printed in the Convention proceedings. One must rely on reports in the local press for information on the contents of the speech by Kidd.

Trades Congress leaders, together with the AFL official representative, discussed, behind the locked door of a hotel room, crucial issues affecting the future of the Canadian movement. We have only the report of the Executive to the reassembled delegates to clue us in on what took place at that secret gathering. However, there is a wealth of circumstantial evidence available to aid us in arriving at substantial conclusions as to the essence of the secret deliberations.

It has been clearly established in Volume I that in the heat and crisis of the years immediately preceding, and during, the Spanish-American War, the American Federation of Labour advanced from domestic support for United States capitalism to open aid for foreign expansion. The Federation

46

undertook the task of garbing United States foreign policy with trade union "respectability," and dragooning workers in the colonies into the acceptance of "liberation," the American way. In this regard, the declaration that appeared in the *American Federationist* in September 1898, bears repeating: "The nation which dominates the markets of the world will surely control its destinies. To make of the United States a vast workshop is our manifest destiny, and our duty, and thus . . . no obstacle can be placed to the attainment of the highest pinnacle of national glory . . . the gates of any country in the world cannot long be closed against our constantly growing industrial supremacy."

A few weeks later Samuel Gompers reinforced this declaration of union support for imperial destiny with a statement that the Federation did not "oppose development of our industry, the expansion of our commerce," nor the power and influence which the United States might exercise over other countries. And when we consider that at this time one-quarter of all American investments abroad were located in Canada, it is understandable that the Federation would be vitally interested in the future of organized labour in this country—at least as interested as they were in Latin America, and that was considerable.

Situating the individuals involved is also important to an understanding of the events in 1898. The leader of the Union of Carpenters, P.J. McGuire, whose motion had resulted in the appointment of Kidd as Federation representative at Winnipeg, was a long-time associate of Gompers, dating to the days of the First International and the formative period of the AFL. There can be little doubt but that McGuire had discussed the Canadian problem, and ways to resolve it, with his old associate prior to making the motion. Kidd, and his Woodworkers' Union, were already in the process of becoming a part of the organization of carpenters at the time of his appointment, so there would have been a relationship existing between Kidd and McGuire, and probably with Gompers as well.

John Flett of Hamilton, Ontario, who was slated to play a crucial role in the transformation of the Canadian movement, was a carpenters' union official who had served in every office in his home local, and had represented it at various conventions and conferences. There is no question about Flett's being known to McGuire, and through McGuire he would be made known to Gompers, who was anxious to avoid a repeat of the Loughrin debacle. Flett proved both his loyalty to the Federation and his ability as a union organizer. He was ever ready to proclaim his "Canadianism" as an aid in furthering the interests of the internationals in Canada, but he expressed a preference for union work in the United States.

After 1902, when it was thought that American domination over the movement in Canada had been secured, Flett got his wish when he was used to an increasing degree in New York State and other areas. Although

Flett's expenses and salary were debited to Federation work in Canada, AFL correspondence shows that he was being used to a greater extent in the U.S. than in Canada. During 1913-1914 Flett spent less than a month organizing activities in Canada.

Opposition elements were led by men like Ralph Smith of Nanaimo, British Columbia, a Liberal Member of Parliament who did not oppose international unions but wanted an independent Trades Congress. P.M. Draper, who later became Secretary of the TLC, also had ideas about the Congress becoming a Canadian body similar to, but independent from, the Federation. Draper continued to hold strong views on this subject for some time after 1902. Like Smith, Draper did not oppose international unions (he was a member of the ITU), but unlike Smith he came around to the AFL viewpoint. His conversion was the subject of comment by the head of the Shoemakers' Union in a letter to Gompers written in September, 1910:

> While at one time Draper's loyalty to the American Federation of Labour was of a very doubtful character, I believe that of recent years he has been developing and has seen the error of his former ways. The last time I saw him (in 1909) . . . he told me how much he had learned during recent years and that he had gotten entirely over his idea that Canada should have a Federation co-equal with the American Federation.

Kidd kept his 1898 rendezvous with destiny at Winnipeg, simultaneous with news of the resounding victories of American arms at sea and on land. According to reports in the *Winnipeg Free Press* on September 19, the American was the centre of attraction in the prairie city, and guest of honour at a banquet where civic officials entertained the Convention delegates. An Alderman proposed a toast to the American Federation of Labour, the band played "Yankee Doodle," and Kidd responded with a speech in which he lauded the success of American expansionist policies.

But in the Convention proper, Kidd was compelled to confront nagging differences in Canadian-American relations—conflicts that he hoped were of a minor character. The *Voice*, a labour newspaper in Winnipeg, in its issue of September 23 commented on Kidd's Convention address, saying that he "expressed the hope that the trade unionists of Canada and those of the United States would be brought closer together. He noticed some little differences of feeling that existed. One of these was that on the other side there was opposition to workers crossing the line; and there was talk of retaliatory legislation . . . There was feeling that Canada was being neglected; this was to be removed by sending fraternal delegates from each body to the other."

Correspondence that had passed between the Congress and the Federation regarding financial affairs and relations between the two organizations was referred to the President and the Secretary of Congress, to study and bring in recommendations. These two, together with Kidd, discussed the situation and a report was presented to the Convention:

> Your Executive Committee, to whom was referred the question of our relation with the American Federation of Labour, beg to report as follows:
>
> Your committee met and invited the presence of Mr. Thomas Kidd, fraternal delegate to this meeting. After considerable discussion it was decided to recommend to this Congress that steps be taken to petition the American Federation of Labour that a sum of money be granted by said Federation yearly for the purpose of carrying out our system of seeking legislation and also for the purpose of assisting, so far as possible, the organization of workingmen in Canada. At the conference Mr. Kidd promised his assistance and support, in his report as fraternal delegate to the annual session at Kansas City, to have the aims and objects of our Congress brought prominently before that session.
>
> Your committee would also strongly recommend that this Congress elect a fraternal delegate to the coming session at Kansas City.[1]

In order to assist Kidd's case on behalf of the Congress, a platform committee of the Convention introduced a thirteen-point statement of principles and objectives, calculated to assure the Federation officers of Congress loyalty to conservative union principles. The platform was adopted, and President David Carey was elected the first fraternal delegate to the Federation. In his report to the Convention of the AFL in 1898, Kidd touched upon the problems in Canadian-American trade union relations, intruded on Canadian domestic affairs with a comment on Canada's Alien Labour Law, and closed with a statement regarding Canadian loyalty to the Federation. The following highlights from the report are of particular significance:

> It may not be inappropriate to here refer to the radical difference between the Labour Congress and the American Federation of Labour. The aims of the two organizations are practically dissimilar. The Congress does not take up grievances of the unions against each other, nor does it care about the limits of jurisdiction claimed by affiliated bodies. Its whole effort seems to be directed towards securing favourable legislation from the Federal and Provincial Governments, and organizing the workers of the Dominion wherever it can.
>
> It would be unwise to deny or ignore the fact that a feeling of antagonism obtained among many of the active workers in Canadian

labour circles toward the American Federation of Labour. Many believe that it is unfair for the international unions with which they are connected to pay a per capita tax to the Federation on their account, which they claim goes towards the support of the lobby in Washington. They say that the American Federation of Labour seems to be a purely American organization and cares nothing for labour legislation beyond the United States. That some attention should be paid to legislation in Canada they believe, and this legislation can best be secured by assisting the Congress to obtain it. The Labour Congress is essential to Canadians with a legislation distinct from, and institutions that have nothing in common with, ours. And if labour legislation is to be enacted it will have to come through the influence of a powerful Canadian Labour Federation. As nearly all of the unions affiliated with the Labour Congress are likewise affiliated with the AFL, the former thinks the Federation should aid it in trying to secure remedial legislation.

In his report to the thirteenth annual session of the Trades and Labour Congress which was held fifteen months ago at Hamilton, Ontario, President Carey, referring to an act to restrict the importation and employment of aliens passed by the Federal Parliament of Canada, and which he claimed called for more than mere mention, asserted that the law did not cover the ground, nor did it embody the aim of organized labour, although it appeared to meet with popular favour for the moment. He contended that what the working man wanted was a law with a provision that the term "alien" should apply to any person from outside Canada, the present law having no practical effect except against persons from the United States, and is thus simply as a retaiatory measure. As the law states "This act shall apply only to such foreign countries as ever enacted and retained in force, or as enact and retain in force, laws or ordinances applying to Canada of a character similar to this law." Mr. Carey contended that retaliation is not a dogmatic principle of organized labour in Canada, and the Congress favours the passage of a measure that will refer to all alike. The principle objection to the present immigration law is that it admits to the Dominion many whom the Canadians consider undesirable: and excludes many who are by no means obnoxious.

I think it eminently proper that mention should be made at this time of the loyalty of the Canadian trade unionists to their respective International Unions having headquarters on this side of the line, and the same laudable interest is taken in the growth of our movement upon American soil as well as upon their own.[2]

Convention delegates received Kidd's report, and voted a $100.00

grant—doubled to $200.00 in 1899—for the purpose of "securing legislation in the interests of labour." But the important money was in organizational work, not in legislative lobbying. In a single year, from 1888 to 1889, Federation expenditures in the United States had increased five-fold. But the Trades Congress was not going to get its hands on important funds like these.

During 1899, when organizing expenses were climbing in the United States, Gompers limited activities in Canada to the appointment of volunteer organizers, all of whom were international union officers, some of their expenses being rebated by the Federation. But it was not until 1900 that the AFL appointed its second (after Loughrin) paid organizer in Canada, and the appointment went to John Flett, who had been elected Vice-President of the Congress in 1898, and had proven his loyalty to American unionism. Flett had at his disposal all of the volunteer organizers to aid him in spreading the message of international unionism, while the Congress was still crippled for lack of sufficient funds. When calls for organizational assistance arose in the Congress, officials could not respond due to a chronic lack of finances. But Flett and his international union volunteers, with the money appropriated from Canadian dues income at their disposal, were able to arrive post haste to advance the cause of American union domination. The situation elicited bitter protest from a British Columbia unionist, who was undoubtedly voicing the sentiments of many others: "What do we find? Canadian organizers paid by the American Federation of Labour organizing members of local unions and drawing their charter from a foreign country."[3]

The rash of organizing activity under the banner of "internationalism," which this letter writer belatedly recognized as a material threat to the independence of Canadian unions, had been gathering momentum for some months, and was paying off in handsome dividends for the Federation and its international craft structure. The balance of forces was visibly moving in favour of American domination.

While increasingly dominated by the Federation, the TLC nevertheless continued to operate with at least a minimum of independence until after the turn of the century. During this period the Trades Congress and the AFL were each proceeding to issue charters to central labour bodies in the districts. Prior to 1902 the Congress did not follow the Federation policy of craft exclusiveness, and the industrial Knights of Labour, the British Amalgamateds, and distinctively Canadian locals affiliated to the Congress and to Congress-chartered centrals, were on an equal footing with the craft unions. In Gompers' correspondence with Canadian volunteer organizers and officers of international locals, there is evidence of an awareness of this "unpleasant" situation. The issue surfaced as early as 1897 in connection with the situation in Montreal, which was drawn to Gompers' attention by local craft unionists, and in which he directly intervened on the side of craft exclusiveness.

The Knights of Labour, an organization close to extinction in the United States, continued to enjoy considerable strength and influence in Quebec.[4] As a result of their strength in the area, the Knights' Assemblies were in a position to dominate the Montreal Labour Council, which had been founded in 1885. The craft unions were unhappy in their minority role and began to make plans for the establishment of a rival centre in 1897, for which purpose they petitioned the AFL to issue a charter. Gompers agreed with P.J. Ryan, a leading figure in the secession movement, that mixed assemblies of the K of L had no place in the labour movement, but his initial response was to advise the craft unionists to seek a solution in the conversion of the Council into an organization exclusive to the crafts. But in July 1897, coming to the conviction that the craft locals would not be able to seize control of the existing body, Gompers issued a charter to a rival Council. The Federation President wrote that: "It was consciousness of this fact that the old central body of Montreal was not conducted upon craft union lines that prompted me finally to issue the charter to you." The second Federation charter authorizing the establishment of a central Labour Council in Canada was issued to the Revelstoke, British Columbia Trades and Labour Council in 1899.[5] Thus the Federation President, who often accused others of disrupting the unity of the labour movement, intervened in a country not his own to create a dual movement based on craft exclusiveness and "international" domination, this in opposition to the all-inclusive policy of the Trades Congress. And this act was but the lengthening shadow of things yet to come.

Throughout 1899, the corps of volunteer organizers working under the authority of Federation credentials reported considerable success in the formation of new locals and in the increase of membership rolls. By December 1st of that year there were more than ten thousand members of American unions in Canada and, in addition to putting Flett on the union payroll soon after, the Federation increased the TLC "grant" for legislative purposes to $200.00 annually.[6]

By 1902 the AFL was collecting dues and assessments from more than 700 locals of international unions and forty-seven federal labour unions. In contrast with the petty few hundred dollars granted to the TLC for "legislative activities," more than six thousand dollars was spent on organization, with Flett having control of nearly 90 per cent of the total. Thus Canadian dues money was used to finance international union activity, at the expense of Canadian unionism and the TLC.

(In 1900 Gompers visited his labour colony in Canada, and on May 4th the Toronto *Globe* reported him saying that the trust and the company had taken the place of the individual, so the trade unions must also replace the individuals. Linking the expansion of American unions abroad with the expansion of American commerce, Gompers is reported to have declared that when the Yankee capitalist came to oppress Canadian workmen, it was only natural that the Yankee agitator should follow him. Thus Gompers was emphasizing the AFL view of the union movement as an organization designed to restrict the worst excesses of the capitalist system, not as a force for social change.)

With such marked success in the advancement of international unionism and the adoption of United States policies and structure it is not surprising that the AFL view of the Canadian Congress as a State Federation took on credibility and strength amongst the American unionists. The first open and direct reference to the TLC as being in the nature of a State Federation appeared in the November 1900 issue of the *American Federationist,* where it was contained in a report by W.D. Mahon, fraternal delegate to the Trades Congress that year. Mahon wrote that "the Congress compares more nearly to our State Federations than it does to the American Federation of Labour, as the object of the Congress is to secure legislation for the workers, and it does not deal with any trade disputes."

At the Convention of the AFL, held a month later, Gompers stressed the sameness of the two national bodies to the point of wiping out the existence of the TLC as an independent national centre. In his officer's report Gompers said that:

> The labour movement in Canada is part of our own; and we have endeavoured to encourage our fellow-workers by advice and such practical assistance as was within our power. Not only have a number of officers and representative trade unionists, including the President of the American Federation of Labour, undertaken organizing tours throughout several parts of Canada, but we have made money contributions to aid and encourage the movement there, as well as made the appointment of a permanent organizer for the Dominion, brother John A. Flett, besides the corps of voluntary organizers in the various industrial centres.[7]

There are several important points left out of this report by the Federation President: 1. The organizing work in Canada was carried out by Canadian unionists—mostly unpaid volunteers; 2. Any expenditures incurred were taken care of—more than amply so—by union dues collected in Canada; 3. The Canadian visits by American union leaders were strictly in the nature of empire building.

This 1900 Convention of the AFL was treated to a report by the fraternal delegate from the TLC that was both a distortion of Canadian reality and a remarkable example of the colonial mind at work. The delegate informed the Convention delegates that "The Canadians are a people separate and apart from those of the United States, but through the medium of the trade unions they all are now a united people . . . The memberships of the trade

unions have increased beyond every expectation during the past year, and
it is all due to the fact that the American Federation of Labour placed a
Canadian organizer in the field. I understand that the success has been of
such a character that the AFL has instructed him to go forth in the
Province of Quebec among the French people, and they appreciate what
has been done for them. It is true that there was a time when there were
some who wished to disrupt the International Union, but their efforts
resulted in their own stultification and created a stronger bond between the
workers."

The reality of the time was in contradiction with this sanguine view of
Canadian-American trade union relations, and it would not be long before
open hostility would turn AFL attention to more direct action to bring the
Canadian movement under control. There was general hostility in Canada
towards the American attitude of domination, but it was Quebec, where
Flett was ordered to "go forth," that most clearly demonstrated the
imperialist and racist aspects of the American unions in Canada.

The secret of the longevity and strength of the Knights of Labour in
Quebec—after the order had been destroyed almost every other
place—was not only its effective industrial union structure, but was
especially due to the fact that the Knights had paid particular attention to the special needs of the Quebec situation, which included the
establishment of several French language Local Assemblies. This
consideration for French-Canadian sensitivities and needs was in sharp
contrast with the openly racist attitudes displayed by Gompers and other
international union leaders.

Flett did indeed "go forth" but his efforts were largely frustrated by the
flagrant Anglo-Saxon biases of many Federation leaders, compounded by
Flett's personal inability to speak French. Aware of his shortcoming in a
difficult situation, the organizer was most anxious to secure the services of
several capable unionists in the province who were fluently bilingual, but
Gompers curtly refused to finance any such appointment, a refusal which
followed hard on the heels of his boasts of "financial aid" to his
fellow-workers in Canada.

But the Federation leader's cavalier treatment of the French presence in
Canada went beyond the casual dismissal of a Francophone appointment
for Quebec; he instructed his French-Canadian correspondents to write to
him in English. When bilingual union leader George Warren wrote
suggesting Federation endorsement of an international language,
Gompers retorted, "I find my time too fully crowded to say one half of
what I want to say in the English language."

This exchange took place in an era when Toronto newspapers were
gaining notoriety for their references to French Canadians as "inferior
people."[8] To sensitive Quebecers a union message in a foreign language
was a mark of contempt not likely to win many converts to the movement.

The result was that, outside of cosmopolitan Montreal, the AFL and the internationals failed to register any significant gains in Quebec.

Contributing to Federation difficulties in this period was the presence of the Provincial Workmen's Association (PWA) in Nova Scotia, a Liberal-sponsored proposal for the "nationalization" of Canadian unions, and the emergence of a radical industrial union movement in British Columbia and the western states at the turn of the century. These opposition elements would converge in the Conventions of 1901 to confront the AFL with its most formidable challenge in nearly two decades of activity.

6

DIVIDE TO CONQUER

A variety of complex problems began to descend upon the Federation at the turn of the century, taxing the ingenuity of the leaders that had guided the movement through the complexities of labour's supportive position in the Spanish-American War. It seemed, at times, that the centralization that had been so painfully achieved would fall apart and the movement throughout the continent split into a thousand parts.

At the instigation of the Western Federation of Miners—which had broken with the Federation over the failure of the latter to support the Leadville strike—the Western Labour Union was formed at Salt Lake City in May 1899. By 1901, the new national centre began to show signs of evolving into a continental organization that would challenge the AFL in all areas. Early in 1902, this continental status was accomplished when the organization crossed into western Canada, and changed its name to the American Labour Union (ALU).

The coal miners' union base, upon which Ralph Smith depended, seceded from the Trades Congress and Smith had to attend the Convention in 1902 as a delegate from a Vancouver local union. The deal to send Smith as a delegate was arranged by the B.C. organizer for the Congress, J.H. Watson.

As the Canadian union movement entered the twentieth century and moved toward the fateful Berlin (now Kitchener), Ontario Convention in 1902, membership was fragmented on a score of different issues. Liberal Party supporters such as Draper, Smith, and Watson were for "nationalization" of the unions; socialists cared nothing about whether the unions were Canadian or American-based, so long as they stood for social reform and general socialist goals; and then there were the dedicated supporters of "international" unions and American hegemony. The "nationalization" camp was divided between those on the one hand who, like Draper, accepted international unions but sought independence for

56

the Trades Congress, opposed policies of exclusion, and wanted the Congress to represent all elements of Canadian labour, and those on the other who demanded total independence.

The defection of many western radical unionists to the American Labour Union weakened considerably the forces favouring nationalization, and surrendered the initiative to the pro-Federation element, who were then able to prepare the ground for the amending of the Congress constitution to exclude non-craft and non-international unions, much to the satisfaction of Gompers and his colleagues. Under attack from radicals in his own western constituency and accused of being a Liberal Party labour-faker by the Phoenix, B.C Labour Council, retiring President Ralph Smith, in what he must have known to be a losing cause, stated the case for nationalization. Smith told the delegates at the Brockville Convention in 1901:

> It is of vast importance that this Congress should adopt some method of increasing its own usefulness. There ought to be a Canadian Federation, for, while I believe that unionism ought to be international in its methods to meet the necessity of combatting common foes, this usefulness is only assured by the strength of national unions. A federation of American unions represented by a national union and a federation of Canadian unions represented by a national union, each working with the other in special cases, would be a great advantage over having local unions in Canada connected with the national unions of America.

Discussion on the proposition for an independent Congress, which was linked to issues like arbitration, political action, and organizational forms, was tabled until the next Convention, scheduled to meet at Berlin in 1902. Gompers' address to the AFL Convention in 1901 reflected the fact that the officers of the Federation were still hoping for a favourable outcome in Canada. The Presidential report said that:

> Much progress is reported in the organization of our fellow-workers of the Dominion of Canada. Our fellow-unionists there are not only growing in number, but are plainly giving evidence of their intense devotion to the trade union movement, and are reaping the benefit of the results of their organization. They recognize, too, that despite geographical division our interests are one and the same, that it is the constant purpose of our International Unions and the American Federation of Labour to render them every financial and moral assistance we do to the workers of the United States, and that we are one and the same in spirit, in fact, in union, with one common quality and policy, with identical principles, hopes and aspirations.

But the complacent and optimistic tone of the Gompers report was rudely shattered by fraternal delegate P.M. Draper, who reviewed the proceedings of the recently concluded Convention of the Canada Congress, emphasizing the climate of independence that prevailed there. Addressing the AFL delegates Draper said, "I desire to state that a very strong feeling is growing in Canada arising out of the criticisms of our opponents, who say that Yankee labour leaders are responsible for many strikes in Canada." Draper then went on to quote Smith's remarks which followed the passage cited above: "I think the greater success would be accomplished in the settlement of disputes in each country if the leaders of each were the representatives of their own national grievances. I do not reflect on any American officials who have handled our labour troubles in Canada, but I am certain of this, that there are such distinctive differences in the condition of each that a presentment of Canada matters by Canadian leaders and vice versa by American leaders would lead to a greater success and would not in any way prevent a Federation of the National Bodies."

Impressed by Draper's warning of imminent trouble, and possibly acting under the delusion that loyalty could be purchased, the Convention voted to increase the legislative grant by 50 per cent, raising the amount authorized to $300.00, and the Executive Committee of the Federation was instructed to meet with opposition elements in Canada, "with a view to bringing about the unity so essential to the toilers of America." Just what was meant by "unity" was soon to be demonstrated at the forthcoming Trades Congress Convention in Berlin, Ontario.

Electoral activity by organized labour in Canada, Britain, and Australia encouraged support for the adoption of similar policies in the United States. In 1899 a Federation delegate from Cleveland moved a resolution urging a recommendation that American unionists "use their ballots, their political power on independent lines from the capitalistic parties, in harmony with the action of our brother trade unionists of Europe, Australia, Canada and other civilized communities, based on their class interests as wage-workers."

The resolution was referred to the Committee on Rules, which brought in a substitute motion recommending close adherence to the established policy of "no partisan politics." Unionism "pure and simple" was digging in its heels and refusing to advance one step forward.

A few years later, when Draper was warning Convention delegates of the threat of independence sentiment in Canada, politics was still an issue, and the problem of forms of organization also took a prominent place in Federation debates when a resolution was introduced proposing reforms that posed a serious threat to the craft union structure of the American movement.

Confronted with technological advances and mass production methods that submerged the crafts in a mass of unskilled and semi-skilled workers, some unionists recognized the critical need for forms of organization that could more effectively challenge new industrial processes. Delegates were urged to support a proposition that the Federation strike out in new directions, and a resolution was introduced calling for the amalgamation of the various trades employed in a single industry "so as to present a solid front and increase the solidarity of all workmen irrespective of trade." This constituted a demand for the replacement of craft unions with industrial type organizations. But the craft union bureaucracies feared the instability and the tendencies towards political action that invariably accompanied industrial type unionism, and they succeeded in sustaining their stand that the laws of trade unionism—apparently immutable—dictated organization on the basis of craft alone.

Industrial unionism was much more of a material threat than a defeated Convention resolution. The Western Federation of Miners had abruptly ended a one-year affiliation with the AFL and had taken the initiative in founding the Western Labour Union—soon to expand into Canada and become the American Labour Union, posing a *continental* challenge to the Federation. The new departure in the west was on industrial union lines, with strong political overtones, and constituted an open challenge to the jurisdiction of the Federation. The Convention delegates in 1901 took note of the new situation and saw it, coupled with the rising tide of nationalism in Canada, as threatening the position of the AFL in the labour movement throughout the continent. Reviewing this growing problem the Committee on the President's Report commented: "It is to be regretted that our fellow-workers, organized as the Western Federation of Miners and Western Labour Union, still hold aloof from the general movement and that there seems to be a tendency towards severance among our Canadian brothers. Movements of this character not only vitiate labour's forces but cause general confusion, friction, and sometimes bitter antagonisms—all resulting in injury to the cause and danger to our integrity."[1]

Events in the months immediately following the AFL Convention—which concluded its deliberations in December 1901—only served to confirm the worst fears of craft unionists concerning the industrial union challenge and the strength of "dual" union sentiment. The United Brotherhood of Railway Employees (UBRE), an ALU affiliate which had been founded in San Francisco in January 1901, established affiliates in British Columbia in June 1902, and expanded into Alberta in the fall. The challenge to craft unionism represented by the invasion of craft jurisdictions was later commented on by members of a Royal Commission, who reported that

The purpose of the organization was to include all classes of employees, whether members of other orders or not. For example, men were being taken into the Brotherhood from the shops at the several divisional points on the Canadian Pacific Railway, although the mechanical departments to which these men belonged had organizations which had agreements with the company; one or two train baggage men, members of the Order of Railway Trainmen, with which the company had an agreement, also joined . . . In December instructions were given . . . the organizer . . . to endeavour to organize the bridge and trackmen . . . although they belonged to a union of the maintenance-of-way men.[2]

In a letter dated December 1902—made public by the Royal Commission—the general organizer for Canada was advised to

carefully word . . . articles so as to develop a public sentiment for the UBRE—the Industrial Union plan—the ALU and against the reactionary and capitalistic party now temporarily in control of the AFL, but not against the masses of members comprising the AFL. Continually separate the administration of the AFL from the AFL itself, and give all possible praise to the masses of the AFL, but without being personal or vindictive condemn the temporary capitalistic administration of the AFL in the strongest terms you can possibly employ.

In this way you will constantly stimulate and augment a great public sentiment for the UBRE—for Industrial Unions, for the ALU and for socialism (but don't use the word) and against capitalism and Gompers' faction . . .[3]

The development of so formidable a challenge to AFL hegemony had to be met with a strong counterattack. Not only must the threat of industrial unions and socialist politics in the west be contained and ultimately destroyed, but Canada, seemingly the Achilles heel in the continental craft union movement which could provide a haven for dissidents and a base from which industrial-political unionists might launch an attack against the Federation, must be brought under control. To the AFL craft union leaders it appeared necessary for Canada to be reduced to the status of a State Federation of Labour, and they set about accomplishing this task at Berlin, Ontario in 1902, and followed up with consolidation measures during the following year.

7

THE CRUCIAL YEARS:
1902 - 1903

The emergence of an industrial and radical union movement in the west played a significant part in the outcome of the Trades Congress Convention which was called to order at Berlin, Ontario in September 1902. The defection of a number of Congress unions to the ALU reduced sharply the number of delegates that could be counted upon to vote against craft union policies. Financial considerations and travel problems had always been a serious disadvantage to western representation, and unions west of Ontario had been perpetually under-represented at Trades Congress Conventions, which had always been held in the east under the watchful eye of conservative craft unionists. Due to the many defections in British Columbia, this fateful year of 1902 was particularly notable for the shortage of western delegates. President Ralph Smith was unable to attend as a delegate from his home local, not only because the members had denounced him as a "labour-faker," but more directly because they had repudiated the Congress and joined the ALU. Referring to this particular episode, The *Canadian Annual Review* commented: "Mr. Ralph Smith, M.P., of Nanaimo, B.C. was in the chair as President of the Congress, for his fourth year, although he had found some slight difficulty in being elected a delegate. His local union refused to send him, and he had accepted the telegraphed representation of a Vancouver body. Mr. J.H. Watson, the well-known Labour official of Vancouver, told the *Province* of September 7th that the cause of the trouble was Mr. Smith's opposition to the control of Canadian Unions by American organizations."

Certainly Smith's opposition to American control constituted the main reason for his defeat in the Trades Congress. But in the west, where there was a rising tide of anti-AFL feeling amongst unionists, it was his inability to relate to militant industrial unionism and radical politics that was the immediate cause of Smith's downfall. In any event, the defection of the unions in the west had consequences far more significant than Smith's failure to receive credentials from the union of coal miners that he had traditionally represented. The absence of a large delegation of militant unionists from western Canada strengthened the hand of pro-American delegates for the important work at hand.

Simultaneous with the radical-oriented rift in the west came aggravation of the long-simmering conflict between the TLC and the AFL, the focal point being the disputed autonomy of the Trades Congress. An issue contributing to the sharpening of this conflict concerned a matter of union organization in Prince Edward Island.

The TLC chartered the first union local on the Island, with the formation of Federal Labour Union No. 10 composed of railway workers. In 1901 this Federal Local requested the assistance of a Canadian organizer to aid with the establishment of additional locals. However, because of the critical shortage of funds the Trades Congress was unable to respond to the appeal, but within a short time John Flett arrived in the area financed by the AFL and, taking advantage of the work done by the existing local union, set up several "international" unions. These "internationals" banded together to form a Trades Council, chartered by the Federation, and when the Federal Local presented its credentials and requested a seat on the Council, the AFL-chartered organization, acting on direct advice from the Federation Secretary, rejected the application "on the grounds that they did not belong to an International Union of the American Federation of Labour and, consequently, could not form part of the general labour movement."

The PEI local informed the TLC officers about the unpleasant situation prevailing in Island labour circles, and expressed the hope that the Congress Convention in 1902 would remedy the situation. Officers of the local stated, "we are strongly of the opinion that Canadian Trades and Labour Councils should be chartered by our Trades Congress."[1]

Passing comment on the general significance of the PEI developments, P.M. Draper told the Convention delegates that the time had arrived "when the powers, rights and privileges of the Congress, as the national organization for legislative purposes of the Canadian wage-earner, must be defined." It was Draper's opinion that it would be useless for Congress to spend time and energy on organizing activities until its chartering rights were established and recognized, and he believed that the TLC, as a minimum, must posess the power to charter central bodies and federal labour unions.

There are many such examples of the Federation organizer catching a free ride on the coattails of Canadian local unions and, in view of later developments, it is worth noting another example from the opposite end of the country. A Vancouver local of railway freight handlers were encountering some success in their attempt to form a national union of freight handlers. The Vancouver organization had spent much time and money on the project when they got the news that Flett was taking advantage of their pioneering effort in the field by issuing charters from the International Longshoremen's Union to railway freight handlers in Ontario and the Maritimes, thus sabotaging the attempts by the Vancouver group to establish a Canadian union on a national scale. The west coast unionists were furious, and they advanced a strong argument that Flett could not serve two masters, and should resign either the Vice-Presidency of the Congress or his post as AFL organizer for Canada. The Secretary of the Vancouver union warned the Trades Congress that there was little time left for the founding of a Canadian Federation of Labour: "If we are going to do anything for the trade union movement in Canada, we must do it at once, or else all our organizations will become American organizations, which I, for one, do not wish to see."[2]

What the Vancouver organization and all of the other defenders of Canadian autonomy appeared not to realize was the fact that, so far as the TLC was concerned, the year 1902 was already too late. They seemed to be unable to grasp the fact that control was being exercised through Canadian locals of international unions and, consequently, had taken no steps to curb Flett's exclusive use of Canadian dues money in the interest of advancing American control over Canadian unions. Throughout a stretch of about six years—nearly four of them as the paid agent of the AFL in Canada—Flett had taken full advantage of his control over organizational expenditures in forming numerous international union locals, with the result that the majority of the delegates that put in an appearance at Berlin in 1902 were representatives of American unions.

Besides Flett's busy schedule there are other solid reasons for concluding that the events at the Berlin Convention were far from spontaneous in character. "Dual unionism" as a formidable challenge to the continental supremacy of the AFL was discussed at length by Draper, Flett, and Gompers—as per instructions from the Federation's 1901 Convention—and by delegates to the Toronto Trades and Labour Council only a few months prior to the convocation of the Congress Convention in 1902.

In an interview with the Toronto *Globe* on September 17th, 1902, E.S. Jackson of the Toronto Typographical Union said that he had been "instructed" on how to vote on the issues, and two Winnipeg delegates told the *Voice* on October 3rd that the Convention had been "packed with delegates who through their respective internationals are affiliated with the AFL, and further organizing and lobbying had been going on for months" to accomplish the desired ends.

International President John Tobin of the Shoemakers' Union travelled from Boston to lead his union's twelve delegates—the largest delegation at the Convention—in the battle against Canadian unionism. Tobin's union had a material interest in the outcome of the struggle in that it faced a

serious challenge from Canadian locals, especially in Quebec. Gompers'
own union of cigar makers, with eleven delegates, was second in size to the
shoemakers, and these two together accounted for more than one-quarter
of the eighty-seven votes that split the Congress and subjected it to
American domination.

Debate on the most contentious issue confronting the delegates—
American domination versus an independent Canadian movement—began
when the Committee on Credentials presented its report. The motion to
adopt the report was challenged by an amendment calling for the exclusion
of delegates elected by the Trades Congress-chartered Montreal Central
Trades Council. The complaint, repeated from the previous year, was that
the Central Council was a "dual union" by reason of not being a body
chartered by the AFL, and, therefore, not a part of the legitimate
international union movement. President Smith ruled the amendment out
of order and, in the opinion of the *Globe* of September 16, "what promised
to be a lively debate was averted." Smith then appointed the Credentials
Committee as a special Convention Committee, charged with the task of
examining and recommending constitutional changes calculated to resolve
the differences. The Committee was instructed to report on its findings on
the following day, the General Assembly of the Convention standing
adjourned in the meantime.

The Committee appointed by Smith was heavily weighted to the
advantage of the internationals. Of the nine members on the Committee,
six were committed to the internationals; two—one from Montreal and one
from Quebec city—defended Trades Congress autonomy and an
all-inclusive labour movement; the ninth member—a bilingual French-
Canadian printer from Ottawa—tried to steer an impossible middle course
between the main contenders.[3]

When the delegates reconvened to receive the report, they were told that
the special Committee had altered the constitution "to obviate, in the
future, questionable representation calculated to injure the work which
should be fostered." But included in the recommendations were two
extremely controversial changes that stripped the officers of the Trades
Congress of the right to charter local unions in sectors of trades jurisdiction
occupied by the internationals, and specifically instructed them to channel
members of federal labour unions into the appropriate international craft
union servicing their trade. This constitutional change, which was adopted
after a full day of debate, said that the TLC

> shall form organizations in localities where none at present exist into
> local unions, but in no case shall any body of workingmen belonging
> to any trade or calling at present having an international or national
> union be granted a charter. In the event of the formation of an
> international or national union of the trade or calling of the unions so

chartered being formed, it shall be the duty of the proper officer of the
Congress to see that the said union becomes a member of said
international or national union. Provided, that no national union be
recognized, where an international union exists.[4]

This change clearly barred the Trades Congress from recognizing *any*
non-international in a trade or calling over which an international union
claimed jurisdiction. That could, and in later years in fact did, mean that
an international union with no members in Canada, and without ever
having expended any effort in organizing, could claim the result of work
done by others. The proposal sparked a bitter debate, causing the *Globe* to
report that "there was a determined fight in which many hard things were
said by delegates on both sides, especially in connection with the
unfortunate situation in the Montreal council by the existence of rival
trades councils . . . French-Canadian members led the fight for recognition
of national organization. Delegate Horan of Montreal gloomily predicted
that the changes in the constitution would 'destroy and wreck the labour
movement in Quebec.'"[5]

The other controversial change in the constitution restricted Congress to
recognition of a single central body in any city or town, suggesting that
such bodies might be chartered by the Trades Congress. The change
allowed that "the Congress shall be composed of delegates duly elected
and accredited from trades councils, trade unions, federal labour unions
and national trade unions in the Dominion of Canada. But in no case shall
there be more than one central body at any city or town, such central body
to be chartered by the Trades and Labour Congress of Canada."[6]

The limitation contained in this proposed constitutional "right to
charter" was made obvious by an accompanying instruction to Congress
officers that the Montreal dispute be settled by exclusive recognition of the
Central Council chartered by the AFL. The delegate from Quebec City
proposed an amendment that would have allowed Congress recognition of
any organization accepted for affiliation by local Trades Councils
chartered by the TLC. In effect, this amendment would have been
tantamount to conceding a form of "local option" in matters concerning
affiliation.

But the only acceptable amendment was the one proposed by P.M.
Draper, who tried to salvage some of the tattered dignity of the Trades
Congress without really changing any of the substance of the terms of
surrender. Draper suggested that since it was the object of Congress "to
unite all labour organizations of the Dominion for legislative purposes,"
therefore it should henceforth "consist of such trade unions, federal
unions, Trades and Labour Councils, and National Trade Unions, as shall
conform to its regulations." But, clearly, "conforming to its regulations"
meant obeying the dictates of the American Federation, and further debate

made abundantly clear the fact that any "rights" accruing to Congress would consist only of those agreed to by the AFL. Debate on this question focused on a resolution which summed up the relatively narrow demands of delegates who found themselves in a similar position to Draper:

> Resolved, that as the Trades and Labour Congress of Canada has placed itself squarely in accord with the principles of international trades unionism, and as such action will entail the loss of revenues from former affiliated bodies debarred from membership under the amended constitution, it is the opinion of this Congress that, being the National Legislative organization of labour in the Dominion of Canada, all Federal Labour Unions and Central Trade and Labour Councils should be under the jurisdiction and control of the Congress; and the incoming Executive is hereby instructed to take immediate steps to make such arrangements with the American Federation of Labour, looking to the consummation of this object. It is the opinion of this Congress that the existence of dual Federal Labour Unions, holding charters from the Congress and the American Federation of Labour, is not conducive to the solidarity and effectiveness of the labour movement in Canada.[7]

It was evident that the Convention had surrendered the last vestiges of independence enjoyed by the Canada Congress. With its capacity to function as an independent national centre thus effectively destroyed, Congress turned its attention to the task of petitioning the conqueror for the right to a limited existence. It seemed to be of little concern to the assembled delegates that what the AFL could give, the AFL could also take away—and that, in essence, has been the historical experience of the Canadian union movement ever since the fateful convention at Berlin, Ontario in 1902.

During the debate on the resolution some delegates suggested that only the American Federation could offer adequate protection to Canadian unionists, therefore no firm stand should be adopted pending consultations between the two national centres. The mover of the resolution, on the other hand, unmindful of the fact that Congress had already seriously compromised its independence of action, declared that Congress should insist "upon being supreme within the Dominion." In support of that argument Draper offered the comment that it was "absolutely necessary to come to some agreement with the AFL in order to prevent injurious competition between the two bodies in the matter of issuing charters," following which observation the resolution easily passed.

The resolution undoubtedly set forth the position of Congress on the charter question. But in the minds of all the delegates, including Draper and the mover of the resolution, there was a clear understanding that the final decision rested entirely in the hands of the American Federation, and there was absolutely no guarantee that the AFL would recognize the legitimacy of the claims advanced by Canada. How the problem would be resolved was now a matter for decision at the forthcoming Convention of the AFL. The Canadians might *propose*, but it was the sole right of the Americans to *dispose*.

Before confronting the AFL Convention delegates with a plea for a spirit of cooperation and understanding, Congress took one more decisive step in the direction of demonstrating its total capitulation to American domination. The final act manifesting Congress subservience came with the election of John Flett, chief runner in Canada for the American bureaucratic aristocrats of labour, to the top post of President of the Trades Congress, a position he combined with that of Federation organizer in Canada. There seems to be no record extant of the opinion held by the Vancouver organization that had suggested the impossibility of Flett's being able to serve two masters. But of course Flett was serving only one master—the American one.

In a survey of opinions and happenings after the Congress Convention, the *Globe* took note of the existence of continuing debate concerning decisions made at Berlin. The reporter commented that "the far-reaching effect of the sweeping amendments to the constitution have hardly yet been realized by the rank and file, but where it has the changes are subject matter of keen discussion."

The *Globe* survey then went on to point out that the Trades and Labour Congress had been originally formed for the specific purpose of uniting *all* Canadian labour organizations in order to exert pressure on Canadian legislative bodies for the passage of measures favourable to union labour. The paper also noted that several of the Congress affiliates had "resisted the persistent efforts which have been made in recent years to persuade them to throw in their lot with the international organizations or with the American Federation of Labour."

The *Globe* reporter correctly assessed the new policy that had been adopted as being designed to "crush out the Canadian organizations as such or force them to identify themselves with the international organization."

Uppermost in the mind of this commentator was the problem of the disastrous effects the Berlin decisions would have on such continuing problems as unity with the Nova Scotia Provincial Workmen's Association, relations with the unions of miners, railway workers, and freight handlers in British Columbia, and the case of the rival union centres in Prince Edward Island. And a major question, already in the process of emerging into prominence, concerned the relationship with French-speaking workers in Quebec—especially significant in view of the expressed racist attitudes

of AFL officials. The writer for the *Globe* justifiably concluded that:
"There unfortunately appears to be a probability, unless wiser counsels
prevail, that in Toronto and other places there will shortly be two councils.
The labour movement must necessarily be considerably injured by such
division, and friends of labour everywhere hope that this may be
avoided."[8]

Flett hastened to inform his American employer on the Berlin
proceedings and to request an early appointment to discuss the
outstanding issues which the Convention had referred for consultation.
Gompers replied with an expression of pleasure on the results, saying that
he wanted to congratulate Flett "and organized labour in Canada upon
the splendid stand taken by the recent Congress of the Trades and Labour
Unions of the Dominion. The policy declared for, and the officers elected,
demonstrate beyond question that the spirit of the labour movement is
growing toward the recognition that our interests are identical regarding
the arbitrary geographical lines."

But the request for an early meeting was curtly rejected with the excuse
that the Federation president was "too busy for the moment" to see his
Canadian agent, who also happened to be the new President of the Canada
Congress. Having already surrendered themselves to domination by the
AFL, the Canadian representatives were not in a favourable position for
bargaining on concessions. No doubt Gompers wanted to allow himself
plenty of time to reflect on future relations with the TLC, in the light of the
Berlin decisions.

The Federation Executive Council met in October 1902, with the
Canadian question high on the agenda as an item for discussion. Flett
submitted a lengthy report in which he told the Council that the "spirit of
unity" between the unions in Canada and the United States had been
strengthened by the decisions made at Berlin. Council members responded
with a resolution instructing AFL officers "to give every assistance to the
end that continental fraternity among all wage earners may be more firmly
established." The Council then ordered that an investigation should be
made into the dispute concerning the authority to issue charters in
Canada.[9]

With the Council deliberations behind him Gompers was prepared to
make a studied comment on Canadian-American trade union relations,
which he proceeded to do in the November issue of the *Federationist*:

> We realize that it is essential that organized labour shall have full
> authority in determining the questions which affect it particularly in
> the Dominion. We aid our Canadian members not only through our
> National and International Unions, but the American Federation of
> Labour makes a yearly financial contribution to aid in the legislation
> or parliamentary work.

Not only did Gompers neglect to tell his readers that the "financial contributions" he referred to represented but a partial return of money collected in Canada, he also spelled out the limitations on Canada Congress work with the declaration that the relationship was "substantially the same" as relations between the AFL and State Federations of Labour. It was within that context of State Federation relationship, and within the framework of the Executive Council discussions, that the AFL Convention met in December 1902, where Gompers proudly acclaimed the victory won at Berlin a few months before. Commenting on the Canadian situation Gompers told the assembled delegates:

> For the past few years, notwithstanding our most strenuous and continued efforts, some of our fellow-workers of Canada have endeavoured to divide the labour movement of the Dominion from the rest of our continent. I am gratified to report to you that at the last Congress of the Dominion Trades and Labour Union of Canada . . . a clear-cut declaration was made and inserted in the constitution of the organization in favour of the closest bonds of unity and fraternity with us. The future is, therefore, assured that no schism or geographical lines of demarcation will enter into the labour movement of the United States and Canada.

With studied disregard for the actual situation in Canada, the fraternal delegate from the Trades Congress danced to the tune played by Gompers. Ignoring the deep divisions and antagonisms introduced into the Canadian movement, the Congress representative hailed the Berlin decisions as the bright herald of unity. Pledging the allegiance of the Federation's Canadian subjects he easily took up the role of mendicant, emphasized with an appropriate reference to Oliver Twist. In his address, a virtual beggar's song, the fraternal delegate declared:

> I am pleased to abe able to say to this Federation that in the aggregate the utmost unity prevails in our organizations in their relations to the international heads. The assurance of the utility and value of the broader international connection in comparison to the local organization has long since dispelled all speculation and doubt on this question; but while this is true, there is a strong feeling of the legislative value of our Dominion Trades Congress. That its value has also been recognized for your body is evidenced by your repeated financial assistance. I trust you will not doubt our gratitude and appreciation if we, like Oliver, "ask for more." Rather would we have you regard it as a weaker brother appealing to the stronger.
>
> We trust you will not lag in your interest towards us. We would have you still continue in maintaining and keeping in the Canadian

field organizer John A. Flett, a gentleman eminently fitted for the work.

Acting on the earlier suggestion advanced by Gompers the delegates appointed an eleven-man Committee to examine and report on the question of jurisdiction in the issuing of charters in Canada. The Committee submitted a report which said:

> We concur in the report of the President of the American Federation of Labour regarding the movement in Canada, and recognize the wonderful progress in organization and labour legislation. We also congratulate the Dominion Trades and Labour Congress in their clear-cut declaration along the lines of international organization, and hope that no geographical lines may ever separate the close fraternal feelings that now exist in the North American continent. We recommend that the American Federation of Labour continue to maintain the services of a general organizer and to secure as many volunteer organizers as may be determined by the President of the American Federation of Labour.

Despite the flowery phrases about brotherly love and fraternal solidarity, the Committee members were not about to trust the unpredictable Canadians with authority to issue charters in their own country. Consequently, the Committee reported it as the unanimous opinion of the members

> that the granting of charters by the Labour Congress of Canada to federal labour unions would have a tendency to divide the labour movement of the United States and Canada, and possibly retard the formation of national or international organization. Realizing the per capita derived from the federal labour unions of Canada, we still believe that the present form of organizing and legislating of the American Federation of Labour reimburses the Canadian Labour Congress, and, with these facts in view, we recommend that the American Federation of Labour appropriate the sum of $500 to the Canadian Labour Congress for legislative purposes.

There is evidence here of a fear that, given an alternative source of funds, the TLC might be tempted to follow an independent course of action better designed to fill particular Canadian needs. The Federation was to maintain control of the purse and dole out funds as they thought fit. The recommendation gave the delegates an opportunity to voice their opinions on the matter, and these were duly taken note of by the Federation officers and the Canadians present at the Convention. This accomplished, and in order to soften the blow for the TLC officers who stood instructed to negotiate the right to issue charters, the question was referred to the Federation's Executive Council for final decision.

In April of 1903, the Executive Council met with their own employee President Flett and with Secretary Draper of the TLC at Toronto to discuss the Congress resolution regarding the issuing of charters, and to settle other outstanding issues in relations between the two bodies. The results of this meeting were reported in the *American Federationist* for June 1903:

President Flett and Secretary Draper of the Trades and Labour Congress of Canada appeared before the E.C. in the interests of the Canadian Labour Congress.

President Flett and Secretary Draper said they were willing to concede the issuance of charters of federal labour unions to the AFL, as they realized that the AFL, on account of the defence fund, was in a better position to support their members in case of strike or lockout, and held that inasmuch as central labour unions were legislative bodies, they should be affiliated to the Congress; and that the AFL should require central bodies to be affiliated with the Congress as one of the conditions requisite to their receiving charters from the AFL.

They both urged the waiving of the fifty cents dues required by the constitution of the AFL from trade and federal labour unions if they desire to receive assistance from the defence fund. They held that it was almost impossible to have the members pay fifty cents dues, and urged the E.C. to recommend to the next Convention that the provision in regard to the dues be eliminated from the constitution.

In the matter of the resolution adopted by the Trades and Labour Congress in Canada, held at Berlin, to submit to the AFL the advisability of the Congress chartering central Trades and Labour Councils of Canada for distinctly legislative purposes, and also for the chartering of federal labour unions, a conference was held with the President and Secretary of the Congress and the request for the chartering of federal labour unions was withdrawn. The E.C. therefore declared as follows:

1. That the AFL will make it a qualification of issuing charters to Trades and Labour Councils in Canada, that they will affiliate with the Trades and Labour Congress, and central bodies throughout the Dominion now holding AFL charters will be instructed to take similar action.

2. That trade affairs in the central Trades and Labour Council in question shall be transacted as heretofore along the lines of international trade unionism.

3. That all local unions in the Dominion of Canada affiliated through international unions or holding charters direct from the AFL

be notified to become affiliated with the Trades and Labour Congress of Canada for the purpose of making it a more potent factor to secure the adoption of favourable legislation for the members by the Federal and Provincial Parliaments.

Despite the appearance of sweetness and light in the contents of the report published by the Executive Council, there exists solid evidence to the contrary. A Toronto *Globe* report in the issue of April 24, 1903 establishes the fact that Secretary Draper did not hesitate to differ with Gompers before a mass audience. The occasion was a public meeting where Draper, in the presence of the Federation President, re-affirmed Canadian support for international unionism, but insisted that Canadian members should be allotted "proper representation" on the Executive Committees of international unions, which would have meant granting the Canadians "special status," not in accord with State Federation standing harped upon by Gompers. Draper also demanded for Canadian unions the right to "absolute and complete liberty of action in the conduct of their own affairs." He noted the desirability of Congress possessing the authority to issue charters to federal labour unions, central bodies, and dissident elements in Canada which the internationals could not or would not deal with. In contrast to Gompers' repeated descriptions of the Canadian Congress as similar in status to a State Federation, Draper argued that the TLC was equal to the AFL.

Further evidence of the internal dispute, which lasted for several days with Flett supporting his paymasters and Draper being gradually whipped into line, is found in the correspondence of AFL Secretary Morrison for June 1907. Reviewing the events of 1903, Morrison wrote:

> When the Executive Council of the Federation met at Toronto, a discussion was brought about through an objection lodged by myself against the [Congress] officers issuing charters to Federal Labour Unions and Trade Unions. This controversy arose through a Federal Labour Union in Prince Edward Island, which, upon investigation, proved to be nothing more or less than a political organization, and which was refused representation. I contended that the Canadian Trades and Labour Congress stands in the same relation to the American Federation as do the states of Illinois, Ohio, and New York, etc., and had no right to issue charters, the issuance of charters being the special province of the American Federation of Labour and International Unions. Secretary-Treasurer Draper persisted in his determination to issue charters to Federal Labour Unions and City Centrals without their first being chartered by the AFL. I called his attention to the fact that the Congress was not in a financial condition to protect the members of the local Trade and Federal Labour Unions in the case of strike and lockout, that the AFL had a substantial

defense fund and was able to furnish financial protection. The contention on my part appealed in particular to President Flett, of the Canadian Trades and Labour Congress, and, after a great deal of discussion, President Flett and Secretary Draper conceded.

In effect, Morrison was underscoring an old adage: "He who pays the piper calls the tune," and it made not the slightest difference that the piper in this case was being paid out of union dues collected in Canada. Instead of resisting the American invasion, the Trades Congress had capitulated on all important points in dispute, and had gradually surrendered its freedom of action to the Federation.

United States domination of Canadian labour should have been fought at its foundations—the international unions. But this crucial point the Canadian unionists seemed not to comprehend.

Agreement by the Executive Council to recommend that all trades unions and central councils in Canada be instructed to affiliate to the Trades Congress may have appeared in the form of a concession, but it had no meaning within the context of Congress freedom of action. If the AFL and the internationals could successfully order their Canadian affiliates to pay tribute to the TLC, it is obvious that they would be just as successful in ordering them to cease, and that has been a constant material threat hanging over the Canadian union movement. The initiative is clearly in control of the Federation. Officers of the Trades Congress might employ inducements such as the advantages of united labour action on the legislative front, but they possessed no powers of enforcement such as were available to the AFL. In essence, Congress had surrendered control over the structure and organization of Canadian unions and had been reduced to little more than an official and subsidized lobby, responsible for the defense of the interests of international unionism in the Canadian political system.

The Executive Council submitted a report to the AFL Convention in 1903, accompanied with a comment by Gompers on the Toronto Meeting:

> During the session of the Executive Council held at Toronto, Canada, and having in mind the conclusion reached by the New Orleans Convention regarding the relations of the Canadian labour movement to that of the remainder of the American continent, we had two conferences with the officers of the Dominion Trades and Labour Congress for the furtherance of the best interests of the working people of both countries. It was decided that all Canadian local central labour bodies affiliated to the American Federation of Labour should be attached to the Congress, and that a prerequisite to the issuance of a charter to any central body in Canada be its attachment to the Dominion Congress.

The general provisions of the Toronto agreement were endorsed by the Convention delegates, but the funds available to the Congress were kept within strict limits through a decision that Canadian locals must pay the fifty cent assessment as a condition of receiving assistance from the defense fund. Thus a concession crucial to the operation of the Trades Congress was denied by the Federation Convention. It is evident that there would be no guarantee that international union locals or AFL-chartered federal labour unions in Canada would agree to accept the burden of paying the extra dues required to join the Congress. Nevertheless, Canadian members of these organizations were required to continue the payment of a per capita tax to the AFL through their international affiliation.

The Convention at Berlin, which ended on a note favourable to the masterminds of the AFL, represented no signal of final and conclusive victory for international unionism in Canada. The constitutional changes endorsed at Berlin, and the agreements made subsequent to that historic affair, guaranteed that the Trades Congress would not harbour enemies of the Federation and international unions. But it was beyond the capacity of those who engineered these events to conjure all such enemies out of existence, or to ensure that the internationals would remain forever free from challenge. In fact, the last rap of the gavel had not yet rung out over the Convention before it became evident that challenges to United States domination would be a permanent feature of the union movement in Canada. As evidence of this we have a report in the *Canadian Annual Review* for 1902.

> On September 18th, the day before the Congress adjourned a new and rival organization was formed at Berlin, Ont.—partly as a consequence of the exclusion of the Knights of Labour and other independent organizations numbering some 10,000 men from the Congress, and partly because of the attitude of the American Federation of Labour in maintaining a superior rather than a parallel jurisdiction in its relations with the Dominion organizations. The new body called itself the National Trades and Labour Congress of Canada, declared itself purely Canadian in character and policy and elected Mr. Omer Brunet, of Quebec City, as President, together with various other officers.

That the AFL Convention delegates were alive to the threat of an independent Canadian movement is apparent from a resolution calling for counter-action that was passed by the delegates. The resolution, which ignored the divisive activities of the internationals and put the newly-established national centre down as a plot by employers, read as follows:

Whereas, there is a movement in Canada by the Employers' and Manufacturers' Association to foster and aid an organization known as the "National Trades and Labour Congress," which was organized in Berlin, Ontario, in September 1902, as a protest to an amendment to the constitution of the Trades and Labour Congress of Canada, excluding dual organizations, known as Independent Canadian Unions and local assemblies of the Knights of Labour, which were organized in opposition to the legitimate international trade union movement and are at the present time operating a policy diametrically opposed to the principle of trade autonomy, by issuing charters to all tradesmen in Canada, as well as placing upon the market a label consisting of a maple leaf surrounded with the following words: "Canada for Canadians" as a substitute for the union label of the various trades, thereby seeking to disrupt and destroy the international labour movement in Canada, and having in mind the Trades and Labour Congress of Canada has placed itself squarely on record in favour of the operation of the trade union movement along international lines and with a view of strengthening the Congress, as their legislative mouthpiece of the legitimate international wage workers of Canada before the Dominion and Provincial governments of Canada, thereby making it a more powerful factor for legislative purposes in the interests of the wage earners of that country; it is resolved, that the Executive Council of the American Federation of Labour take the necessary steps after the adjournment of this convention to have all international unions affiliated with the American Federation of Labour insist upon their local unions in Canada affiliating with the Trades and Labour Congress in Canada with the least possible delay.[10]

Considering the fact that the American unionists had manifested a blatantly nationalistic attitude in support of United States aims in the Spanish-American War, and seeing that it was the founders of the American Federation of Labour who took the lead in institutionalizing class collaboration as the basis of employer-employee relations, the criticism of the Canadian unionists verged on the obscene. No one wants to claim for the Canadians the role of saints in confrontation with American evil. Canadian workers suffered from all of the disabilities that afflicted their American counterparts. But they were correct in demanding an end to United States interference in their internal affairs, the right to make their own decisions—whether those decisions were right or wrong. Far from being outrageously nationalistic and employer-oriented in their attitudes, the NTLC adopted a generally correct stand on the controversial question of Canadian-American union relations, as evidenced at the organization's Quebec City Convention in September 1903, when President Omer Brunet told the assembled delegates:

> For a long time past, the necessity of a national union has been felt, and in order to prove it we have only to quote here the words of an eminent man who possesses, we may say, a true insight into the future and who is an ardent as well as enlightened patriot, Mr. Ralph Smith. In his address to the delegates of the Congress of Canada during its session of 1899, he expressed himself as follows: "The necessity for a national union, even for an international one, is urgent."
>
> Well, is not your presence here in the opening of the first session of the National Congress of Trades and Labour of Canada, the realization of that great idea expressed by the eminent and distinguished compatriot?
>
> It should be well understood, that in refusing to accept the flag of the American Federation, we had no desire to issue an ultimatum or to make a declaration of war. What we did desire, and what we still desire, was to affirm our national autonomy, not to change our allegiance, though keeping for our brother workmen on the other side of the line all the sympathies they deserve, and according to them on this side all the advantages which we consider as prejudicial to the interests of Canada.
>
> Do not forget it, many before us have said and repeated it: It is only by a reform of our laws, and in no other way, that we will be able to improve our conditions. And in order to obtain that end, we cannot do better than unite ourselves closely under the protection of the national flag of which the motto is and must remain "Canada for Canadians."[11]

A critical feature of the Berlin Convention decisions is found in the racist consequences flowing from them. Seventeen of the twenty-three unions expelled under the provisions of the constitution as amended were mainly French-Canadian in membership and language. In Montreal, the Central Trades and Labour Council, five assemblies of the Knights of Labour, four locals of a Canadian union of shoemakers, a barbers' local and a union of coopers—twelve organizations in all—were expelled from the Congress in order to satisfy American demands for the outlawing of "dual unionism." Five Quebec City locals suffered a similar fate to that of Montreal, while American Federation officials turned a deaf ear to pleas for appointment of a French-speaking organizer. The Americans insisted that an organizer who spoke only English could perform adequately in Canadian union circles.

The negative attitude towards appointment of a French-speaking representative was predicated on the assumption that the workers of

Quebec, sooner or later, would have to accomodate themselves to the English-speaking majority in America. Flett, who also timidly suggested a need for an organizer who spoke French, did not press the issue to the point of endangering his own employment, nor did he attempt to learn French so he could communicate. The movement in Quebec went into decline—especially outside the city of Montreal, and by 1908 TLC delegates had to be told that the movement was dead in Quebec City. Shortly thereafter, and as a direct result of the TLC failure, Confessional Unions were established in Quebec. The predictable response to that development was a taunting of the French-Canadian worker with being "priest ridden," as well as employer-dominated.

In the Maritimes, where the Provincial Workmen's Association dominated the labour scene, the AFL made very little headway until the United Mine Workers, assisted by Flett, launched a heavily-financed raid aimed at the destruction of the PWA. This raid was not unrelated to the fact that the Maritimers were cooperating with the British owners of the mines in efforts to protect the Pennsylvania-supplied Ontario-Quebec market for Canadian coal.

The traditionally radical west also held enormous problems for the AFL-TLC combination, and the years immediately following the Berlin Convention—particularly the year 1903—produced events on the labour front that were to clearly establish employer-government preferences for the type of "responsible" unionsim represented by the American Federation and its officers.

8

WESTERN RADICALISM
PRECIPITATES A CHALLENGE

The strength of the American union establishment was located in the region of central Canada, chiefly in southern Ontario and the Montreal district, which together comprised the main centres of concentration of United States branch plant industry. Of eighty-two American branch plants established between 1880 and 1887, fifty were located in Ontario alone, twenty five in Quebec, and just one in all of Canada west of Ontario.[1]

Nova Scotia, where British capital was long dominant, featured the distinctively Canadian Provincial Workmen's Association, which could not fail to take note of competition eminating from the Pennsylvania coal and steel districts, especially during periods of economic crisis.

Quebec, outside of cosmopolitan and Anglo-dominated Montreal, was a particularly difficult area of resistance to the intrusion of American unions. Language, culture, religion, constituted almost insuperable obstacles to the realization of American union domination, which was fortified by openly expressed racist attitudes on the part of United States labour spokesmen.

Western Canada occupied a distinctive place in the Canadian-American union mosaic, different from both Nova Scotia and Quebec in its resistance to craft union conservatism. Until the closing years of the war, which saw the emergence of the One Big Union, western unionists did not adopt independent Canadian organizations as their chosen weapons to combat the American Federation.

The main considerations in the minds of western unionists consisted of a conviction of the crucial importance of independent labour and radical political action, and ideas on the forms of economic organization appropriate to their needs—industrial unionism as opposed to craft unions. Even conservative union members in the west supported the idea of one or another sort of political action, an outlook which was in conflict with the "no partisan politics" policy of the AFL. Since they could find a satisfactory expression for their opposition in American-based radical unions, the unionists in the west experienced no irresistable urge to form independent Canadian labour organizations and, accordingly, joined such movements as the ALU and the IWW.

In his outline of the western situation at the September 1903 Convention of the TLC, P.M. Draper told the delegates that the Western Federation of Miners, the ALU, and the UBRE were dedicated to "international, semi-political, industrial socialism," and were actively opposing the Trades Congress and the AFL in British Columbia. The two chief representatives of Congress policies in B.C., J.H. Watson and George Bartley, put a large share of the burden of responsibility on the failure of the Federation to respond to appeals for a full-time organizer to work in the area.

The ALU had placed organizers in the field and they were experiencing a large degree of success during 1903. A crisis in relations was precipitated when the ALU locals in Victoria, B.C. applied to the Trades Council for the admission of delegates representing their organizations. Citing the Berlin amendments, craft union delegates challenged the eligibility of the ALU locals and the authority of the Council to admit them.[2] The Council Secretary wrote to Draper for advice on the issue, and in an incredible demonstration of colonial mentality and dependence on the American Federation, Draper forwarded the letter to Gompers with a request for instructions on how to answer it.

Gompers drafted a reply, leaving a space for Draper's signature, before passing it along to the Victoria Council. The letter declared that the applicant for affiliation—an ALU local of lumber workers—was not eligible for a seat because it had failed to join the craft union that held jurisdiction in the industry. ALU activities in the area were stigmatized as "inconsistent, unfair, and unfraternal, and should be discountenanced and discouraged, rather than accorded representation. If these woodworkers are earnest thorough-going trade unionists, they will attach themselves to their international union, and be in full accord with the spirit and purposes of the labour movement of the continent of America."[3]

Obviously the issue was not one of Canadian unions versus American unions in this case. The fundamental transgression committed by the British Columbians lay in their challenge to the monopoly claimed by the AFL in continental labour matters.

This period of bitter altercation was also marked by the withdrawal of the Vancouver Trades Council from the Congress in April 1903. The AFL representative, J.H. Watson, who sat on the Council, had come under attack for a public statement that "every socialist must be thrown out of our trades unions if we mean to uphold their integrity." Council members who had unsuccessfully demanded Watson's removal from office then declared their support for industrial unionism and voted to withdraw from the Trades Congress.

Strikes in British Columbia in the early months of 1903, and in Montreal in April, sparked a torrent of criticism which was mainly directed at international unionism. The meeting of the Federation's Executive Council in April (previously referred to) was constrained to take note of the public and official reaction to these strikes, and to plan some response to it. The B.C. strike movement in particular—which was organized and led by the ALU rivals of the Federation—was an especially critical event in the view of the Federation officers. This particular strike wave was the subject for investigation by a Royal Commission appointed by the Liberal Government of Wiflrid Laurier, the Report of which supplied material in abundance for anti-union propaganda.

Gompers and his colleagues tried to gain advantage from the attacks by asserting that they were aimed at the AFL, thus using the situation as the basis of appeals for public sympathy and support. Certainly there were those in employer and government circles who sought to seize the opportunity to restrict all union activity. But the main focus of the attack was the radical and political industrial unionism in the west, and, in the final analysis, events proved that the employers and their political representatives, far from wanting to outlaw *all* international unions, were quite ready to do business with the "responsible" leaders of the American Federation.

The attack on the union movement, which won the attention of the lawmakers in the Senate, was precipitated by the Report of the Royal Commission. The Report (written by Mackenzie King) focused on the ALU-led strikes in B.C., with the Montreal strike movement as a secondary factor. But the specific *type* of union under attack from the Commission constituted a significant feature of the Report. This aspect of the submission could scarcely fail to attract the attention of Gompers, and was probably the reason for his confident attitude during this critical period in Canadian-American union relations. Having made some comments on the AFL-type of craft union, which could not be construed as unfavourable to those conservative organizations, the Commissioners went on to describe the western radical unions in the most hostile terms possible:

> There is, however, a class of so-called union developing rapidly in western America, which is really not a trade union at all, but a secret political organization whose members are bound by an oath so strong as to be considered a shield against giving any but forced testimony before the Commission. The primary object and common end of this class of organization is to seize the political power of the state for the purpose of confiscating all franchises and natural resources without compensation, and to this class belong the American Labour Union,

the Western Federation of Miners, and the United Brotherhood of
Railway Employees. . . . their leaders were engaged in a conspiracy to
sweep all the employees of the Canadian Pacific Railway into the
United Brotherhood, and all the coal miners into the Western
Federation.[4]

The Commissioners claimed that all of the organizations named by them
had "declared for socialism," and as evidence of this and of the alleged
despicable character of such associations, the Report cited a resolution
endorsed by a Convention of the WFM, held at Denver, British Columbia,
which read as follows:

Whereas, the natural resources of the earth upon which humanity
depends are being swiftly concentrated into the hands of the
privileged few; and
Whereas, political independence is a bauble and a delusion while the
toiling millions bear the yoke of wage slavery in the industrial field;
and
Whereas, no man among the vast army of labouring humanity can
successfully assert his manhood while his necessities make him a
suppliant at the feet of another for a job which he must have to sustain
life; and
Whereas, the privileged few who own the jobs which the many must
have must necessarily own the man; and
Whereas, capitalism can never be dethroned and wage slavery
abolished until the natural resources of the earth and the machinery of
production and distribution shall be taken from the hands of the few
by the political power of the many, to become the collective property
of all mankind, to be utilized for the use and benefit of all humanity;
and
Whereas, the Socialist Party is the only political party in any nation
of the world that demands that the land and the machinery of
production and distribution shall become the common property of all,
and that labour shall receive the full product of its toil;
Now, therefore be it resolved, that the delegates of the Western
Federation of Miners in their eleventh annual Convention assembled,
reaffirm the political policy of the tenth annual Convention, believing
that the principles enunciated by the Socialist Party will make man
the "noblest work of God," women the queen of the home, and the
child the bud and blossom of an emancipated generation.[5]

Addressing themselves to the specific objects of their vituperation and
condemnation, the Commissioners went on to propose that:

With regard to these organizations we think they ought to be specially declared to be illegal, as their leaders . . . at all times preach the doctrine of confiscation of property without compensation, and that society is divided into two classes, the toilers and the spoilers . . .

There is an additional reason in the case of the United Brotherhood of Railway Employees, which is that it is the aim of this body to force all classes of railway employees, from the highest to the lowest, together into one organization, in opposition to the wishes of virtually all of the existing railway unions.

In a passage which openly endorses AFL-type international craft unionism the Commissioners, in reference to the railwaymen, take particular note of the fact that:

They have their own class organizations with contract on their behalf with the company, and with which they are satisfied, as, on the one hand their grievances are passed on by a Committee of their own number who fully understand them, and, on the other hand, they deal directly with those officials of the railway who are in control of the Department to which they belong. It is obvious that a Committee of car labourers or freight handlers could not deal as intelligently with a trouble arising among the conductors or engineers as the latter can themselves; in fact the latter (who are, according to one of the sympathetic strikers, the aristocrats of unionism) would not submit to have their movements dictated by the former. To allow an organization like the United Brotherhood of Railway Employees to gain any foothold among the employees of a great railway system like the Canadian Pacific Railway, would be to introduce the bitterest dissensions among them, and at the same time make it impossible to carry on the proper management and discipline of the railway, which is just as necessary as in a ship at sea. The best evidence that the United Brotherhood of Railway Employees is not wanted by railway employees as a whole, is that the engineers, conductors, firemen, trainmen, etc., of the Canadian Pacific Railway, although appealed to, refused to come out in aid of, or to render financial assistance to, that organization . . . it is not a trade union at all, but in reality a one-man despotism.

It is most unlikely that Gompers himself could have argued a stronger case than this for craft unionism before a body of employers, and the bitter condemnation of politically-oriented industrial unionism would certainly have been approved of by the Federation President. In brief, while their methods might necessarily differ, the Commissioners and the AFL desired essentially the same thing; the total destruction of the industrial union movement and the preservation of the conservative crafts.

With a view to strengthening their case against the western radical union movement, the Commissioners cited some examples of what they referred to as "incendiary and scurrilous literature," several of which follow here: "Organized labour has been fighting on the industrial field to maintain a wage compensation that enables the human family to obtain some of the necessaries of life, but organized labour is arousing from the hypnotic spell of fake leaders, and moving towards the political battlefield where capitalism will be assassinated for once and forever."

And further on, this example: "The courts are recognized today by organized labour as partial to capital. Nearly every labour law that passes a legislative body is declared unconstitutional. What justice can be expected from tribunals which, upon the slightest pretext, grant injunctions to corporations which shackle the power of organized labour in its struggle for justice?" And a final example of "scurrility": "The minister of the gospel who is not in sympathy with organized labour should be placed on the 'scab' list."

Having thus unburdened themselves of their strongly biased attack on militant industrial unionism, the Commissioners proceeded to reveal both their intentions and where their sympathies lay in the field of union organization. In their recommendations to Parliament the Commissioners said, "We think, then, that legitimate trade unionism ought to be encouraged and protected, and that organizations of the class just dealt with ought to be prohibited and declared illegal, and that there ought to be strict enforcement of the law relating to the administration of voluntary oaths."

The "alarming" rise of militant unionism in the west, the threat of a spread eastward, the extremely biased Report submitted to Parliament by the Royal Commission, and AFL opposition to all forms of industrial unionism, formed the basis for a common outlook among the foes of industrial unions, despite differences over methods employed.

One of the first to respond to the raising of the alarm was the Nanaimo "labour" M.P. and former President of the Trades Congress, Ralph Smith, who wrote a letter to Laurier warning the Prime Minister that society was on the verge of breaking up into two hostile camps "just as Marx had predicted."[6] Responding in a manner less rhetorical and more direct, a conservative Senator and leader of the Calgary bar, James Lougheed, proposed an amendment to the Criminal Code of 1892, which would allow for the arrest and imprisonment of anyone who "not being a British subject and not having been continuously domiciled and resident in Canada during one year before the commission of the act complained of, does in Canada counsel, incite, urge, or induce any strike or lockout, or a rise or fall in wages, or the imposition of additional or differential conditions or terms of employment or impairing the exercise of industry, employment or labour.''[7]

Naturally there were in Canada, as elsewhere, employers who would welcome the destruction of the trade union movement. The fear of western radicalism and the public clamour over international unionism gave such employers the opportunity to attack, and they were quick to seize advantage of the opportunity that seemed to be tailor-made for them.

Gompers was alert to the dangers inherent in the situation and took steps to combat them. On his return to the United States, he kept abreast of the situation in Canada through detailed reports prepared by Flett and Draper. The Federation President directed the campaign against the bill from his American office, ordering Flett to remain in Ottawa to lead the fight, and issuing instructions that a circular be distributed to all locals in Canada urging members to adopt resolutions, write letters, and forward protests to Members of Parliament.

The American Federation offered to underwrite the cost of a brochure which would consist of articles supporting international unions and attacking the Lougheed bill. To avoid being accused of meddling, it was suggested that the booklets should be printed in Canada under the seal of the Trades Congress.[8]

But in spite of the apparent atmosphere of crisis, Gompers gloried in the limelight and, from the start, seemed to be quite confident that the bill would suffer defeat—at least so far as it concerned the AFL. The American unionists no doubt knew that the employers would prefer to do business with the reliable conservative craft unions than to take an uncertain chance on the probable alternative.

Confidence oozed from Gompers as he made a regal tour through central Canada following adjournment of the meeting of the Executive Council that had plugged the gaps in the Berlin decisions. In Ottawa the President conferred with labour spokesmen, including two Members of Parliament, Puttee of Winnipeg and Smith of Nanaimo, who most likely told Gompers about the letter to Laurier. In the evening the AFL spokesman addressed a meeting attended by Conservatives Borden and Mulock, and Senator Templeman, a presence which could scarcely be construed as disapproval for "responsible" international unionism.

The Ottawa meeting received only perfunctory attention from the press, the headlines of the day being given over to a strike of longshoremen in Montreal and an accompanying threat by carpenters to call a general strike in the same city. Thirteen hundred troops occupied the Montreal docks and the President of the Board of Trade linked the strike to the international unions, declaring that, "The outcome of the present dock struggle will mean either the freedom of the port of Montreal or its manipulation to the detriment of Canada from Washington.''[9]

Gompers, in seeming disregard for the storm breaking around his head, left Ottawa for Montreal, arriving on the eve of May Day. As he moved through the crowd in his carriage, the Federation President bowed to the left and right in acknowledgement of cheers, "just like the Prince of Wales," according to one admirer.[10]

Gompers addressed an outdoor meeting, triumphantly announcing settlement of the carpenters' dispute "to the satisfaction of the union," and, in a move calculated to enhance his image as a "responsible" union leader, he warned the striking longshoremen: "If you value your honour, your liberty and your future, keep the peace. Do not allow your enemies to provoke you to breaches of the law."[11]

According to the Toronto *Globe* it was the largest demonstration ever in Montreal, with Gompers being given ample opportunity to denounce the oppressive provisions of the Lougheed bill. But the Montreal *Herald* of May 1st, claimed that a large part of the mainly French-speaking audience drifted away early, which the reporter attributed to a blunder committed by Gompers, who boasted of being born a Londoner, but in possession of the sanctifying virtue of American citizenship.

On June 4, public hearings were held on the legislative merits of the Senate bill. The Trades Congress lawyer appeared, accompanied by Flett, Draper, and several other union representatives. Basing his approach on the long-established policies of the AFL, the lawyer asserted the identity of interests between capital and labour. He conceded that there were those who taught a different philosophy, some of whom undoubtedly made their way into the ranks of the labour movement. But so far as the radical unionists were concerned, he concluded that "we declare that they are a menace to the society in which we live."[12]

The Royal Commission Report made its appearance in print soon after the Senate hearings had concluded. British Columbia workers were under severe strain at the time, and one of the founding members of the ALU, the Western Federation of Miners, was engaged in bitter struggle in the "Colorado Labour War." These embattled workers on the west coast needed all the aid they could muster. But all they got from Gompers and the AFL was opposition and condemnation. The Federation, the employers, and the Government shared a common aim—the destruction of the radical union movement.

Gompers quickly came into possession of a copy of the Report and, far from expressing any sympathy for the striking workers in British Columbia, he set about the task of drawing a clear line of distinction between the "responsible" Federation and the "irresponsible" radical unionists and socialists. Gompers protested that it would be the grossest sort of injustice for the Canadian Parliament to include the AFL in the same category with "the irresponsibles and those who want to tear down." He charged—most illogically—that the UBRE was backed by corporations intent on blackening the name of organized labour, and declared, "It must cause a feeling of indignation and outraged injustice to think that despite the straight-forward course the honest, legitimate trade unions of the American Continent have pursued, and which is acknowledged in the Royal Commission Report, that we should be classified and come under the category of such concerns which the Commission has exposed to the contumely of the civilized world.''[13]

At the Convention of the Trades Congress, Flett gave prominent place to outrageous expressions of hostility toward the radical unions, and soon after, at the Convention of the AFL, Gompers revealed that while in Canada he had conversed with Mackenzie King, the Deputy Minister of Labour and author of the Commission Report. During the conversation with the Deputy Minister, Gompers had been assured that the Commissioners entertained no feelings of animosity for the Federation. In his report to the Federation Convention in 1903, Gompers commented on the situation in Canada:

> The Dominion Government some months ago appointed a Commission to investigate a number of strikes that had occurred in the far west. From the Commission's investigation and Report, reflection is made upon some, but we can proudly declare that not one scintilla or shadow could be thrown reflecting upon the honour, integrity, and faithfulness of any organization affiliated to the American Federation of Labour or upon any of its men. Recently I had an interesting conversation with the Hon. Mackenzie King, Chief of the Bureau of Labour for Canada, a member of the Commission, and he substantially repeated this to me.
>
> We have the right, then, to insist that the bona fide labour movement and its men shall not be ostracized or outlawed, particularly when it is the aim and work of the American-Canadian trade unionists of Canada and the remainder of the American continent to make for the well being, the good citizenship, loyalty, and the fraternity of all.

In the King-Gompers conversation which was referred to in the President's report, the Deputy Minister no doubt had in mind the favourable references to craft unions contained in the report. A number of the crafts had refused to lend any aid to the strikers, and this attitude received high praise from the Commissioners.

Commenting on the ''attitude of the Railroad Brotherhoods toward the UBRE,'' the Report of the Commission says: ''The attitude of the several existing railway organizations towards the Brotherhood in its conflict with the Canadian Pacific Railway is important as illustrating the difference between methods pursued by legitimate and responsible unions . . . and the purposes and methods of working pursued by an organization like the UBRE. Although urgent appeals were made by the Brotherhood to all of the several railway organizations . . . for their cooperation and assistance, it does not appear that the United Brotherhood received a single cent from the local lodges or members of any of these organizations. In fact there is direct evidence to show that as an organization it was discountenanced from the outset by the several existing orders of railway employees."

The blacksmiths at Revelstoke, B.C. at first struck in sympathy with the UBRE, but intervention from American headquarters of the blacksmiths' union forced the men back to work. The Commissioners were most favourably disposed towards this kind of "international" intervention about which they had this to say:

> A number of men who were on strike at Revelstoke were members of the International Brotherhood of Blacksmiths, which order had, at that time, an agreement with the Canadian Pacific Railway covering the terms and conditions of employment of its members in the shops at Revelstoke. They had, however, become members of the United Brotherhood of Railway Employees as well. When the latter went on strike there at once arose a conflict of jurisdiction as between these two orders, the executive officers of the blacksmiths' union taking the ground that no members of a local union belonging to the international order had any right to violate a contract which they had with their employers.
>
> As soon as it was brought to the notice of the headquarters Executive of the blacksmiths' union at Moline, Illinois that the local at Revelstoke had gone out in violation of its contract, a member of the Executive Board came to Revelstoke, investigated the matter, and ordered the men back to work immediately, on penalty, if they refused, of being expelled from the union. This action on the part of the member of the Executive was reinforced by messages from headquarters stating that the men "must religiously observe agreement with company." The men thereupon returned to work.

Of course expulsion meant loss of employment and blacklisting, since the international would cooperate with the employers by bringing in workers from other parts of the continent to fill the positions. In view of such a "responsible" attitude on the part of the officers of the international, it is obvious that the employers would not be at all inclined to "rock the boat" of amicable union-employer relations for to do so would have the probable result of opening the floodgates to radical unionism and socialist agitation. The Commission had got the message, and so did the Senate, with the mover of the bill stating his preference for "responsible labour organization," during the debate on second reading: "Now, the conditions between labour in the Dominion of Canada and the United States are vastly different. We know very well that certain classes of labour in the United States are becoming very largely tainted through the importation of those anarchistic classes from southern Europe that have [contributed]" to the very many upheavals of industrial life in that country." The Senator went on to say that his bill was not aimed at the American Federation of Labour and "the more responsible classes of labour organizations of an international character."[14]

The Lougheed bill, with some amendments, passed through the Senate on July 22, and was subsequently delivered to the House of Commons for consideration and debate, going down to overwhelming defeat there. In any event the bill had become very much an exercise in futility, since the western radicals, at whom the provisions of the bill were aimed, had suffered serious defeat in British Columbia. Momentarily at least, there was only the AFL left in the field to represent "international" unionism, and the conservative craft unionism promoted by that body presented no very exciting nor rewarding target for attack.

However, over the following years several Senators, with nothing more important to occupy their time, sounded off about the dangers and immorality represented by international unions. In 1907 Senator McMullen introduced a measure modelled after the Lougheed bill, but most of the Senate members had changed their minds about international unions, and the McMullen proposal was given a six months' hoist.

During the Parliamentary session of 1908-1909, McMullen tried again, with no greater success than had greeted his first effort. Then, in 1910, there was a renewal of effort, instigated by the Canadian Manufacturers Association. In 1909 the CMA endorsed a resolution calling on the Government to enact legislation that would bar American union organizers from operating in Canada. The cause was taken up in the Senate in 1910 by Senator Belcourt, who introduced a bill to amend the Criminal Code, declaring trade unions whose members were not all British subjects to be a criminal conspiracy in restraint of trade. But the Senator's amending bill met with so much opposition that he asked Senate leave to withdraw it.[15]

In a report to the delegates attending the 1910 Convention, the Trades Congress Executive Council confidently reported that Senate antagonism toward international unions had at last evaporated, leaving only a few lingering traces of the former bitter animosity held by a few prejudiced individuals. Employers were not overjoyed about any type of union's remaining in existence. But if there was to be unionism as a fact of industrial life, then they much preferred to cooperate with the "responsible" and conservative craft unions of the American Federation.

From 1906 until the start of World War I, the Federation was confronted with competition in a rebirth of industrial unionism, in the form of the Industrial Workers of the World (IWW). Once again the WFM, as in the case of the ALU, had acted as midwife at the birth of a radical industrial union movement, when leaders of that union presided at the founding of the IWW in Chicago in 1905. By 1906 the new organization in the industrial union field had established its first Canadian locals in British Columbia.

Almost from the start of its existence the IWW was torn with internal dissension that reduced its effectiveness and its ability to survive in the face of Federation opposition.[16] But a possible coalition between socialists and "wobblies," along with the first ever scheduling of a Trades Congress Convention in B.C.—the heart of socialist and IWW strength in Canada—disturbed the peace of mind of the AFL leaders.

Eastern Socialists: The Threat from Within

James Simpson, a Toronto socialist and member of the ITU, was being mooted for President of the Congress. AFL Secretary Morrison had doubts about Simpson's loyalty to international unionism, and directed Flett to put pressure on the Toronto socialist with a view to having him "modify his support of the dual organization." Simpson swore that he was "in favour of the American Federation of Labour, first, last, and always," but Morrison, who distrusted Simpson's protestations of loyalty, insisted in his correspondence with Flett that "our friend James Simpson is a socialist, and is probably wrapped up in the Industrial Workers' organization. All the socialists are, or nearly all of the them. Brother Simpson is fully aware of the position he occupies. He is a member of the ITU, but a socialist first, and like all other men of that ilk stands for that which is nearest to his heart."[17]

As the date for the Convention approached, Draper and other international unionists in Canada warned Gompers that the British Columbia locale for the gathering might well mean the Congress' falling under the control of the socialists. Gompers was immediately galvanized into action, notifying the heads of the international craft unions to make sure that their Canadian locals sent "loyal and trustworthy delegates" to the Trades Congress Convention "so that the continuity and safety of the Canadian trade union movement and particularly in its international aspect may be guaranteed beyond peradventure." Flett he had already dispatched on an organizing trip across western Canada, and during his travels Gompers confidently expected that Flett would be in a good position to help assure the election of non-socialist delegates.

There had been speculation that central locals would not send a full quota of delegates to distant Victoria in 1906. But liberal financial assistance, and pressure from international headquarters of the Canadian affiliates, resulted in a normal attendance from the centrally located organizations. Of course no one would openly admit that the international officers had manipulated delegate attendance in order to ensure that the position of the internationals in Canada was protected. No one would actually say that Flett and Draper had been used by the AFL leaders to prevent the capture of the Trades Congress by socialists, who in Gompers' mind were guilty of the "crime" of supporting dual unionism.[18]

In a move calculated to out-flank the socialists, Flett and Draper and their supporters moved for the formation of a labour party composed solely of members of trades unions. Following an extended and sometimes bitter debate on the advantages of forming a labour party versus endorsation of the Socialist Party, the Flett-Draper combination won a resounding victory on behalf of moderate trades union politics.

James Simpson declared his intention to be bound by Socialist Party loyalty to vote only for Party candidates. Nevertheless, Simpson won re-election as Congress Vice-President,[19] a result that was criticized by Morrison who, in a letter to Flett in October, asked the rhetorical question: "What process of reasoning caused the delegates to the Convention to vote for a man who declared that he could not vote for a single trade unionist for office? . . . I say he forfeits the right to hold office in a trade union."

But while they were successful in their manipulation of the Convention, the Flett-Draper-AFL cabal failed to win the west. A B.C. conference summoned to implement the Convention decision to form a labour party was dominated by socialists and radical unionists who carried the day with a resolution to endorse the Socialist Party as "the political expression of discontent among the British Columbia workers."[20]

In Ontario, the election of Allan Studholme as labour member for Hamilton sparked a widespread demand for the formation of a labour party. Draper responded with the issuing of a call for a conference to assemble in Toronto on March 29, 1907. Gompers and Morrison were concerned for the possible outcome of such a conference, and warned Flett that he "should by all means be present. It will be unfortunate if the effort to commit the Convention to a declaration in favour of socialism succeeds."[21]

Just as Flett, Draper, and the unionists "pure and simple" expected, the verbal fireworks began immediately after Draper had submitted a motion calling for the formation of an Ontario labour party. Simpson touched off an uproar by moving an amendment demanding endorsement of the Socialist Party in place of forming a new political alignment. The Toronto *Globe* of March 30, 1907 reported that the Simpson amendment was received with

> about the same courtesy that a hornet would be by ladies at an afternoon sewing circle. The mover being widely known amongst unions, and being capable of making himself heard, was given a good hearing when he first rose, but when he came to the clauses which

dealt on the ethics of the Socialist Party, into the fray went the six hundred.

Delegate Drake of Hamilton (said) . . . "I see there's going to be a split here . . . I say that if this meeting was called by the Congress then we have no right to listen to a Socialist."

Delegate Flett . . . followed, and stated that he could not understand how any man could get up and try to square the principles of trades unions with those of Socialists.

Uncontrollable excitement prevailed till nearly half-past five. Delegates from various parts of the province spoke, some in favour of socialism, some denouncing it in the most vigorous way, and others admonishing their fellows for taking up so much time. Both the Liberal and Conservative Parties were opposed, and the methods of the politicians were called bunco games, trickery, and several other names that are known to everyday parlance. The result of it all was a vote which recorded 34 for the amendment of Mr. Simpson, and the remainder of the Convention as in favour of the main resolution.

But the victory scored by the moderate unionists could scarcely be rated a resounding success outside the Convention hall. Efforts at meaningful political action in Toronto failed miserably. While Socialist trade unions were stormed at, Congress did nothing to prevent union officers from appearing on platforms in support of Liberal and Conservative candidates, and refused financial and other aid to independent labour candidates in Ontario communities.[22]

The continuing threat from western-based radicals was still apparent at the Congress' Winnipeg Convention in 1907. A B.C. delegate moved a motion to allow each province freedom in working out political policy. Draper insisted that it would be incorrect for Convention delegates to endorse a position that was in advance of trade union opinion in the east. Although defeated the Socialist element demonstrated considerable Convention strength, losing by a fifty-one to thirty-nine vote.[23] Simpson was easily re-elected to office, which caused Morrison to comment in a September letter to Flett: "I notice that . . . my fellow craftsman, Mr. James Simpson, has been re-elected with loud acclaim."

Problems continued into 1907, with the Canadian carpenters objecting to a "double taxation" system of dues payment. Carpenter delegates at the AFL Convention that year submitted a resolution that they be exempt from paying a per capita tax to the Federation. The intent of the resolution was to have the Canadian members pay the tax directly to the Trades Congress, thus effectively removing Congress finances from AFL control, and simultaneously raising the Canadian body above the status of a State

Federation. Several Canadians present at the Convention, including Socialist James Simpson, ably defended the proposition, but the decision went against them.

An alternative proposal endorsed at the Trades Congress 1907 Convention instructed Congress leaders to negotiate an agreement with the AFL, "whereby the moneys devoted by that body for organization and legislative purposes in Canada shall be paid over to the Executive Committee of this Congress and expended under their supervision."

The effect of the proposal would have been not only to enhance the authority and autonomy of the Congress in Canada, it would also have brought Flett's job directly under Congress control. It mattered nothing to Flett that the resolution was accorded unanimous endorsation from the Canadian delegates; he had no desire to be placed under the control of the Trades Congress, and set about arranging its defeat in the Federation.

Flett alerted Gompers and Morrison to the fact that it was the intention of Congress officers to send James Simpson to the AFL Convention to press the case for Flett's transfer to direct Canadian control. He requested that he be allowed to be present at the meeting should the Executive Council of the Federation consider entertaining so "impudent a proposition." Morrison concluded that he could not imagine the Council receiving Simpson, well known for his socialist views, with any degree of favour. But in a letter of November 14, Morrsion instructed Flett to be on hand for the encounter with Simpson.

At the Trades Congress Convention in 1908, Simpson gave a detailed account of his experiences at the AFL Convention, as he did in discussions with officers from a variety of international unions. His report, published in the proceedings of the Convention, dealt with attitudes of the international unions toward the Canadian Trades Congress:

> I decided to go to Norfolk by way of Washington, with a view to meeting the delegates as they assembled at the AFL headquarters . . . In taking this route I was enabled to do considerable work among the representatives of international unions. I found that the real work of the Congress was not clearly understood, and I was afforded a splendid opportunity to dissipate many erroneous impressions that were entertained with reference to its status as the legislative mouthpiece of the wage workers of Canada . . . I wish to refer to an impression that the Congress should be classified with the State Federations of Labour in the United States, and for that reason should receive no special recognition from international organizations that are now paying per capita tax to the American Federation of Labour for legislative purposes. It was only necessary to point to the special field of opportunity open to the Congress because of geographical boundaries that are entirely closed to the AFL . . . In one specific case I

was met with the objection that the Congress was fostering a national sentiment in the trade union movement in opposition to the international sentiment. I endeavoured to trace the source of the information but was unsuccessful . . .

In concluding his report Simpson briefly reviewed conversations with leaders of twenty-seven different international unions, citing the example of President Tobin of the Boot and Shoe Workers Union, who "classified the Congress as similar to a State Federation and therefore he did not think it advisable that the International Executive Committee should take any action."

For some unexplained reason, when he finally appeared before the Federation Council after the Convention, Simpson failed to ask for Flett's transfer to Trades Congress control, requesting only that the AFL "either place an additional organizer in the field or re-organize the districts of organizers who were engaged near the frontier, so that they could make more frequent visits to Canadian territory." Gompers promised to give the request careful consideration. But it was filed away and studiously ignored.

Immediately after Simpson had completed his report, Draper took the floor to accuse Federation officers of not placing any trust in the elected officials of the Trades Congress, for the reason that they believed Draper to be a confirmed nationalist and Simpson a socialist.

It was widely acknowledged that the Federation leaders did not entirely trust Congress officers—their many actions and words firmly established that fact. Gompers had told Simpson to his face that it was impossible to be a loyal trades unionist and a socialist at one and the same time, and while Draper's politics were considered "safe," his recognized desire and drive to build the Canadian Trades Congress into a strong and autonomous national trade union centre was looked upon with suspicion by the American unionists. The American union leaders were not going to stand idle, watching the equivalent of a State Federation grow into an independent power centre in North America.

The conflict over chartering rights—especially as it concerned the chartering of central bodies—was by no means permanently settled by the Executive Council meeting at Toronto in April 1903. Draper was understandably ambitious for the extension of Congress control by means of direct chartering and payment of dues to the Trades Congress. At the 1906 Convention he advised the delegates:

My aim and ambition is to have a Trades and Labour Council established in every town and city in Canada, operating under a charter from this Congress. By this method we can federate and consolidate our movement in Canada . . . and possibly evolve a

scheme whereby this Congress could select and finance the election of
trade unionists to the Federal Parliament and Provincial Legislatures
in the industrial centres that would be likely to elect labour men, the
same as is now done in Great Britain.

In contrast to the many claims stated by international union leaders that
the Canadian Congress was similar in structure and authority to a State
Federation, Draper reiterated his concept of equality at the Congress
Convention in 1908. "The Trades and Labour Congress of Canada," he
said, "is co-equal with the British Trades Union Congress and the
American Federation of Labour. It is to the Canadian organized
wage-earners what the British Trades Union Congress and the American
Federation of Labour are to the organized workers of the British Isles and
the United States, a sovereign and supreme body within the confines of its
own territory, the Dominion of Canada, for legislative purposes."

Draper's concept was obviously within a much broader context than the
strict and narrow limits of simple legislative action. The sharpening of the
differences over chartering rights brought into the open the divergent
opinions on the extent of "legislative purposes," as viewed from the
conflicting perspectives of Canadians and Americans.

Canadians generally accepted the phrase as one embracing chartering
rights, organizing work, and independent politics of a labour or socialist
character. The Americans, on the other hand, argued that it meant
nothing more than the lobbying of politicians in the corridors of the
various legislative buildings. Moreover, the Americans gave every
indication that they had a vested interest in Canada that was in need of
protection, and they many times demonstrated their determination to
maintain control over the finances and organizing activities of the
Canadian movement. The Canadian leaders seemed to be reluctant to
tackle the problem at its base—the control of Canadian locals by the
headquarters of the various international unions. Thus they were
constantly falling short of the capacity to take any independent action.

However, Draper had remarkable success in his drive to enlarge the
number of central bodies chartered directly by the Trades Congress. While
only a handful of these organizations had bothered to apply for a charter
from the Federation, an increasing number were affiliating to the Congress
during the several years immediately after the Toronto meeting which had
agreed that either national body possessed the right to charter. But
Federation officials were fully aware of the strategic importance of these
chartering rights, which signified both a degree of loyalty and control.
Consequently, in a letter addressed to Flett in February 1905, Federation
Secretary Morrison instructed the Canadian organizer to take steps to
enlarge the list of central bodies in Canada chartered by the AFL. "It is
our desire," Morrison wrote, "to keep the unions we now have in good

standing intact by getting as many central bodies affiliated with the AFL as possible."

At the AFL Convention the following year Gompers outlined the thinking behind Federation policy respecting central bodies. He pointed out that both the international unions and the AFL were dependent upon these organizations to carry out policies decided upon by the American union leaders. Central bodies enforced jurisdictional decisions "of the highest court in the realm of labour"—the AFL. Gompers concluded that: "No central body should under any circumstances give representation or encouragement to any local organization which for any reason has seceded, or has been suspended from, or has demonstrated its hostility to, a bona fide international union, and especially when such an international union is affiliated with the American Federation of Labour."[24]

In short, the American unionists looked on the central Councils as the first line of defence in the struggle for hegemony, and against "dual unions." Within Canada, starting from 1902, the application of this concept of "bona fide international unions" compelled the Canadian movement to duplicate every split and schism that developed in the United States, thus keeping the unions in Canada perenially at odds with each other on the basis of splits originating in the American Federation and having no relationship whatever to the Canadian situation.

The designs of the Berlin Convention and the Toronto meeting of the Council were the reduction of the status of the Trades Congress to that of a State Federation, but the forty-ninth parallel kept getting in the way. Similar business union philosophies and shared cultural roots, combined with expanding American industrial interests in Canada, were important factors that drew the two organizations together. But during the first quarter of the twentieth century Britain still constituted a major economic and cultural influence in Canada. Political attitudes, and national and economic realities, were important sources of conflict between the Congress and the Federation. The result of these conflicting factors of attraction and repulsion was an obviously ambivalent attitude on the part of Canadian union leaders towards Canadian-American union relations. The problem was capable of resolution only by means of a correct and undistorted policy of international solidarity based on a relationship of equals. This, in essence, is what the Congress leaders were demanding, but the American unionists were unwilling to concede.

An economic crisis between 1910 and the opening years of the War promoted political action to a position of priority in the labour movement. The AFL continued to do business at the old stand of "no partisan politics," spiced with a paranoid distrust of anything that even remotely resembled socialist philosophy. Ever present in the minds of the Federation officers was the fear that the socialists might gain favour in the eyes of the workers and "take over" the trade unions for political purposes.

The Americans always viewed this as an important problem in connection with the movement in Canada, and always dreaded the possibility that "nationalists" and socialists might unite to end AFL domination. In Canada, British and Australian successes with independent labour political action constituted a major influence, and under the impact of the crisis the Canadians turned more readily to united action based on a radical political outlook.

The Toronto District Council was one of the more important central bodies outside of the western region where union and socialist groups managed to maintain a solid basis of cooperation. James Simpson could remain a leading figure in the Council while maintaining that: "The state only protects the property interests of the ruling class, and if the working class is ever to become the only class in society, it must capture the state and all that is comprehended in the state and use it in the interests of that class alone."

In the United States that statement would have been sufficient to justify Simpson's expulsion from the union movement—or, at the very least, his disbarment from union office. In Canada it got him elected to the Toronto City Council with the support of the Trades Council, and 20,000 votes. Clearly the Federation was unable to exercise *total* control over the Canadian movement. There was always a challenge to American domination.

The expanding influence of "left" politics was evident at the Trades Congress Convention in 1912, when Scottish independent labourist Keir Hardie was the featured speaker. In an address that drew prolonged applause from the Canadian unionists, but must have given Gompers fits, Hardie told the delegates:

> While the strike may secure small reforms for the worker, it can never solve the industrial problem. The conquest of political power alone can do that . . . Don't be ashamed of being called a Socialist. The capitalist class will make you proud of being called a Socialist. The railways and land of Canada should be owned by the people of Canada instead of by the people who even don't live among you. See to it that you hand over to your children a nobler life than you yourselves have entered into.

But Gompers insisted that European experiences did not apply to America, where universal suffrage prevailed and there were no aristocrats or enemies of democracy. In an article featured in the *American Federationist* for March 1910, Gompers harangued his readers: "Fellow working-men of all countries, the American Federation of Labour is on the right political road, at least for America."

In this same period a strike situation in the Vancouver Island coal mines, while not constituting any challenge to AFL hegemony, showed that it was not solely an interest in the welfare of Canadian workers that brought American unionists to Canada and caused them to stay in spite of the many evidences of their unpopularity. The strike was led by the United Mine Workers of America, an AFL union that was simultaneously working for the destruction of the Nova Scotia Provincial Workmen's Association—assisted by Flett and the AFL. In an article published in the UMW *Journal* in 1912, union agent Frank Farrington suggested that the organization of the British Columbia mines was required in order that the competitive position of B.C. coal in the United States market be reduced. Farrington said:

> These mines are located so that the output can be dumped from the tipple to ocean-going vessels and, with the long haul around the Horn eliminated, can be freighted without transfer from the mines to the Atlantic seaboard at a transportation cost that will allow it to become a strong competing factor in the markets now supplied by the union-mined coal of the eastern states.
>
> So it is not beyond reasonable conjecture to expect that within a comparatively short time we will find this coal bidding for markets on the Atlantic seaboard as well as on the Pacific coast. This feature in itself would not be so bad if there could be an interchange of competition but that cannot be, for the reason that the much superior quality of this coal will always bar outside competition from its own zone.
>
> The duty devolving upon the United Mine Workers of America because of this condition is to organize Vancouver Island and adjacent territory, raise the standard of employment and act as a balancing medium in the establishment of equitable competitive mining rates. This will be a herculean task, but it must be done, or we must suffer from inequitable competition—and the job can be easier done now than after the task gets bigger.

It must be assumed that this is internationalism at its very best. Only the Trades Congress would be guilty of nationalism and aim to break the bonds of "internationalism." And on the other side of the continent this same union was intent on sustaining conditions that shut Nova Scotia coal out of the Quebec-Ontario market to retain it for the Pennsylvania product.

The variety of issues touched upon here kept alive the conflict arising from the contradictions inherent in Canadian-American union relations. The next serious challenge to American hegemony would erupt during the war and immediate postwar years.

9

WAR AND CONSCRIPTION:
THE INTERNATIONALS
ON THE SIDE OF MILITARISM

During the last two years before World War erupted, some additional steps were found to be necessary in order to consolidate American domination over the Canadian unions.

Readers will recall the references to British trade unions that expanded into North America in the mid-nineteenth century. Two such unions—the Amalgamated Society of Engineers and the Amalgamated Society of Carpenters and Joiners—operating from headquarters in New York, established organizations in Canada, the former in 1850 and the latter in 1860. Shortly after the founding of the American Federation of Labour the Engineers were absorbed into the jurisdiction of the International Machinists, and the Carpenters into the International Brotherhood of Carpenters and Joiners. In Canada the Engineers automatically adopted the policy set in New York, but a large number of British artisans amongst the carpenters chose to maintain their traditional contacts with British unionism and remained members of the Amalgamated.

This was still the situation at the 1912 Convention when the American unionists undertook to close the loophole that allowed such things to happen. The result was a rather astonishing revelation of the AFL criteria for what, in their view, constituted internationalism.

The first move to be made in the plot to exclude the Amalgamated as "non-internationalist," was to initiate an amendment to the Trades Congress constitution of 1902, which read as follows:

> Further no national union or local unions comprising said national union shall be entitled to membership in this Congress when there is in existence an international union of their craft, nor shall any local union attached to a national body separated from their international organization be entitled to delegates in any central body chartered by this body.

Now, if having affiliates in more than one country makes an organization "international," then surely the British union qualifies. In fact, by reason of having affilates in a number of countries, the Amalgamated could be considered to be more international than any of the AFL unions, which had only Canadian connections abroad. But to apply the criteria in that way would undermine the authority of the American unions and open the door to "dual unionism." That such a situation could not and would not be tolerated was made very clear when, after adoption of the above amendment to the constitution, the following resolution was placed before the Convention by the Executive Committee of Congress:

> Whereas, there are now two rival organizations of carpenters and joiners, each being affiliated with this Congress, and as the charter of the Amalgamated Society of Carpenters and Joiners has been revoked by the American Federation of Labour, resolved that the United Brotherhood of Carpenters and Joiners be the one union of carpenters affiliated and acknowledged by this Congress.

However, Convention delegates in 1912 did not subscribe to the strange idea that Americanism and internationalism were synonymous, and the Resolutions Committee brought in a recommendation of non-concurrence which, after a bitter and protracted debate, was endorsed by 124 votes to seventy-six.[1]

Undeterred by such a minor thing as a majority vote by Congress delegates, the Executive officers defied the Convention decision by refusing to accept per capita payments transmitted by the Amalgamated. At the 1913 Congress Convention the Executive defended their bureaucratic action, with the explanation that, "It will be remembered that the United Brotherhood is an international organization having its headquarters in the United States, while the Amalgamated Society is a British Trade Union, which has established branches in the various British dominions, and also in the United States."[2]

Accepting the "explanation" and the consequences implicit in its intended application to Canadian union organization, the Congress Convention in 1913 fully endorsed the argument that Americanism and internationalism are synonymous.[3] The *Labour Gazette* for October 1913 reports that "the Committee on Officers' Reports . . . complimented the various officers on the work accomplished and upheld the decision of the Executive Council in refusing per capita from the Amalgamated Society of Carpenters and Joiners."

Following this act of abject surrender of all semblance of autonomy, the Trades Congress delegates adopted yet another amendment to the constitution of 1902, that had the effect of forever removing all doubt about the point that only American-based unions could qualify as international organizations. The *Labour Gazette* reports that the Committee on Constitution and Law "reported favourably on the proposition to amend Section 2 of the constitution by adding the words 'or any organizations which have been expelled or rejected by the American Federation of Labour.' The effect of the amendment is to debar local unions not affiliated with the American Federation of Labour from representation in Trades and Labour Councils."

These clarifying amendments in 1912 and 1913 were to be later applied to a Canadian union of railway workers that had originated in the Maritimes in 1907. In the midst of other wartime activities—to be detailed later—this Canadian union was to be ordered to submerge its identity in an American-based union that had previously done nothing of an organizational character in Canada.

In 1907 a group of freight handlers on the Intercolonial Railway in Halifax struck spontaneously for shorter hours and improved working conditions. As a result of this spontaneous action, an independent local union was formed and became known as the Freight Handlers' Union of Halifax. Shortly thereafter, the head of a United States union of railway workers based in Boston, who made very attractive promises as to what his organization could and would do to improve the conditions of workers on the Intercolonial Railway, impressed the Halifax group and some other railway employees so favourably that they agreed to affiliate with the American union.[4]

However, results fell far short of the promises made and the Canadian workers became disenchanted with the practical work of the highly articulate President of the union. In October 1908, a representative group of the discontented unionists met in Moncton to determine what action they might take to better this situation. The minutes of this meeting state:

> Considerable discussion took place with reference to the actions of Grand President R.P. Neil, and practically all delegates voiced their objection to the delay in starting the preparation and presentation of a schedule. It was claimed that he had deserted the membership on the Intercolonial Railway in time of need, and had not given his personal attention to important Brotherhood matters. Other complaints of a serious nature were made, and it was the opinion of all delegates that, in order to advance the interests of themselves and their fellow-workers, it was necessary to relinquish our membership in the International Brotherhood of Railroad Employees and form a Canadian union. It was accordingly moved . . . and seconded . . . that all those present withdraw from the International Brotherhood forthwith and form a Canadian railway workers' organization . . . This motion being put was carried unanimously.

The organization that emerged from the meeting at Moncton became known as the Canadian Brotherhood of Railway Employees (CBRE), the members of which held, and expressed, strong opinions on the greater effectiveness of an industrial form of organization, and on the desirability of an independent Canadian movement. Commenting on this latter point, Greening says:

> It was the firm conviction of the Brotherhood officers and members that Canadian workers should form their own unions, directed by Canadians who were fully familiar with labour and industrial conditions in this country. In their view the dependence of Canadian workers on the United States labour leadership represented a humiliating type of dependence on foreign influence and authority. They felt that Canadian workers should have full autonomy and national sovereignty in the field of labour organization, and that the existing reliance on and directions from unions controlled in the United States represented an undesirable form of colonial servitude and subjection.[5]

And an article in the April 1909 issue of the union journal, *The Canadian Railroad Employee,* commented on the fact that there was plenty of organizing work for the American unions to do in the United States, and went on to say: "We have just as good union men in Canada as any other country can produce. Not that we have any quarrel with our American friends, but it is time that we made up our minds to run our own business. Let our American friends get themselves together instead of coming over here to disrupt us. We can look after this end of the country. That is more than they can do for their end of it."

The February 1911 issue of the journal pressed the case for industrial unionism against the craft form of organization, as a more effective method to employ in the contest with the employers: "We believe in the amalgamation of the various crafts, bringing them under one head, thus avoiding the complication that rises in the time of trouble . . . we consider that it is far better to have a national organization with the fifteen different crafts under one head . . . than an international organization with only one craft at your back."

In 1917, despite opposition from some of the affiliated railway crafts, the CBRE became an affiliate of the TLC. But the organization was not to be left in peace for long to pursue its objective of Canadian industrial unionism. Within a year of its affiliation, the jurisdiction of the CBRE was fated to be challenged by an American union whose application for affiliation was accepted by the TLC, despite the prior affiliation of the Canadian organization.

A hitherto small American union, the Brotherhood of Railway and Steamship Clerks, Freight Handlers, Express and Station Employees, took a new lease on life as a direct result of Government operation of the railways after the United States entered the war. During 1917 and 1918, the American union greatly increased its membership, and consequently had the funds, and could afford the organizing personnel, to embark on a large-scale campaign among Canadian railway workers, with the cooperation of the Trades Congress.

The BRSC made important gains on the western lines of the Canadian Pacific Railway, and by virtue of its affiliation with the AFL and TLC claimed sole right to represent in Canada as well as in the United States the classes of railway workers that the CBRE had been fighting to organize. The Canadian organization was placed in a very difficult situation because the BRSC had the support of the officers of international unions in Canada as well as the support of the TLC.

The BRSC claim to jurisdictional rights came up for discussion at the 1918 Convention of the TLC. In a CBRE resolution that began, "Whereas the Canadian Brotherhood of Railway Employees is an international organization . . .,"[6] the Canadian union laid claim to legitimacy as an organization that was international in scope. At least the claim was legitimate, since the CBRE had locals in the United States and in Newfoundland, which was not then a part of Canada. But the Canada Congress, which refused to concede the "international" legitimacy of the British Amalgamateds, was not likely to be swayed by such arguments from the CBRE.

The Congress officers, wishing to avoid administrative action if at all possible, suggested negotiations aimed at effecting a merger between the two unions. The CBRE agreed to discussions and put forward the following proposals as the minimum for agreement:

1. The degree of national autonomy proposed must be acceptable to the Canadian membership;

2. The Canadian members of the merged organization must have the right to elect the Canadian officials who would have charge of the administrative work in Canada;

3. An Executive office of the merged organization must be maintained in Canada, through which Canadian business would be transacted;

4. Past membership in the CBRE must be considered as past membership in the BRSC;

5. Provision for the employment of the present officers and the field forces of the CBRE, subject to constitutional procedures.[7]

The granting of such far-reaching demands for Canadian autonomy might have set an example to others who held similar views. Consequently, the only "concession" that the American union was prepared to make was the inclusion of all the CBRE members in the BRSC without having to pay initiation fees.

Formal expulsion of the Canadian union actually occurred near the end of 1920 when the CBRE received a letter to that effect from TLC President Tom Moore. Moore informed the union's officers that there was nothing more that the Congress could do toward promoting a merger, and that, in the circumstances, it had been decided to annul the charter of affiliation which the Congress had issued. But the simple demand for autonomy made the decision unpalatable to Congress elements who favoured some independence for Canadian unions, so Moore tried to justify the unpopular action with a series of unsubstantiated accusations directed at CBRE officers. Moore claimed, for example, that in 1919, the CBRE had made an effort to get the TLC involved in the Winnipeg strike, that the official journal of the union had vilified Gompers, and had attacked the League of Nations.

TLC officers were understandably anxious to see that the CBRE did not attend the next Congress Convention, where they could argue their case before the assembled delegates. But the expelled union applied for an injunction, contending that the Congress had no greater responsibility to promote international unionism in Canada than it had to promote national unionism, as represented by the CBRE. The Trades Congress Executive advanced the argument that the matter was not one of jurisdiction, but of dual unionism. The CBRE was dual to the BRSC, a recognized international organization, and, according to the Congress constitution, international unions had preference over Canadian national unions. The Congress Executive, it was argued, was only carrying out the policies laid down at the Congress Convention in 1902 not to allow any organization dual to an international union to be in affiliation with the Congress.

As a result of the court action, the CBRE was able to appear at the 1921 Convention, where it had 150 credentialed delegates. In reply to criticisms for having taken the Congress officers to court, the President of the union said:

> It is true that a great many of the representatives of international unions have found fault with our organization for taking the Congress into court. I am not ashamed of the action we took. It was the only possible way of bringing the matter before this Convention, and at the same time protect the rights of our organization. The law was used for that purpose. I took exception to the statement made before the court by President Moore that the aim of the Congress is to promote international unionism. The Congress exists for the sole purpose set forth in the preamble of the constitution and no other.

Constitutionally, the CBRE is a national body. It is composed of
Canadian workers, who will not stand for any dictation from outsiders
and it will always claim the right to elect its own officers and conduct
its own business as it sees fit. Sections (2) and (3) of Article 1 of the
Congress constitution do not enable the Executive to expel our
organization.[8]

The presence of the CBRE delegates at the Congress Convention was
very useful in that it compelled the supporters of American union
monopoly in Canada to once again, with fervour, expose the shallowness of
their claims to "international" status. One union local from Point St.
Charles, Quebec castigated the Congress officers for having "discrimin-
ated" against international unions by issuing a charter to a Canadian
union. The resolution declared that: "[We] go on record protesting
against such discrimination to all bona fide international unions affiliated
to the above Congress through the American Federation of Labour."[9]

After four years of trying to convince the CBRE to commit
organizational suidice, the Congress passed its resolution of expulsion at
the Convention in 1921: " . . . be it resolved that the thirty-seventh
Convention of the Trades and Labour Congress of Canada, in Convention
assembled, in the city of Winnipeg, Manitoba, do hereby revoke the
charter of the Canadian Brotherhood of Railway Employees on the
grounds that there is a bona fide international organization affiliated to
this Congress, covering this class of workers; and on the further ground
that a continuation of the affiliation of the Canadian Brotherhood of
Railway Employees with the Trades and Labour Congress would be
recognition of a dual organization, a policy which the Congress
emphatically declared against at its annual Convention in the city of
Berlin, Ontario, in 1902."[10]

Labour Leader or Recruiting Sergeant?

At the same time that the American Federation was conducting open war
on "dual unionism" through its Canadian agency, the Trades Congress, a
war of vast proportions for the redivision of the world was being fought in
the European arena. Changing attitudes towards the War by the Canadian
unionists played an important part in shaping the labour movement, as
well as in the determination of further developments in Canadian-
American union relations.

By the end of the century's first decade, war in Europe
seemed imminent, and the Canadian union movement initially took steps
to express its opposition to any such conflict. The first clear
pronouncement against the projected war was proclaimed at the
Convention of the TLC in 1911, when the delegates declared that war was

fought solely in the interests of the capitalists and resolved to support a general strike to prevent the outbreak of war, "so that the workers may see the pitiful exhibition of fighting of those capitalists that seem so fond of it." Again, in 1912, Convention delegates voiced firm opposition to war with the prophetic declaration that "the only result war between Germany and Great Britain would achieve would be the degradation of the toilers."

But the following year, under the ominous cloud of impending conflict, the former anti-war stand was modified and the TLC, while still voicing opposition to any participation in international war, resolved that it was "not a war of Great Britain's choosing," and expressed their determination and confidence in seeing that "despotism in Europe will be hurled to its final destruction, to make way for constitutional freedom in all the countries in Europe in preparation for the last and great struggle of the working class to their own actual freedom."

The Convention that was held in Vancouver in 1915 signalled a considerable change in Congress policy regarding war. Delegates endorsed all previous resolutions opposing war "in principle," but proceeded to take issue with militants and socialists who maintained that since the war was not the business of the working class, it was a matter of indifference to them which side won. In contrast to the socialist position, the Convention offered "voluntary" assistance in an endeavour "to secure early and final victory for the cause of freedom and democracy."

In accordance with its new policy declaration, the TLC now vowed unyeilding opposition to any form of compulsion in its support for an Executive recommendation calling for "unchangeable opposition to all that savours of conscription either here or in the empire." The principle inherent in this anti-conscription resolution was again endorsed at the 1916 Convention. Congress had gone from opposition to war itself as inimical to the interests of the working class, to a formal declaration against compulsion, i.e., against conscription. But Government policy, affected by heavy casualities in war and the consequent need for troop reinforcements, introduced an element of crisis in Congress policy.

In 1916, the Government established a National Service Board with the power of supervision over national security and labour selection. The Board proceeded to draw up plans for the registration of workers, said to be for the purpose of collecting basic information as to the location and distribution of manpower. The feeling was that the registration scheme was preliminary to the institution of conscription, and was met with considerable opposition on the west coast and in Quebec. While on a national tour Prime Minister Borden and R.B. Bennett, head of the National Service Board, were challenged by a delegation of unionists in British Columbia who demanded assurance that conscription would not be instituted, but no such assurance was forthcoming. The British Columbia *Federationist* for January 12, 1917 reported that the interview with the Government officials was followed by a joint meeting of the Vancouver and

Victoria Trades Councils along with the B.C. Federation of Labour, where delegates declared their continuing and unanimous oppostion to the registration scheme and conscription.

Later, on their return to Ottawa, Borden and Bennett were greeted by Trades Congress officers who requested an undertaking that under no circumstances would conscription be carried out. The Prime Minister evasively expressed the hope that conscription would not be necessary, but "if it should prove the only effective method to preserve the existence of the state and of the institutions and liberties which we enjoy I should consider it necessary to act accordingly."[11]

In the face of the uncompromising attitude of the Government, Congress officials retreated one more crucial step. Abandoning the Trades Congress declaration of "unchangeable opposition" to compulsion, the representatives called for the conscription of wealth as well as manpower, to which Borden unctuously replied that "the Government accepted and acted on the principle that the accumulated wealth of the country should bear its due proportion of contributions and sacrifices in the War." Despite Borden's failure to disavow manpower conscription or to agree to the conscription of wealth, Congress made the final gesture of total capitulation when Executive officers urged union members to cooperate with the registration campaign. An Executive circular recommended that "all members of affiliated unions fill in the answers according to their conscientious opinion and return the cards as directed."[12] The recommendation met with agreement in the east, but was greeted with a storm of protest throughout the west. When Borden announced on May 18, 1917 that the plan for national registration would not be sufficient to meet Canada's commitment to the empire and that conscription was imperative, the worst fears of the western radicals were fully confirmed.

By the time the Trades Congress met in Convention at Ottawa in 1917, conscription was the law of the land, and western advocates of "direct action" responded to the controversial legislation with a proposal for consideration of a general strike against the measure. But Congress Executive officers laid the responsibility for the situation on the German people alone, in a statement that said: "Let it be made clear to the German people that they themselves are the masters of the situation, that they themselves have the power to stop the War and establish permanent peace by overthrowing their own and the world's enemy."[13]

Having thus judiciously laid the foundations for a "justification" of their own blatantly militarist stand, the officers of the Congress presented their position on the conscription law—a position that represented a complete reversal of all previous Convention resolutions on war, and labour's response to it. The officer's report stated that:

In 1915 the Trades and Labour Congress of Canada, at the annual

Convention held in Vancouver, declared an unqualified opposition to conscription as a method of military enlistment. Last year, at Toronto, the same resolution was reaffirmed in all its emphasis. Since then the question of conscription for Canada has agitated the public mind to an unprecedented degree . . . within the past few months the issue has been before Parliament and a most drastic measure . . . has been . . . carried through the Commons and Senate. That measure is now law and, as such, contains provisions that impose heavy penalties upon all and sundry who make use of any form of opposition to the principle that might frustrate the carrying into effect of the Act now in existence. While the Congress cannot stultify itself to the degree of either contradicting or withdrawing this year its firm and carefully thought out views on the question of conscription, as embodied in the resolutions of 1915 and 1916, still, under our representative form of Government, it is not deemed either right, patriotic, or in the interests of the Dominion or of the labour classes, to say or do aught that might prevent the powers that be from obtaining all the results that they anticipate from the enforcement of such law.[14]

Western and Quebec delegates to the Convention denounced the Executive report and its accompanying recommendations as an unconditional surrender to the tyranny of the state. A delegate from Edmonton submitted an amendment to the report, proposing that pending the conscription of wealth no support be given to the principle of conscription of men for war purposes. Debate on the amendment elicited from Congress Vice-President James Simpson the statement that labour's claims on the Borden Government had not been satisfied by the appointment of International Brotherhood of Railroad Telegraphers' Gideon Robertson to the Senate. Simpson claimed that "no member of organized labour appointed to the Senate by either the Liberal or Conservative Government is free to serve the working class as they should be served in the Upper Chamber, and therefore, in my judgement, the action of the Government cannot be regarded as a concession to labour."

An Executive officer who intervened in the debate as an opponent of "direct action" pointed out that the Trades Congress could not promote independent action because the international affiliations of Canadian unions prevented it. In his revealing statement the Executive member said:

It is just as well, at this time, that I should point out that the organized workers of Canada stand in a position that has no parallel in any other country of the world. This Congress can only exert its moral influence in the enforcement of its decisions, and the economic powers to support legislative demands is not vested in our movement, but is under the control of the international officers of our representative unions. When the Executive Council of the American Federation of Labour reaches a decision, members of that Council, being heads of powerful international trade unions, can use their influence effectively. The same applies to the Parliamentary Committee of the British Trade Union Congress, but in Canada we cannot use our economic power without the sanction of the heads of our international unions . . . In cases where our decisions are at variance with decisions taken by the American Federation of Labour regarding important national issues, it is difficult to secure that sympathy, that support in the exercise of our economic powers, as we otherwise would recieve if the Executive of the Congress were composed of heads of powerful economic organizations.[15]

Replying to this humiliating confession of complete inability to take decisive action in a crisis, one delegate remarked, "President Gompers had committed the workers of the United States to conscription, therefore a general strike was not feasible." But that complaint was only partly true. The Trades Congress members had acquiesced in the destruction of their own effectiveness at Berlin in 1902 and had gradually undermined their initial stand against war by surrendering to state pressure and jingoistic militarism. However, it is also true that Gompers and the AFL were already moving to take a direct hand in the Canadian situation, in opposition to the opponents of war.

It was not until near the end of 1916 that United States capitalists, concerned for the ultimate safety of their extensive investments, made their decision to intervene on the side of the Allied Powers. The situation at the time was all the more urgent in view of the imminent collapse of bourgeois authority in Russia and the spread of Bolshevik influence throughout the country. It was apparent that Russia was about to cease being a factor in the prosecution of the war against Germany, and the Americans felt the necessity for action to fill the vacancy created by a disintegrating Russian army.

In the period of "war preparedness" that preceded the actual declaration of hostilities, Gompers felt free to make public pronouncements in opposition to compulsory military service. This corresponded approximately to the point in time when the Congress was abandoning its clear-cut anti-war stand, and retreating to a position of protesting conscription measures. In its June 1st, 1917 issue the *Industrial Banner*—a labour journal endorsed by the Toronto District Labour Council—printed a statement by Gompers critical of conscription proposals in the United States and protesting that voluntary institutions had not been given an effective and conclusive test to prove their worth.

But Gompers and the Federation colleagues, sighting war clouds on the horizon, were even then in the process of changing policy. Consequently, in the June 15 issue, the *Industrial Banner* printed an article in line with the new Federation policy wherein Gompers addressed himself to demands for Government recognition of labour's role by appointing AFL representatives to War Service Boards, and to recommendations regarding methods of exemptions for "essential workers" under the provisions of the Conscription Act. The *Industrial Banner* quoted Gompers as proposing that:

> The fundamental demand which labour makes in connection with the Conscription Act is that representatives of wage earners must be upon every Board, national, state, and local, which has to do with the administration of the law. This demand is in accord with the methods found necessary in Great Britain and is founded upon justice and democracy. The wage earners will be vitally affected by selective conscription and they ought to have representatives in such strategic positions.
>
> The spirit of labour in the nation's emergency has been generous and patriotic. The workers are willing to do their part and to give that which is part of their lives. They must be met in the same spirit of fairness and cooperation by both the Government and employers in order that the ideals of the nation may be maintained in the contest in which we are now engaged.

The Convention of the AFL in November 1917 was held in Buffalo, New York, close enough to the scene for Federation leaders to get a sense of the growing restiveness in Canadian union ranks. The "direct action" amendment moved at the 1917 Assembly of the Trades Congress had been defeated by the narrow margin of ten votes—111 to 101—and Borden's Government was confronted with a serious challenge from socialist and radical unionists. It was urgent that the Federation respond with some material measure of support for their beleaguered conservative union brothers in Canada.

The Toronto *Globe* reported from Buffalo that the Convention had unanimously approved of an investment of $10,000 in Canadian War Bonds, as a tribute to the heroic brothers in the Dominion. In addition, it was decided that the President himself should be rushed into the breach, and at the conclusion of the Buffalo Convention, Gompers swept into Toronto to play the part of recruiting sergeant on behalf of the Canadian bourgeoisie.

On November 30, the *Industrial Banner* reported that Gompers' first act on arriving in Toronto was to make application for $10,000 worth of Victory Bonds in the name of the AFL. In the same issue the *Banner* reported on a Victory Bond meeting held on November 26, where Gompers was featured as the star attraction:

He claimed that Labour should recognize that a war was on and that the cause of democracy was at stake and it was up to labour to back the Government in every effort to help win the War.

He was an anti-militarist and had opposed conscription in his own country but after it had become law he had done everything in his power, and the labour movement behind him, to uphold the hands of the President and the Government . . . He also demanded that when flesh and blood was conscripted wealth must also be levied on to the fullest possible extent.

The pro-Government and pro-war Toronto *Globe* provided a more extensive report of the meeting that retained the full flavour of the Federation President's propaganda for war. The November 29 edition of the *Globe* reported Gompers as saying, "I hold it to be the first duty of every Canadian, by birth or citizenship, to do everything within his power to unite the people in the winning of this War. Regarding politics and religion I say that all the people should stand united to bring victory to Canada . . . Men of Canada, . . . volunteer and don't wait to be drafted. Go and fight!" The *Globe* went on to say of Gompers that "while he had opposed conscription and used his influence to defeat it when it was before Congress, he had done his part since to make it effective when Congress decreed that it was to be enforced. He considered it the duty of every man to do the same thing."

Ignoring his militaristic record during the period of the Spanish-American War, Gompers went on to boast of his previous firm stand for peace. Continuing, he said, "Then in August 1914 came the proof that the world had been befuddled and fooled by a schemer and deviser unparalleled in the history of the world in the shape of a declaration of war from the Imperial German Kaiser." The *Globe*'s account went on as follows:

The Imperial German Kaiser, the Prince of Kultur, had broken the laws of God and man in creating this present world-conflict. Most severely he scored world Socialists generally, and German Socialists in particular. "If you read the philosophy of the German Socialist school," he said, "you will find that, after all, it is patterned after the autocratic power of the German Imperial Government. It is at variance with, and is not akin to, the great labour movement as expressed by the trade unions of the world. In our trade unions we represent in fact and in philosophy that fundamental principle of voluntarily and individually yielding a certain amount of our rights in order that our other rights may be protected and advanced. In the scheme of the German school of Socialist philosophy there is the thought that everything must be done by the Government, and the individual loses himself.

"From the facts of the world war, as can be laid before everybody, any man in England, the United States, Canada, Australia, or the other free democracies who does not arise at this hour and fight for his country is a coward and a poltroon."

He apologized for seeming to interfere in any way with Canadian political issues, but reminded his hearers that only a people undivided by party lines could hope to successfully wage a huge war.

A federal election was in progress at the time of the Gompers' visit to Toronto. It was obvious that the precarious situation of the Borden Government, occasioned by the widespread opposition to conscription, had more than a casual relationship to the Gompers' safari into Canada at a time of great stress in the United States as well as in Canada. There was a rumour abroad that the American recruiting sergeant would journey to Winnipeg to lend support to the Government campaign against two strong socialist contenders, one of whom was an Executive officer of the Trades Congress. This rumour caused the *B.C. Federationist* in December 1917 to comment editorially: "Gompers might as well be told that the labour movement in Canada requires none of the sort of assistance that he is intellectually qualified to give."

The rumour may have been just that—a rumour. In any event Gompers never got to participate in the Winnipeg campaign. But he did intervene directly in the election on the side of the Government and its war policies. This intervention took the form of an outrageously racist and scurrilous advertisement which occupied a half page in the *Industrial Banner* on December 7, 1917. The ad, which reiterated the propaganda content of the recent Gompers recruiting speech, read as follows:

SAMUEL GOMPERS SAYS:

"I hold it to be the first duty of every Canadian to do everything within his power to unite the people in winning this War . . . Having entered the War, the people of Canada, without regard to politics, or religion, or any other difference, should stand as one phalanx."

TO BRING VICTORY TO CANADA

This is the urgent message of Samuel Gompers, President of the American Federation of Labour, at a mass meeting of workers held in Toronto, November 26th, 1917.

SUPPORT UNION GOVERNMENT

There was a time when Gompers was the strongest of the peace advocates. German treachery, German brutality, Germany's plan of world domination opened his eyes. He says so himself. Today he just as strongly advocates war on Germany and German methods. He is proud of the union brothers in the Canadian lines in France. He has placed the union label on Union Government!

QUEBEC MUST BE MADE TO DO HER SHARE

You know Canada's needs even better than Gompers. You know that Quebec has not done her share in this War—either in men or money—and does not intend to do it. She trusts in Laurier and Bourassa to effect Canada's withdrawal from the War. In other words Quebec is a quitter. And she is looking for other quitters from Halifax to Vancouver to get her into power. Now is the time for *men* and *women* with red blood in their veins to express themselves on the ballot paper. Union Government alone will react to Quebec slackers, with the arm of the law.

WOMEN WHO CAN VOTE

Every woman may vote who is a British subject, 21 years of age, resident in Canada one year and in the constituency 30 days, who is the mother, wife, widow, daughter, sister or half sister, of any person, male or female, living or dead, who is serving or has served without Canada in any of the Military forces, or within or without Canada in any of the Naval forces of Canada or of Great Britain in the present War, or who has been honourably discharged from such services and the date of whose enlistment was prior to September 20th, 1917.

Unionist Party Publicity Committee

The strictly limited vote for a select number of women was obviously designed to allow Borden's female supporters to vote for the Unionist Government. In this restricted franchise there was no universal franchise for women.

Note that the ad was inserted in a journal of the labour movement, endorsed by the Toronto District Labour Council, *and in no other paper.* It was solidly based on the theme of Gompers' address to the Victory Bond rally; it could only have been published after it had been cleared with Gompers personally; and it was never repudiated by him. On the contrary, the Federation President responded with alacrity to a personal invitation from Borden to address a joint session of the House and Senate in April 1918. This was an honour previously extended only to two other personages—Arthur Balfour, ex-Premier of Britain, and Rene Viviant, ex-Premier of France.

The *Globe* of April 27, referred to Gompers as the "Great Commoner," and reported that he had stirred Parliament. The correspondent for the paper reported that "There was bite and sting to the contemptuous satire in which he spoke of 'Kultured' Germany and Austria." There is no doubting that Gompers gloried in being surrounded by the apparently attentive and fawning aristocrats and capitalists present for the occasion of his Canadian triumph, and he spoke in a manner calculated to delight his audience.

Speaking to delegates at the 1918 Convention of the AFL, that once staunch defender of Canadian autonomy, now turned servile flatterer, P.M. Draper pompously informed the Federation assembly of how their President impressed the Parliament of Canada:

> I will refer before I close to the honour that was shown to the President of the American Federation of Labour in Canada. The Government of the Dominion of Canada conferred upon President Gompers . . . an honour which has been conferred upon only two other persons. They asked him to speak to the legislative representatives of both the Upper and Lower Houses of the Dominion . . . They were so impressed by the stand he took that they ordered his speech printed and distributed by thousands throughout the entire Dominion of Canada.

Draper could have better employed his time with a recital of the splits in the Canadian labour movement, occasioned by American interference in Trades Congress affairs, ever since the first "fraternal" delegate of the Federation appeared on the scene in 1898. He could have informed them of how AFL domination had again set the stage for yet another crisis of Canadian labour at the just recently concluded Trades Congress Convention in Quebec city.

The war was winding down but the bitterness of the conscription issue and AFL involvement on the side of arch-conservatism still lingered on when the Trades Congress Convention was called to order in the city of Quebec in 1918. The fading conscription issue alone would probably not of itself have been sufficient cause for the deep divisions that emerged from the Convention. There were numerous other factors that went into the making of the crisis, of which class collaboration and a world in crisis were not the least. And the appointment of an "international" union officer to the post of Minister of Labour in Canada, at the very moment when resentment against the AFL was intensifying, was surely calculated to antagonize the radical and socialist unionists, not least in the always radical west.

Alliance Against Canadian Industrial Unionism

At Quebec, manifestations of blatant class collaboration were opposed by the unionists from the prairies and the west coast. The westerners also brought with them the ever contentious issue of industrial versus craft unionism. The Winnipeg Trades and Labour Council submitted the following resolution calling for a referendum on the question of organization:

> Whereas, in the past the capitalist class have used every means at their disposal to defeat the workers in their attempt to ameliorate the conditions under which they work; and, whereas, the present form of craft organization leaves us in the position whereby the capitalist class can successfully defeat us in any attempt we may make; therefore, be it resolved, that we call upon the Trades and Labour Congress of Canada to take a referendum vote on the question of organizing the Canadian Labour Movement into a modern and scientific organization by Industry instead of by Craft.

Obviously, giving practical effect to a resolution of this nature would have necessitated a clean break with the AFL and "international" unionism. As the Transcona Trades and Labour Council pointed out in a motion submitted by that body, joint strike action in Canada was impossible because it was "necessary for each craft to obtain sanction from its international." The Transcona position was echoed by several locals of the International Union of Machinists in a resolution which read:

> Whereas, to successfully conduct a strike all Crafts in an industry must act together and realizing that the present organization in Craft unions, whereby it is necessary for each Craft to secure sanction from its International, tends to defeat this object of a successful strike, therefore be it resolved, that the Executive of the Trades Congress be instructed to take a referendum vote of all Crafts affiliated on the following question: are you in favour of reorganizing the workers by Industries instead of by Craft.

The radicals present at the Quebec City Convention had thrown down the gauntlet, and the conservative custodians of craft unionism and class collaboration did not hesitate to take up the challenge. Every resolution on organization and policy proposed by the western-based locals and central bodies was defeated by a solid phalanx of eastern delegates from the international craft unions. It had been traditional for the west to nominate a member to the Executive Committee, and heretofore the nominee had been assured of election by acclamation. In 1918 the conservative bloc defeated the candidate chosen by the western caucus, electing instead a nominee of their own choice. Also defeated was a proposal that would have made possible larger and more representative delegations from the western region to the Conventions that were almost always held in eastern—mostly central—Canada.

In the face of these many defeats, the bloc of western delegates in caucus decided on the holding of a western conference at Calgary, Alberta in March 1919. The purpose of the proposed conference was to arrive at a united policy on western attitudes towards the Trades Congress and international unionism in Canada. It appears that the caucus at the time had in mind no other objective than the elaboration of a common policy that would enable them to play a more effective role in Congress affairs. Two items bear witness to the fact that the participants in the caucus meeting at Quebec did not anticipate any definite or final break with the Trades Congress. The *Western Labour News* for October 4, 1918 expressed the prevailing outlook and intentions of the western delegates:

> The only other alternative is for us to bring the east and south in harmony with the spirit of progress and fair play. This will be done in one of two ways. Either we shall persuade them to step alongside of us; or we shall compel them so to do. The former is well nigh hopeless, therefore the latter must be our task. This means a solid and intelligent west. This means a united and intelligent platform and policy. This means a Convention of the west to formulate plans and policies.

In a letter circulated to every affiliate of the B.C. Federation of Labour, and published in the *B.C. Federationist* of October 25, 1918, Federation Secretary A.S. Wells was careful to point out that the west was not advocating "dual unionist" policies: "It must be fully understood that the idea of holding this conference is not a secessionist movement, but a movement to give expression to the aims and objects of organized labour in the west . . . . some means must be provided for the western movement, which is so different to that of the east, to give expression to its sentiment. This is most important in view of the serious situation that is likely to develop in the near future as a result of the cessation of hostilities in Europe, and the period of reconstruction that must follow."

However, world crisis and the maturing of class contradictions and crisis conditions in Canada, with their natural accompaniment of repressive measures by the state, proved to be important influences in pointing the Calgary conference in a direction not anticipated by its sponsors. The conference met in Calgary on schedule, and British Columbia unionists gave evidence of the significance with which they viewed the historic event when, for the only time ever, they arranged to hold the annual Convention of the B.C. Federation outside of the boundaries of the province.

Federation delegates met in Calgary for two days prior to the opening of the western conference, and then attended its sessions in a body.

By the time of the opening of the conference, events of international import had developed which had an important influence on the deliberations and decisions at the gathering. The Bolshevik Revolution was victorious in Russia; the Spartacist Revolution in Germany was not yet defeated; there was mutiny, or near mutiny, in the armed forces of both France and Britain; and already critical economic conditions in Canada were worsening while the cost of living was rising dramatically. These events exercised a tremendous influence on conference delegates, turning Calgary in March 1919 into a breeding ground of all those policies that were anathema to the AFL and the international unions: direct political action, radical opposition to policies of class collaboration, industrial unionism, and an independent Canadian movement. Resolutions spelled out policy on these questions in a way that left no margin for error as to the intentions of the assembled delegates. A comprehensive resolution on the central theme of the conference stated that:

> Realizing that the aims and objects of the labour movement should be the improving of the social and economic condition of society in general, and the working class in particular;
> And whereas the present system of production for profit, and the institutions resulting therefrom, prevent this being achieved,
> Be it resolved that the aims of labour as represented by this Convention are the abolition of the present system of production for profit, and the substituting therefor production for use, and that a system of propaganda to this end be carried on.

Having thus stated the general aims and objects of the movement, the conference delegates proceeded to resolve the organizational methods by which they were to be achieved. This was accomplished in a resolution which read as follows:

> Whereas great and far-reaching changes have taken place during the last year in the realms of industry;
> And whereas we have discovered through painful experiences the utter futility of separate action on the part of the workers, organized merely along craft lines, such action tending to strengthen the relative position of the master class;
> Therefore, be it resolved, that this Western Labour Conference place itself on record as favouring the immediate reorganization of the workers along industrial lines, so that by virtue of their industrial strength, the workers may be better prepared to enforce any demand they consider essential to their maintenance and well being;

And be it further resolved, that in view of the foregoing, we place ourselves also on record as being opposed to the innocuity of labour leaders lobbying Parliament for palliatives which do not palliate.[16]

The conference adopted a strong internationalist position which, besides proclaiming support for revolutionary struggles currently in progress, left no shadow of doubt on how the delegates viewed political action required for the resolving of Canada's many social problems. A resolution formulated on these lines read as follows:

Whereas, holding the belief in the ultimate supremacy of the working class in matters economic and political, and that the light of modern developments have proved that the legitimate aspirations of the labour movement are repeatedly obstructed by the existing political forms, and clearly show the capitalistic nature of the Parliamentary machinery, this Convention expresses its open conviction that the system of Industrial Soviet Control by selection of representatives from Industries is more efficient and of greater political value than the present form of Government;

Be it resolved that this conference places itself on record as being in full accord and sympathy with the aims and purposes of the Russian Bolshevik and German Spartacan Revolutions, and be it further resolved, that we demand the immediate withdrawal of all Allied troops from Russia; and further, that this conference is in favour of a General Strike on June 1st should the Allies persist in their attempt to withdraw the Soviet administration in Russia or Germany, and that a system of propaganda be carried out and that a referendum vote be taken.

That this Convention declare its full acceptance of the principle of "Proletariat Dictatorship" as being absolute and efficient for the transformation of capitalistic private property to communal wealth and that fraternal greetings be sent to the Russian Soviet Government, the Spartacans in Germany, and all definite working-class movements in Europe and the World, recognizing they have won first place in the history of the class struggle.

That the interests of all members of the working class being identical, this Body of Workers recognizes no alien but the capitalist; also that we are opposed to any wholesale immigration of workers from various parts of the World and who would be brought here at the request of the Ruling Class.[17]

The *Manitoba Free Press* for March 14, 1919 described the decision of the conference as "an automatic declaration of war on the part of the labour people against the capitalistic classes of the world." But it was also a declaration of war on international craft unionism and AFL domination over the Canadian labour movement. This was clearly recognized by the delegates, who passed a resolution calling for a complete break with the internationals:

> Resolved, that this Convention recommend to its affiliated membership the severance of their affiliation with their international organizations, and that steps be taken to form an industrial organization of all workers;
> And be it further resolved, that a circular letter outlining a proposed plan of organization be sent out to the various organizations and that a referendum be taken on the question at the same time.[16]

The referendum was an overwhelming success in the region west of Port Arthur, Ontario and was followed with the calling of a constituent Convention, which assembled at Calgary on June 11 to 16, 1919. A constitution comprised of 39 clauses was adopted, the Preamble to which read as follows:

> Modern industrial society is divided into two classes, those who possess and do not produce, and those who produce and do not possess. Alongside this main division all other classifications fade into insignificance. Between these two classes a continual struggle takes place. As with buyers and sellers of any commodity there exists a struggle on the one hand of the buyer to buy as cheaply as possible, and on the other, of the seller to sell for as much as possible, so with the buyers and sellers of labour power. In the struggle over the purchase and sale of labour power the buyers are always masters—the sellers always workers. From this fact arises the inevitable class struggle.
>
> As industry develops and ownership becomes concentrated more and more into fewer hands; as the control of the economic forces of society becomes more and more the sole property of imperialistic finance, it becomes apparent that the workers, in order to sell their labour power with any degree of success, must extend their forms of organization in accordance with changing industrial methods. Compelled to organize for self defense, they are further compelled to educate themselves in preparation for the social change which economic developments will produce whether they seek it or not.
>
> The One Big Union, therefore, seeks to organize the wage worker, not according to craft, but according to industry; according to class and class needs; and calls upon all workers to organize irrespective of nationality, sex, or craft into a workers' organization, so that they may be enabled to more successfully carry on the everyday fight over

wages, hours of work, etc., and prepare ourselves for the day when production for profit shall be replaced by production for use.[19]

International union reaction to radical union action in the west, was both immediate and predictable. A labour journal in Edmonton, *The Soviet*, in the number for July 31, 1919 reported on action taken by the AFL Convention at Atlantic City, as follows: "The Constitution of the Federation had been amended to make it illegal for any organization or members of the organization to advocate a general strike or industrial organization without the consent of the General Executive Board of the American Federation of Labour."

The Trades Congress was quick to follow the Federation lead with yet another amendment to the much-amended Article 1, Section 2, of the constitution. Passed by the 1919 Convention, the amendment read:

> The Congress Executive Council shall have power by a majority vote of its members to suspend or revoke the charter of any Provincial Federation of Labour, Trades and Labour Council or Federal Union chartered by the Congress where the officers have encouraged or advocated secession from international unions or assisted in forming independent or dual organizations, and the books, papers, funds, and property shall be surrendered by the organization against which action is taken to the Executive Council, to be held in trust pending the restoration of the charter suspended or revoked or the granting of charter in the place of the one suspended or revoked, when it shall be restored to the original or the new organization. Provided that where the interests of the movement can be better served, the Executive Council shall have power . . . to suspend the officers of any chartered organization, and appoint a commission of not more than three members who shall take charge of the affairs, funds, and property for a period not to exceed six months, or, in the case of a Provincial Federation of Labour, until a regular Convention can be held . . .

An issue that affected relations between radical unionists and officers of the Congress concerned repressive measures directed against militants and anti-war elements. State repression had intensified as the war dragged on and the toll of casualties mounted. As the real cost of the war, in terms of shattered lives, became widely known, opposition to the continuation of the conflict grew—and not least among the workers who bore the brunt of its burden.

To the extent that they cooperated with Borden's War Cabinet, the Trades Congress officers shared responsibility for the repressive measures instituted by the Government. And, more significantly, international unionism and the AFL were directly represented in the War Cabinet, in the person of Senator and Minister of Labour Gideon Robertson, who was simultaneously a member of the International Executive of the Commercial Telegraphers Union. As early as February 1918, Robertson was personally calling for joint action by the Departments of Labour and Justice to ferret out radical industrial unionists in British Columbia. The Minister was not at all hesitant in making known the fact that, in addition to the "safety of the state," he was concerned for the protection of the American union movement in Canada. In a letter to cabinet colleagues dated February 20, 1918, Robertson recommended prosecution of suspected radicals ". . . on behalf of and in the interests of the bona fide labour organizations of Canada who are at the present time endeavouring to cooperate with the government and lend their assistance to the end that every man available should be employed in some productive capacity, and because the IWW activities are diametrically opposed to such policies."[20]

C.H. Cahan, a Montreal corporation lawyer appointed by Borden to conduct a survey of public attitudes, submitted a report that denied the existence of any activities of a special or significant character on the part of radical unionists or alien saboteurs. He informed Borden that he viewed the general situation in the country, although troublesome to the Government, to be in the nature of a natural response to the problems caused by protracted war. The report prepared by Cahan, concurred in by the commissioner of the RNWMP, said, "I am convinced that the unrest now prevalent in Canada is due to the weakening of the moral purpose of the people to prosecute the war to a successful end; to the fact that the people are becoming daily more conscious of the bloody sacrifices and irritating burdens entailed by carrying on the war; and to the growing belief that the Union Government is failing to deal effectively with the financial, industrial, and economic problems growing out of the war which are, perhaps, incapable of any early satisfactory solution."[21]

But intensification of the national and world crises, and the growth of radical unionist and socialist activities influenced by the example of the revolutions in Russia and Germany, became reason for serious concern among the Canadian ruling class, with the result that repressive measures were increased. On September 25, 1918, a Department of Public Safety was created by Order-in-Council, with Cahan as Director. In October, despite the fact that the war was nearing an end, another Order-in-Council was passed restricting labour's right to strike. In an issue of March 21, 1919, the *B.C. Federationist*, quoting an OBU spokesman, equated the Government's suppression of civil liberties with the anti-radical repression practiced by the Trades Congress and the international unions:

> Following the last Trades and Labour Congress of Canada in this country, at which certain resolutions were put forward, the movers

were denied access to the floor by the majority of that Congress, and you will note that the Government immediately, upon the adjournment of the Congress, put into effect certain restrictive methods against the workers which had not been done prior to that time, and they had taken their cue from the sentiments expressed by the Trades and Labour Congress of Canada, in spite of the fact the entire western section represented at that Congress had desired that those questions should be threshed out on the floor, and we must notice that all the federated bodies of these Trades Councils of labour serve the purpose of the rulers at the present time by pointing out to what extent they can repress the worker, and know to what extent they can attain their ends.

Members of the United Mine Workers Union at both ends of the country were in revolt against their international, which was industrial in form of organization but arch-conservative and class collaborationist in established policies. A communication over the signature of J.B. McLachlan, Secretary-Treasurer of the union, stated it to be the intention of the Nova Scotia miners to boycott a Government-sponsored labour conference. The statement, published in the Nova Scotia *Labour Leader* in August 1919, said:

The miners of Nova Scotia practically refuse to attend the labour conference called by the Government to meet in Ottawa in September, as a protest against the alleged domination in that proposed gathering of the ultra-conservative labour element. The text of the telegram is as follows: "The following motion was passed on Thursday by the Executive Board of District 26 of the UMWA. That the Board does protest against the hand-picking of labour's delegates by Tom Moore and P.M. Draper for the conference of employers and employees to be held in Ottawa, September 11th, and wish to state that such a conference held when all labour unions in Canada, including the One Big Union, are not allowed to select their own representatives cannot by any process of reasoning be said to represent organized labour in Canada, and that unless such representation is granted all labour unions of Canada, District 26 of the UMWA refuses to take part in the said conference."

The case of the miners of British Columbia and Alberta, comprising District 18 of the UMW, is one of the more clearly delineated examples of the alliance between international unions, employers and Government, in opposition to militant industrial unionism and radical politics.

A referendum vote conducted among the miners of District 18 favoured affiliation with the OBU. In May 1919, 6,200 miners in the District struck

the coal mines under the leadership of the OBU. Attempts to conduct
negotiations failed due to the combined refusal of the members of the
Western Coal Operators' Association to recognize the Executive of the One
Big Union.

In July, the international President of the UMW revoked the charter of
District 18, and ordered it placed under the administration of a trusteeship
appointed by the international Executive Board. The Government,
through its Department of Labour administered by Senator Gideon
Robertson, actively supported the UMW with the application of
Department orders decreeing closed shop conditions in favour of the
American union. According to the 1919 issue of *Canadian Annual Review*,
Robertson contended that it was impossible to recognize two unions
claiming jurisdiction in the negotiation of a wage agreement.
Furthermore, the Minister charged that the One Big Union, by the actions
of its leaders, had shown no tendency to respect or fulfil contracts and
obligations, and that it was wholly unreliable and untrustworthy. The
workers, he said, could expect to enjoy trade union rights "only so long as
the organization to which they belong is not one which has for its purpose
the destruction of industry and of existing legitimate institutions."

In a flagrant effort designed to assist in securing the position of the
UMW, the Department ordered a sizeable increase in wages for those
miners who were members of the American organization. Published in the
Labour Gazette issue for January 1920, the order read as follows:

> ORDER No. 139—An application was made by the international
> representatives of the United Mine Workers of America for an increase
> in wages to their members in District 18 in accordance with recent
> advances made to coal miners in the United States. It was therefore
> ordered on December 1 that all miners of this organization employed
> in or about the mines of District 18 should be paid an advance of 14
> per cent of their gross earnings.

In the same issue of the *Gazette* we read how this agreement was set up
in a conference between the UMW and the operators, assisted directly by
Gideon Robertson, fulfilling his responsibilities to the AFL and the
international unions:

> Early in December last conferences were held in Calgary between
> international representatives of the United Mine Workers of America,
> sent from the headquarters of the organization at Indianapolis to look
> after the interests of District 18, and the coal operators within that
> region . . . Special interest was attached to these conferences, owing to
> the fact that the One Big Union was advancing its claims for
> recognition by the operators . . . The representatives of the United

Mine Workers of America advanced the proposition that all the mines throughout the District should adopt the "closed shop" principle, on the understanding that if this were done the organization would then do all in its power to discourage the organization campaign that was then being carried on by the officials of the One Big Union.

There was evidence of considerable unrest in the District, and on December 16, the Hon. G.D. Robertson, Minister of Labour, arrived in Calgary to inquire into the causes of the unrest among the miners, and the possibility of a strike resulting. Following the arrival of the Minister, further conferences were held between the operators and the representatives of the United Mine Workers, at which the Minister and Mr. W.H. Armstrong, Director of Coal Operations in the District, were present. On December 18, a settlement was reached . . . The 14 per cent increase sought by the miners was agreed to by the operators, and embodied in an order issued by the Director of Coal Operations. The agreement further provides that only members of the United Mine Workers of America may be employed in the mines of District 18. With respect to this provision the Minister of Labour, in reply to a letter from the President of the One Big Union, stated that in view of the probability of increasing agitation and unrest in the near future in the Alberta mining industry . . . it was deemed necessary to take this unusual step to meet the situation before any interruption of output should occur. With respect to the exclusion of members of the One Big Union from participation in the agreement, the Minister stated that it was obviously impossible to recognize two organizations as having jurisdiction to negotiate wage agreements for the same workers; and that the United Mine Workers of America, in contrast to the One Big Union, had a well established reputation for respecting and fulfilling its agreements.

It was patently false on the Minister's part to state, or to imply, that the One Big Union had a reputation for failing to honour agreements. The organization had been in existence less than six months when the dispute arose in the mining District, and it had no agreements to either honour or to break. The sole intent of the Minister, who used the facilities of his Government Department for the purpose, was to preserve the status of an international union—the United Mine Workers of America—by breaking the One Big Union, and through the medium of entering into a conspiracy with the coal operators and the American officials of the UMW.

In order to accomplish this aim the Government had taken the unprecedented step of prolonging the authority of the Director of Coal Operations despite the fact that his office, which was established under the authority of the War Measures Act, was due to end with the termination of the war. The extension of his authority enabled the Director of Coal

Operations to intervene officially in the Calgary negotiations, and allowed the Government, on July 21, 1920, to pass an Order-in-Council requiring all men who worked in and around the mines, who were eligible for membership, to become members of the United Mine Workers and to sign a check-off for all dues, assessments and fines levied by that organization on its members.[22] As a result of further assistance through the intervention of the courts the American union was soon able to re-establish control over the District,[23] but not before a considerable number of miners had registered their resentment in strike action.

There was considerable agitation in the mining District over the fact that the wage increase agreed on would be paid only to members, or those becoming members, of the American union. This flagrantly partisan and repressive measure was authorized under clause (3), of Order No. 141, approved by the Director of Coal Operations on December 18, 1919, which read as follows:

> . . . this contract is made and entered into for the sole use of the United Mine Workers of America and the members of the Western Coal Operators' Association of Canada. All men who work in and around the mines who are eligible to become members of the United Mine Workers of America must join that organization and agree to sign check-off for all dues, assessments and fines . . .
>
> Note—The foregoing clause to become effective whenever the officials of the United Mine Workers of America appear on the ground in each locality and cooperate with the operators in arranging details.
>
> (4) It is agreed that no man will be employed or be permitted to remain in the employ of the Company unless he agrees to comply with the foregoing conditions.[24]

Of course the UMW and the operators could determine who would, or would not, be given employment under the "eligibility" rule. And it is certain that any worker who was considered "troublesome" by one or both of the parties would stand little chance of finding work in the mines. Against such a powerful aggregation of enemies any resistance must be considered nothing less than heroic. But resistance there was. Enforcement of clause (3) was the officially admitted cause of a number of strikes in the District that continued for some months into 1920. The *Labour Gazette* for April 1920 furnishes the following details on the strikes:

> As a result of the reorganizing of District 18 by the United Mine Workers of America and the subsequent agreement between that organization and the coal operators, a wage increase of 14 per cent was established by Order 141. This Order also provided that such increase was limited to members of the United Mine Workers of

America who signed the check-off to that body. Further to offset the active hostility of the One Big Union, it was decided to guarantee the closed shop privilege to United Mine Workers of America by enforcing the compulsory check-off clause so that the mines were closed to One Big Union labour. On March 9, the Director of Coal Operations issued the first "Closed Shop" order against the Bellevue mine. It resulted in a strike of the One Big Union faction at that place. The next day, the Greenhill mine at Blairmore, under the same firm, went on sympathetic strike in protest against the order. On March 22 the "Closed Shop" was put in effect in the mines at Canmore, Coleman, and Hillcrest, and all but United Mine Workers of America members resorted to strike action. In all about 1,800 miners are out on strike at these mines . . . . a patrol of Royal Canadian Mounted Police has been stationed in that district.

It is important to note that the Canadian Government, through its Minister of Labour and the Director of Coal Operations, who functioned under authority of the War Measures Act, was not in alliance only with an American union. Since most of the western coal operations were in control of United States corporations the Government was also in alliance with American capitalists against Canadian workers. This was the classic Latin America alignment, under slightly different conditions and circumstances, and certainly just as effective in Canada as in Latin America.

Having thus disposed of his competitor, John L. Lewis gloried in his victory over the impossible "visionaries" and had the unmitigated gall to speak of the "bitter opposition" encountered by the UMW, who had only an entire Government and capitalist class in its camp to war on the OBU. Goliath slew David, and Goliath boasted of his courage in the conflict. In his address to the UMW Convention in 1918, Lewis thundered:

> The OBU, like its contemporaries, the Industrial Workers of the World, the Provincial Workmen's Association, and the Working Class Union of the South West, is founded upon the day dreams of visionaries and lacks a proper conception of our industrial needs and fails to recognize the prodigious achievements of the legitimate trade union movement. The UMWA has encountered the most bitter opposition ever given to a labour organization, but it has demonstrated the test of experience, the soundness of its principles, and the perpetuities of its structure. There must be no compromise on the part of our organization with any element of our membership that seeks to set up an institution to compete in the field of industry with the UMW.

Lewis was uncompromising in his principles regarding cooperation with working miners who entertained dreams of a better life. But he possessed no firm principles that obligated him to refuse to cooperate with the owners against those working miners.

Two more examples of collusion are worth mentioning at this point, both incidents occurring in the hardrock mining centres of north Ontario. The first incident is related in a report by J.R. Knight, given at the First Semi-Annual Convention of the OBU, held at Winnipeg in 1920. Knight informed the delegates that: "The mining districts of Cobalt and Porcupine are sure prospects for the OBU. So bitter is the feeling against the international that a vote was taken on secession. The result so far is almost unanimous for breaking away . . . However it is essential unless a fight is to be precipitated to act with great diplomacy in this matter. The only hope for the International is that the OBU will jump in and establish a local. In fact the stage has been set in expectation of this . . . Their scheme was to await the formation of the OBU, then through the Minister of Labour approach the Operators and point out to them the menace of the new organization and so get them to agree to employ none but international card holders."[25]

The other incident was noted in the record of hearings held by a Royal Commission on Industrial Relations that was set up in 1919. At the Commission sittings in north Ontario a mine operator emphatically declared that the employers were firmly opposed to recognition of the miners' union because it was too radical, following which statement this interesting conversation was entered in the records:

> Commissioner Bruce: During the war President Gompers came to this country to recommend to the workers what their attitude should be?
>
> Answer: Gompers is a Britisher himself.
>
> Bruce: He is an American citizen.
>
> Answer: That may be, but he is British born and a very clever man.
>
> Commissioner Moore: Then I take it that if you could choose the Chief Executive of the miners' organization, you would be prepared to do business with him?
>
> Answer: Bring Gompers here and we will talk to Gompers. It all rests with the heads of these organizations. In my opinion if you are going to get any place you must have good brains at the head of the workmen.[26]

When discussing the question of American domination of the Canadian union movement, one cannot ignore the strange case of Mr. Gustave Francq and the International Labour and Socialist Conference, held at Berne, Switzerland in 1919 (the Berne Convention).

Samuel Gompers, on behalf of the American Federation, had roundly denounced the Berne Convention and refused to appoint delegates because there would be socialists and nationals of "enemy aliens" in attendance. But for some strange reason P.M. Draper, who was in Paris on other business together with Gustave Francq, appointed Francq to attend the Berne Convention representing the Trades Congress. Equally strange, Francq thought that he actually could be a full-fledged delegate and representative of Canadian labour. Acting on his mistaken belief that the Canadian union movement was free to participate in such affairs, Francq accepted a place on the Permanent Committee appointed by the Convention. This unexpected development precipitated a crisis for Draper and the Trades Congress.

When news of the Francq appointment came to the attention of Congress President Tom Moore, he immediately communicated with Camille Huysmans, withdrawing the appointment and advising the International Secretary that he should substitute for Francq the representative of some affiliated organization, and at the same time Moore declined an invitation to the Trades Congress to appoint a representative to a second international Convention to be held at Lucerne.

The correspondence relating to this affair is included in the 1919 Convention proceedings. A letter from Huysmans to Moore reads as follows: "In reply to your letter of April 21st, I beg to inform you that Mr. Gustave Francq attended the Berne Convocation organized by our Committee and declared he represented the Trades and Labour Congress.

"This Convention appointed a Permanent Committee of which he was accepted in membership, and as such he received my cablegram.

"If there is any confusion I should be very glad if Mr. Francq would kindly send me an explanation, for we have no intention to affiliate anybody without due inquiry."

The cablegram mentioned by Huysmans concerned a cabled request to Francq for the names of Congress delegates who would be in attendance at Lucerne in August. But no one would be present in Lucerne in August, and Moore rather than Francq would give the "explanation," which was communicated to Huysmans in a July letter:

> Mr. Gustave Francq, of Montreal, who represented the Trades and Labour Congress of Canada at the Berne Convention early this year, has forwarded on a cable sent by you under date June 16th and also a letter mailed under date 27th of May.
>
> We extend our thanks for the courtesy of the invitation, but our authority does not extend to the point of being officially represented in the Labour and Socialist Secretariat. The Trades and Labour Congress of Canada is in a unique position in the labour world. Our trade union movement in Canada for industrial purposes is part of the American Federation of Labour; but the same unions are affiliated

with the Trades and Labour Congress, which is a body formed for legislative purposes in the Dominion of Canada. We have not attached ourselves to any political party, though we have created Federated Labour Parties in the different provinces of this Dominion for direct political action.

Our Convention meets in the city of Hamilton about the 22nd of September this year, and it would only be on authority of our Convention that we could enter into such an affiliation as you suggest, and I know you will appreciate that without having a definite policy relative to affiliation it would be both inadvisable and improper to send official delegates.

The last letter in the series dealing with the international conferences was from Huysmans to Moore: "We thank you for your letter of July the 4th and regret that you are unable to send official delegates to the Lucerne Conference. The invitations were sent in execution of decision taken in presence of your delegate at Berne, who told us that, although your organizations are affiliated as unions with the American Federation of Labour, your bodies are completely free to decide alone in questions of political action. We have the impression here in Europe more and more that the labour classes of all countries have to unite and to combine in order to avoid, for the future, the return of the unhappy events of these later years and work in a positive way to construct a new world of liberty and fraternity."

Unfortunately the new world of liberty and fraternity, if it was to be constructed at all, would have to be built without the direct participation of the Canadian union movement. It was the sole prerogative of the American Federation to act in that capacity on behalf of its Canadian labour colony. Moore already knew when he was writing to Huysmans that policy on the matter had been firmly established years before, the policy being that the AFL would represent Canadian unionists at all international gatherings, and if the Federation chose not to attend, then neither would Canada be represented. To European labour we must have appeared as a strange breed of people indeed that would accept a voluntary colonial status rather than choose freedom of action. The decision of the Congress Convention not to participate was a predictable one. The appropriate Committee of the Convention recommended non-participation, and the final word on the subject appears as follows in the Convention proceedings for 1919:

> The Committee recommended the approval of this section and suggested that, at a later date, the Congress might consider whether affiliation was desired. Delegate Trotter expressed the opinion that the Congress should determine its own status in regard to the International Secretariat at this Convention. The Congress ought not

to be satisfied merely to be represented through the American
Federation of Labour, but should be directly affiliated. Delegate
Francq stated that in his report as fraternal delegate to the
International Trade Union and Labour and Socialist Conferences he
had expressed his opinion on the subject of affiliation.

Winnipeg, 1919

Undoubtedly the most dramatic event of the period was the Winnipeg
general strike of 1919. Although the strike was not organized, called, or led
by the One Big Union—only one OBU member, R.B. Russell, was on the
general strike Committee—it is inseparably linked with the emergence of
the new movement, and there is no questioning the fact that it reflected the
organizational principles, and much of the philosophy of the organization.

Aside from any other consideration—and not all aspects will be
discussed here—the strike at Winnipeg stands out as an historic event in
the calendar of labour activites. Though small in comparison to other
general strikes—Sweden 1909; Seattle 1919; China 1925; and Britain
1926—the Winnipeg strike was the longest (May 15 to June 26, 1919) and
the most stubborn general strike in history, and involved 35,000 strikers in
a population of 200,000 and, in addition, sparked sympathetic strikes in a
number of other cities and towns.

The strike was particularly significant for the way in which it crystallized
the strong feelings of class consciousness of the after-war period that
produced such events as the Russian Bolshevik Revolution, the Spartacist
Revolution in Germany, the mutiny in the French Black Sea Fleet, and the
incipient mutiny amongst the British troops alerted for duty in Russia. It
opposed the representatives of the capitalist class in the Citizens'
Committee of One Thousand, and brought the state apparatus into direct
action on the side of ruling class "law and order." In the six weeks of bitter
strife and its aftermath, the American Federation of Labour, the
international unions, and their Canadian agency the Trades Congress—
occupying a strategic position in the Ministry of Labour—lined up on the
side of the capitalists against the working class.

Historian David J. Bercuson, who is no radical in politics, comments on
this alignment of forces against the strikers:

> The government of Canada, under the leadership of Robert L.
> Borden, with Senator Gideon Robertson as Minister of Labour and
> Arthur Meighen as acting minister of justice [who had economic links
> with U.S. corporations—*J.S.*], was from the outset deeply involved in
> the events in Winnipeg. Though the principles which the workers

fought for were well established in Canadian industrial centres, Meighen and Robertson refused, in the face of massive evidence, to admit there were any real grievances at the heart of the dispute. These men feared the imminent rise of radical industrial unionism combined with syndicalist principles embodied in the nascent One Big Union. They were convinced that the Winnipeg strike was, in reality, a test case of OBU ideas and the experiment upon which the OBU revolution was to be based.

The government sidestepped the issue of collective bargaining, took aim at the OBU, and threw its massive military and judicial weight on the side of the employers. The underlying causes of the strike were ignored and the basic issues were questioned by a government determined to bring about a collapse of the general walkout. The fictitious OBU issue was used to alienate the workers of Winnipeg from other possible sources of trade union support and from middle-class and farmer sympathy. In the end the government, defining collective bargaining only in terms of craft union principles, presented disaffected strikers and orthodox trade union leaders with an excuse to return to work. The famous declaration of 16 June 1919, in which the Metal Masters agreed to a form of collective bargaining, was, in fact, a carefully engineered manoeuvre, guided by Robertson, in which a negotiating committee composed of orthodox railway union leaders threw their support against the strikers. Their actions were prompted by fear of the OBU—a fear fed by the contagious anxieties of the federal government.

Bercuson concludes his essay with a comment on the aims and methods of the two Government Ministers chiefly involved: "The mediation process had been twisted by the Government to serve its crusade against the OBU. The collective bargaining issue, paramount to the strikers, was never faced by either Robertson or Meighen. They refused to acknowledge its existence. Their aim was to mount an attack against the OBU. Therefore they could not admit that the strike had legitimate economic roots. Collective bargaining and union recognition were swept aside in Canada's own "'little' Red Scare.''[27]

Concerning Senator Robertson's role as Minister for the American union movement, on June 2, 1919, the *Times* of London reported that the Senator had carried his case to the ultimate court of appeal, to Samuel Gompers and the American Federation. The *Times* published a report on the strike situation in Canada, which was sent by Robertson to Gompers:

A general sympathetic strike involving ninety-five unions was called in the city of Winnipeg May 15, resulting in a complete tie-up of all business and the declaration of the strike committee of control over civic affairs, as well as interference with provincial and federal employees. As in the case of all general strikes of this nature it has already defeated itself, but I feel it is proper to address you, after being on the ground for several days, that in my opinion the prestige and authority of the international unions whose local membership participated in the strike . . . should receive earnest and serious consideration of the Executives of the various organizations concerned . . . The underlying motive in calling the strike is undoubtedly to support what is known as the One Big Union movement.

According to the London paper, an immediate result of Robertson's appeal for help from the American Federation was the appearance of a number of international union officials in Toronto and Winnipeg, for the express purpose of both settling the strike and penalizing rebel locals and members. An example of the outcome of this visit from "friendly foreigners" can be found in the report of the Robson Commission, set up by the Manitoba Government at the conclusion of the strike. The report says:

The lodges referred to above are integral parts of international unions. Their movements in important steps are under the guidance of the international officers. One of their principles is that there shall be no sympathetic strikes by their unions. The determinations to strike must also be subject to the approval or direction of the international . . . international officers came on the ground, held trials and expelled men who had departed from the laws and principles of the respective unions.

The effect of this expulsion was serious for the men affected, as the employer company . . . takes eligibility of its men in large measure from their union status. Certain leaders in the unauthorized strike of the international union members were still out of work at the time of the hearing.

But there was more than one piece of correspondence that passed between the American union Senator and his international leader. Most are apparently now out of sight;[28] at least one other was quoted by Peter Heenan in the House of Commons on June 2, 1926. Discussing Government conduct in the Winnipeg strike, Mr. Heenan stated, "On June 5th, Senator Robertson wrote a letter giving permission for forty-four porters to be brought in from the United States to take the place of the Canadian Pacific Railway men on strike . . ."

United States union officers and United States scabs were mobilized by the Minister of Labour of Canada to break a strike of Canadian workers.

These acts of national humiliation caused a noted French-Canadian
nationalist to pass critical comment on the strange conduct of a Canadian
Minister. The *Times* of June 5, 1919 reported on the comment as it
appeared in *Le Devoir*: "Mr. J.B. Bourassa, in his paper *Le Devoir*,
denounces what he calls the submission of the Canadian Government to
American labour organizations. He asks if it is possible to imagine French
Ministers begging a British or Belgian labour leader to intervene in the
French labour world. He says that what is important is not the merits of the
struggle in Canada, but the subordination of Canadian labour to American
labour as attested by the appeal of Mr. Robertson to the International
Federations."

The Government in the role of general staff of the ruling class and acting
chiefly through the titular heads of the Departments of Labour and
Justice—the former connected with American unions and the latter with
links to American business—arrived at the decision that it was essential
that the strike be broken rather than settled. The Ministers concerned and
their aids resorted to chicanery and double-dealing, not hesitating even to
use illegal methods in order to attain their objective.

The workers not only had grievances regarding wages and working
conditions, they were denied the reasonable opportunity to address their
grievances through an acceptable form of collective bargaining. In private
Robertson admitted that the strike was justified. In a letter addressed to
the Acting Prime Minister, Robertson expressed the opinion that there was
"no doubt merit and justification in the original grievances." But in
public he agreed with the employer's stand on the important question of
collective bargaining.

Later in 1919, when the situation had calmed down considerably, the
Royal Commission on Industrial Relations would draw attention to the rise
of conglomerates in industry, and emphasize the value of larger
bargaining units in the facilitation of negotiations. The Commission
Report criticized employers who balked at meeting larger organizations of
workers, and concluded that an employer's only legitimate concern should
be whether his men were represented, not the kind of body which
represents them.[29]

But Senator Robertson publicly associated himself with the employers'
stand on collective bargaining, which—and only after considerable
pressure had been applied—did not go beyond the narrowest craft union
form of bargaining. In a statement to the Toronto *Daily Star* on May 26,
1919, the Minister asserted: "The kind of collective bargaining through
centralized control like Trades Councils or like the One Big Union
demanded by the Trades Council is utterly unjustified."

The same theme is repeated in a slightly longer interview with the Regina
Morning Leader, in which the Senator stated: "There was no justification
for the general strike at all, and further the metal trades employees were

utterly unjustified in demanding the recognition of . . . the Metal Trades Council. They were justified only in asking recognition of craft unions, which were already recognized by their employers. The right of collective bargaining was inalienable, but the collective bargaining was not justifiable through Councils or combinations of unions.''

Robertson's statements were deliberately designed to cloud the issue. He clarified his personal prejudices in the Winnipeg *Citizen* of May 31, when he characterized the strike as a ''blow at international trade unions, and in support of the Big Union movement.'' The problem of bargaining unit should have been the choice of the workers alone, and it was not true that the employers had conceded bargaining rights of any sort. But the Minister preferred no bargaining rights at all, rather than have an industrial competitor against craft unionism recognized. In the craft tradition of Gompers and the American Federation, he was taking the stand that unions are acceptable only so long as they do not attempt to organize too many of the unorganized and as long as they conform to traditional craft structures and business union practices. The Winnipeg strikers were in violation of these golden rules.

At the very time these statements were being published, there were already Metal Trades Councils conducting joint bargaining in eight Canadian cities, and building Trades Councils in twelve.[30] At Vancouver in 1918, Robertson had personally taken part in a Metal Trades Council settlement of a strike of shipyard workers.

In the 1926 debate recorded in Hansard, Heenan tabled documents that proved the Minister had intervened to *prevent* a declaration in favour of collective bargaining. A Mediation Committee composed of leading officers of the International Railway Brotherhoods was at the point of making known a decision on collective bargaining favourable to the striking workers. Apprised of the impending declaration, Robertson on May 25 dispatched a telegram to Winnipeg with the following instructions:

> This is not an opportune time to make a declaration in favour of principle collective bargaining as it would be grasped as an excuse by strikers to claim they have forced the Government and thereby proved success of sympathetic strike.
>
> I anticipate that the general strike will either be called off very shortly or a last desperate move made to make it successful. If it proves a failure the One Big Union movement intended to be launched at the Calgary Convention on June 4 will I think also fail. These are my personal views expressed in Mr. Meighen's absence and for the information of council.

In Winnipeg Robertson met secretly with the railway union mediators

for the purpose of convincing them to reverse their position. Railway
unionists were already joining in the strike movement and international
officers, supported by the railway bosses, were on the ground threatening
disciplinary action. Under the circumstances, it was a relatively easy
matter to get the conservative leaders of the railway unions to make their
contribution to the halting of the "red menace." The result was a public
statement that fully supported the policy of the metal trades employers.
Signed by the heads of five railway internationals, the statement said:
"The undersigned representatives of the train service organizations . . . do
endorse the policy of collective bargaining—as outlined by the metal
trades employers in their announcement of this date, being in principle
and effect the same as that enjoyed by these organizations."[32]

Despite frantic efforts to avoid it, Robertson and Meighen saw their
problems increasing as strike sympathy spread in all directions. The
greatest fear of the two gentlemen who represented ruling class interests in
the crisis was that the strike wave would spread into conservative Ontario,
and from there into a highly volatile political situation in Quebec. Their
worst fears in this regard seemed to be coming to pass. In a dispatch dated
June 1, the *Times* of London reported:

> A long and exciting meeting at the Labour Temple at Toronto ended
> in the seizure of control by the Socialist element. Mr. O'Leary,
> President of the Trades and Labour Council, Mr. Hevey,
> Vice-President, and Mr. Doggett, Secretary, have resigned office in
> protest against the extreme proposals of the strike Committee. The
> retiring officers represent the conservative forces of organized labour
> and affiliation with international bodies as opposed to the "One Big
> Union" idea.
>
> By this action the leaders of the strike in Toronto establish an active
> alliance with the strike leaders at Winnipeg, and show that there will
> be a determined effort to paralyze the public services and consolidate
> labour throughout the Dominion in support of the demands of the
> Socialists and Syndicalists.

It was this development that brought officers of the internationals post
haste to Toronto, to bring their influence and authority to bear on the side
of conservative policies. The *Times* on June 3, in a further report on the
situation in the Ontario metropolis, said: "In Toronto, where 15,000 men
quit work for a forty-four-hour week and in sympathy with Winnipeg, the
employers refused point blank to make any concessions, claiming that it
was 'not a strike but a Socialist-inspired movement' and a 'rebellion
against capital' . . . After a long meeting the street car men . . . finally
decided not to join the general walk-out in Toronto and this decision
practically settled the fate of the general strike call in that city. The

appearance of 'international' officers in Toronto and the hostility of the more conservative leaders of the Toronto Trades and Labour Council completed its failure.''

In Toronto, spokesmen for the internationals acknowledged the justice of the demands advanced by the strikers, but they insisted that members must abide by the rules and effect a settlement favourable to international unionism. The public declarations made by the American officers of the internationals were also calculated to support employer charges of a "Socialist plot.'' In a comment dated June 4, the *Times* said:

> Owing to the resolute attitude of Mr. Robertson, Minister of Labour, the sympathetic cooperation of the heads of the International Labour Federations, and the hostility of the leaders of the Canadian Trades and Labour Council to sympathetic strikes and the severance of the connection with American labour bodies, the Winnipeg Strike Committee is facing defeat, and the decisive failure of the general strike movement at Toronto is assured . . .
>
> The President and Secretary of the Labour Council . . . explain that they are in sympathy with the aims of the Metal Trades Council, and hope that the trouble will be settled in a few days, but in the interests of the international labour movement.

All the conservative unionists loudly proclaimed their sympathy with the demands advanced by the strikers. But all of them, to a man, worked industriously and in league with employers and Government to obstruct the forging of the only kind of industrial organization that might offer some hope of victory in the struggle.

The very last thing that Robertson and Meighen wanted to see happen was any sort of move that might tend to encourage the strikers and expand the action. In that regard, they faced a crisis just at the crucial point when it seemed that the Toronto events could be turned around. The employers in Winnipeg at last indicated a willingness to make concessions that would prepare the ground for a settlement of the strike well short of a defeat for the workers. Heenan discussed this in the House on June 2, 1926, when commenting on documents in the files of the Department of Labour: "On June 9th evidently there were some members of the Government . . . who did not desire the strike should be called off, because I find here a message from Mr. Meighen . . . that the settlement on the terms proposed would be a triumph for the strike leaders.''

An employer offer to settle had, in fact, been made. On June 7, 1919, Mr. Andrews of Winnipeg, a local lawyer specially appointed to act for the Department of Justice, wired Robertson giving details of such an offer proposed by the metal trades employers. The minister, responding to this unwelcome information, instructed Andrews on June 9: "Feel strongly company should adhere to refusal mediator's proposal collective bargaining and the sympathetic strike should be called off before negotiations are resumed. Understand Citizens' Committee and employers agreed sympathy strike cannot be allowed wholly or partially to succeed."[33]

The prime movers in the affair must have regarded the situation as critical, requiring desperate remedies. The sympathetic movement was already gaining strength in the radical west, and, more importantly, was far from under control in conservative Toronto. It appeared, too, that the employers at the centre of the action at Winnipeg were prepared to make at least partial capitulation to the general strike movement, which could only encourage action in other centres throughout the country. Robertson, then on the scene in Winnipeg, decided on drastic action aimed at turning the tide in a direction more favourable to his cause.

On the night of June 16-17, Andrews, acting on the direct orders of the Minister of Labour, ordered the arrest of ten strike leaders, who were immediately taken into custody and held without bail or formal appearance before a Magistrate. On June 17, Robertson wired the Prime Minister pointing out the importance of providing machinery for the deportation of undesirables, and also advising him of ten arrests on the previous night.

On the same day, Meighen wired his Winnipeg agent, Andrews, questioning the legality of the arrests, and pointing out that they had been made without proper authorization. However, Meighen promised that the formal authorization was being forwarded. In other words, the men had been illegally detained, but the Government would take the necessary steps required to legalize the procedure. A bit worried about his personal status because of the affair, Special Prosecutor Andrews blamed the whole business on Robertson. In a message to his boss, Andrews pleaded, "Everything I have done has been at the suggestion of Senator Robertson, but because it might weaken his position with Labour I have taken the full responsibility for the Justice department."[34]

In the unprecedentedly short time of just twenty minutes, the Government passed through the entire legislative process a notorious piece of legislation that legalized the Winnipeg proceedings, and served the Canadian ruling class until it was finally repealed in 1936. Emboldened by his successes in the prairie city, Robertson cast about for new fields to conquer. Heenan described the Minister's budding ambition to the Members of the House in 1926, in the following words: "Senator Robertson . . . asked . . . that certain amendments to the Criminal Code be hastened, as Commissioner Perry (RCMP) . . . might desire to take general action throughout western Canada . . . Having arrested ten men illegally . . . having conquered Winnipeg, as it were, he was now prepared to attack the whole of western Canada. He therefore asked for certain legislation so that he could get out on the war path again."

This combined assault by international unions, state apparatus, and employers proved to be too much for the strikers to overcome. The strike failed; but only after the Government had demonstrated its readiness to resort to the most repressive measures, even when those measures were in violation of its own laws and judicial processes. Local leaders of the strike were the first to buckle under pressure, calling off the strike on June 26, 1919 without first consulting the workers who, leaderless, resentfully drifted back to work over the next several days.

A few months after the strike had ended (in October 1919) Gompers, following the example of John L. Lewis after the defeat of the coal strike, passed critical, and not very balanced, judgment on the strike and the industrial union movement that he and his international union colleagues, in association with the employers, had helped to break. Purporting to speak on "Winnipeg's Experience and Lesson," Gompers wrote:

> There are great calamities that leave their trails of blessing. There are clouds that in compensation eventually turn their silver linings upon the erstwhile depressed. There are those who insist that there is a law by which good always compensates for evil in some way. Whatever may be the truth of that, there are times when experiments in doubtful ventures prove the worthlessness of those ventures to others who may be contemplating their chimerical virtues.
>
> Such seems to be the case with respect to Winnipeg and the so-called one big union that for a brief time blazed in that municipality with such spectacular effect.
>
> Winnipeg is not without its value today. Perhaps it was even helpful. Certain it is that the wave of adventure, ill-advised as it was, has been receding since the fiasco of Winnipeg.
>
> One big union advocates are being less heard than formerly. There are few today who clamour for this particular road to Utopia. On the other hand, those in western Canada who, under the spell of the Winnipeg frenzy, forsook the American Federation of Labour, are coming back into the bona fide and time-tried movement as rapidly as they can. It is stated that 95 per cent of the miners who left the United Mine Workers have returned to that organization.
>
> In Vancouver, on petition of nine international unions, a new central body has been formed to which those who seceded are making haste to affiliate themselves. In our own northwest the desirability of the so-called one big union is much less ardently proclaimed than was the case earlier in the year.
>
> Winnipeg failed to grope its way into the promised land. For the one big union the loss of Winnipeg was a moral loss of the most damaging kind. The idea could not stand the test and it went down.

That the idea would not stand the test was, of course, a foregone conclusion. Its friends may liken their concept of the one big union to the ant hill with its complete unity, but they would do a better service to accuracy if they would liken their project to a joining of ant hill and poultry yard in one community of effort.

There are fundamental reasons for the existence of the American labour movement in its present form. The movement has grown to its present great strength and ability for service through the experience of the men and women of labour in daily grapple with conditions over a period of years stretching back into the early history of our country. Someone did not sit down and evolve a theory around which he built the movement. The American labour movement is a movement that has grown, molded by the needs of toiling humanity and the conditions under which they work. As such it is the logical and enduring servant of the American working people.

Winnipeg proved only what was proved long ago, but which some chose not to see until it was thrust upon them through adversity.

There are far too many inaccuracies in the Gompers' article for analysis within the scope of this work. Only a couple of points will be touched on. Gompers suggests that the demise of the One Big Union was an inevitability. But it seems that he was not prepared to leave the outcome to chance. Having made the prediction he worked together with employers and Government to make the prediction a reality.

The temporary defeat of the workers in the Winnipeg strike did not do anything to disprove the value of industrial forms of organization. Aside from the errors made in the process of the strike, it proved only that, at that stage of working class development, a combination of conservative craft unions, employers and the Canadian state was sufficient to deprive the Canadian workers of the fruits of what could have been an historic victory for the workers of North America.

Gompers demonstrates an absence of sympathy for embattled workers that is equalled only by his pomposity. As to the vaunted growth of strength—the international union movement at the time represented less than 9 per cent of the total labour force in Canada and the United States.

Gompers would have experienced no difficulty in finding support for his cause amongst the employer class, or assistance in spreading his business union philosophy in their propaganda organs. The Victoria, B.C. *Times*, on June 25, 1919, published an article that could easily have been written by the Federation President himself. In part, it said:

The defeat of the sympathetic strike is not a defeat for the trades unionist movement . . . . no principle of recognized trades unionism was involved. The heads of labour unionism in America . . . were sternly and relentlessly against the strike. They knew it for what it was—a deliberate attempt planned in Calgary to wreck the trades unionist movement and set up the Red oligarchy denoted by the One Big Union idea. They realized that if it had succeeded, organized labour would have been severed from its international connection. . .

The strike, thus, was largely a fight between the promoters of the One Big Union and sane trades unionism and, therefore, one of the chief factors in its defeat was the attitude of the leaders of the great international organizations . . .

The Toronto *Globe*, organ of the mining barons and the American corporations in Ontario, editorialized on June 26: "The outcome should give special satisfaction to trades unionists. The strike was engineered by their enemies in furtherance of the One Big Union, the Canadian counterpart of the IWW. Thousands of trades unionists who answered the call have been loath to believe that they were being used to undermine the crafts unionism which is the basis of the great international Labour organizations . . . "

It would not be fitting to end this chapter without commenting on the political significance of the 1919 general strike movement in Canada, and why the ruling class and the international union heads acted as they did—seemingly panic-stricken by the appearance of a pink cloud on the horizon.

It has become nearly an automatic reflex to protest that the Winnipeg strikers and their leaders had no revolutionary objectives in view, and certainly no firm plans to seize state power. It is generally maintained that the strike was launched and conducted with nothing more revolutionary in mind than the securing of collective bargaining rights. This view of the strike movement was summed up in the House of Commons on June 2, 1926 by A.A. Heaps, a strike participant and one of the ten arrested in the dead of night. On that occasion Heaps said, "I claim, Mr. Speaker, that the strike in the city of Winnipeg was an ordinary manifestation of the workers who protested against the conditions of employment that existed at that time in the city of Winnipeg."

Well, looked at within the context of a "normal" strike situation, the Winnipeg strike was no "ordinary manifestation." Even if Heaps, a participant, could not appreciate that fact, there were plenty of others who did—among them Arthur Meighen.

It is true that the focus of the strike, in its economic aspect, was on the legitimate grievances and just demands of the workers. And it centred especially on the demand for an effective collective bargaining system, capable of satisfying the needs of the workers. To that extent the strike was a "normal" event in working class experience. But to stop there is to see only the economic side of the struggle while ignoring its political implications. It is to reduce the historic significance of the strike and fail to understand the lessons in it.

An analysis purely economic in character fails to explain the decision to break the strike, rather than seeking a satisfactory compromise that could settle it. It does not explain the concentration of forces with the deliberate aim of forcing strikers to capitulate. Just how extensive was the mobilization? A letter from General Mewburn to the Prime Minister contains a clue on how serious a view was taken of the situation. Mewburn's letter—which does not discuss the RCMP forces deployed in the strike zone—says in part:

> The same precaution has been taken in British Columbia as has been taken in Manitoba and other Provinces.
> . . . I, long ago, came to the conclusion that it was up to the loyal citizens of any municipality to link up with the Militia Units and assist in maintaining law and order in any municipality where trouble might arise. We have arranged whereby Militia Units will be commanded by returned Officers and, while the military organization is not as efficient as I would like to see it, yet I believe if serious trouble arose the loyal citizens of any municipality would perform their duty. The bulk of the returned soldiers, I am convinced, will stand ready to preserve law and order and for the preservation of life and property. You can rest assured every possible measure has been taken.
> I should have felt more comfortable had a British cruiser or two paid a visit to British Columbia in an offical way, and I strongly recommended that a request for one or two of the cruisers from the China Squadron should visit British Columbia, but not with the intention of disembarking marines, except as a very last resort, and I am convinced that it would have a good effect if a cruiser or two had been there even temporarily . . .[35]

Are we to believe that these plans were discussed with the sole aim in view of preserving the craft form of unionism, to deny to workers a system of collective bargaining that was already normal in Canadian industry, or even to rescue a handful of employers from an association that was distasteful to them? That scarcely seems credible. Only a political analysis will answer these seemingly unanswerable questions that surround the problem of the Winnipeg general strike.

Undoubtedly Robertson, and even Arthur Meighen, wanted to preserve craft unionism. But organization is a political question. The American unionists are committed to craft unionism and its particular ideology, because they are committed to the capitalist system. Business unionism operates within the context of a "free labour market." It treats labour—especially skilled labour—as a commodity, for which one obtains the best price possible. Efforts are made to limit the availability of the commodity and lessen competition in order to maintain an upward pressure on prices. It does little in the area of social reform, and never seeks to effect any fundamental social change.

Craft unions and capitalism are allied. The capitalists understand the system by which it operates, and they accept it on the basis of both collusion and conflict, which is a natural phenomenon in the market place. In a period of crisis the defence of one is simultaneously the defence of the other. Hence, there was the closest possible relationship between Robertson the international unionist, and Meighen the very class conscious representative of big business. It was not a relationship based on simple class collaboration, but of basic *class solidarity* in the face of political crisis.

The strike should not be looked at separate from its historical context. It was a period of world crisis and revolution. Although not of the intensity that it attained in Europe, the world crisis seriously affected Canada and, as testified in the proceedings of the Calgary conference, Europe's revolutionary potential influenced at least some of the union leaders. In brief, the political and economic conditions in the country were such that even a minor disturbance might have precipitated an irresistible movement for revolutionary social change—and the Winnipeg strike was a little more than a minor disturbance. As Mao Tse-tung once put it: "A single spark can start a prairie fire." Winnipeg was at least a spark. Only concerted and decisive action by the ruling class prevented it from becoming a conflagration.

Soviets were arising as revolutionary beacons all across Europe. (Soviet is simply the Russian word for council.) The original Soviet was the Petrograd Labour Council in 1905, and the Congress of Soviets was a Congress of Workers, Soldiers and Peasants Councils. Even if no one else could draw the necessary lessons from that, the very class conscious Mr. Meighen could, and did. He could see that the Winnipeg Labour Council, functioning as the general strike Committee, was operating on every bit as broad a basis as the Petrograd Labour Council.

What, Mr. Meighen must have asked himself, might the consequences be if decisive action is not taken? Similar strike committees might spring up in all the important cities and towns in the country. Toronto was a key point in the struggle, and Toronto almost went over to the general strike.

The next logical step, after expansion of the general strike, would have been the convening of regional, provincial, and then national conferences of local strike Committees, which would have represented the urban centres of commercial and political power and, by their very nature, as demonstrated in an incipient form in Winnipeg, would have constituted a dual political power of a revolutionary character. From the point of view of the capitalist class, everything must serve to prevent that from taking place. The ordinary mundane affairs of a handful of Winnipeg employers were of minor importance. It was in the interests of the entire class that they were denied the right to settle the strike.

Settlement in Winnipeg could not resolve the problem in the interests of the capitalists, and might well intensify it. Even partial victory for the workers in the prairie city would have lent encouragement to workers elsewhere to take similar action. The only possible solution: Don't settle the strike, break it, and smash the OBU, the movement that might carry the contagion to other places. That had to be the decision consciously taken by the ruling class, and to that end the entire class and the full power of the state were mobilized.

This is not to say that the workers, regardless of the "revolutionary" rhetoric of some of the union leaders, had any immediate aim beyond their stated demand for collective bargaining rights, or any conscious will to exercise political power. Their class consciousness, and consequently their class solidarity, was at a much lower level than that of the capitalist class they confronted. Had the workers possessed such a level of class consciousness, the history of North America would be much different than it is.

But that does not mean that a potential for revolution did not exist. There is a large element of chance and accident in every revolution, and it would be idealistic to think that participants are fully conscious of the end result of their actions. In any case, the level of class consciousness rises in pace with experience gained in struggle. The problem for the bourgeoisie was to stop the struggle short of the working class—as a class—accumulating the political knowledge and experience necessary for them to suppress the capitalists and rule the nation.

In his autobiography, *All My Life*, A.E. Smith, who was attached to the labour church movement in Brandon at the time of the strikes, makes the following well-placed comment on the Winnipeg events: "Objectively here was revealed more clearly than by any other event in Canadian labour history the elemental factors of working-class power. Under conditions of a nation-wide political crisis the Winnipeg Strike Committee would have become an organ of truly democratic power."

But that conclusion was based on hindsight, thirty years after the event. The bourgeoisie and their international unionist allies, on the other hand, acted on foresight. The strike movement was held in check in the west, and the Toronto situation kept well under control. In the end the Winnipeg strike was defeated—not settled.

10

FROM THE WINNIPEG STRIKE
TO THE FOUNDING OF THE CIO

The coal miners of Nova Scotia, mobilized under the banner of the Provincial Workmen's Association, were among the earliest trade unionists in part of what is now Canada. Many of them, especially the Scots miners, had trade union experience before coming to Canada. By the turn of the century they had not only the mine owners to confront, they had also to contend with the bureaucratic mismanagement and divisive policies of the United Mine Workers of America, which accounted for the great difficulties encountered by the miners during the period of some of the most bitter battles fought in the Nova Scotia coal fields.

Partly due to poor economic conditions and partly due to the failure of PWA policies, which rested on a foundation of rather crass class collaboration, the UMW had made considerable inroads in the bargaining jurisdiction by 1909. By 1911 there was an approximately even split between the two organizations, with the UMW making great promises about what an international would do to improve conditions in the mines. The result was constant friction between the two organizations and a consequent fall in production which brought the Labour Department on the scene in the role of investigator and mediator.

One consideration which greatly influenced the thinking and attitudes of both working miners and mine operators was the competition from the Pennsylvania coal fields that confronted Nova Scotia coal in the Ontario-Quebec market. This was particularly acute in a period of economic recession accentuated by the loss of New England markets to the United States product. In the Labour Department investigation that took place in 1909, the operators laid special emphasis on their fear that UMW-control of union affairs would be exercised in order to make it additionally difficult for Nova Scotia to compete against the Americans for the central Canada market.

In August 1909 the *Labour Gazette* published the findings of the Board

of Investigation. The company position at the hearings was reported by the
Board as follows:

> The company contends that it should not be required to encourage
> and help support the foreign labour organization, the main body of
> whose members are working to produce coal to supplant Nova Scotia
> products in Canadian markets to the demoralization of its business,
> and possible annihilation of its property. The company further says
> that owing to the depression in the United States last year and this, a
> determined effort has been and is being made by the American
> operators to capture the St. Lawrence trade, and large quantities of
> American coal have been sold to the extent of depriving Nova Scotia
> companies of their right to important Canadian markets. The result of
> this intrusion is to make local competition in the province keener and
> to depreciate values to such a degree as to either compel Nova Scotia
> operators to cease producing or force them to make a reduction in
> wages. The cost of producing coal in the United States is only
> one-third of the cost of producing coal F.O.B. cars in the deep mines
> and heavy pitching seams on the mainland of Nova Scotia, and the
> result, if this intrusion continues, will be that Nova Scotia operators
> will either close down or the cost of production be reduced.

One cannot ignore the fact that the mine operators would prefer not to
have to deal with any union at all. But if a union must be dealt with, then a
preference would be for a union already tested during a lengthy
relationship, and one, moreover, that shared the owner's concern about
market control. The many declarations by American union spokesmen of
the period, that it was the "manifest destiny" of America to "control the
markets of the world," was material evidence that there were substantial
grounds for concern. And as stated earlier, Farrington had spoken of the
role of the UMW as a "balancing medium" in the control of marketing
conditions: "The duty devolving upon the United Mine Workers of
America . . . is to . . . act as a balancing medium in the establishment of
equitable competitive mining rates . . . it must be done or we must suffer
from inequitable competition."

The "we" referred to was the United States union miners, and the
"equitable rates" were to be so designed as to assure a favourable
competitive position for the United States product. In fact, Farrington was
proposing to do exactly what the Nova Scotia operators were accusing the
UMW of preparing to do by taking over the Canadian union—exclude
Canadian coal from the United States market while holding on to whatever
portion of the market in Canada could be captured by Pennsylvania coal.
Working miners and owners alike would ignore that kind of union policy to
their economic peril. On this point the Board seems to have agreed with the

mine owners, the report stating, "We think it ought to be left to the judgment and discretion of the company as to how far it will officially recognize an organization having its control authority outside the province, and largely under the control of interests that may be at some time in acute competition with the interest of the company."

The portion of the coal District controlled by the UMW was struck in July 1909 to win recognition, but failed of its objective because of the divided layalties of the miners. The strike was called off in April 1910. The only contribution made by the UMW at this time to the miners' cause was to keep them divided in the face of employer resistance to needed improvements. Not even the UMW cause was advanced to any appreciable extent.

When the strike ended the UMW was still in receipt of per capita tax from seventeen locals in the District, but two years later the number had declined to ten, and by November 1915 only eight locals were in good standing with the international. In March of 1915, the UMW headquarters accepted temporary defeat and retrenchment with the dissolution of their District 26, covering the Nova Scotia coal fields. As of November 1917 there was just one local still paying dues to the UMW.[1]

The general militancy that swept the Canadian labour scene in 1917 and for several years thereafter had its effect in Nova Scotia. The main cause of the unrest concerned wages and conditions in the coal mining areas, but was aggravated by the divided loyalties of the miners. A Royal Commission was dispatched to the area and advanced a proposal for a resolution of the problems that arose from the existence of contending union organizations in the mines:

> The Commission was able to persuade the leaders of the two organizations to agree to the establishment of a new organization, which is intended to absorb the membership of the two existing ones, and we believe that in due course this scheme will be carried into effect to the advantage of both employers and employees as well as the community. The Commission gave its unqualified approval to the proposition.[2]

Conferences were organized with the assistance of the Labour Department, and by June 1917 agreement had been reached on the proposition to form a single union of mineworkers in the Nova Scotia coal District, the new body to be called the Amalgamated Mine Workers of Nova Scotia. The UMW headquarters signified agreement, expressing the hope that the miners would set aside "personal feelings and bring about what is best for the great body of mineworkers in the province."[3] Subsequent developments would demonstrate exactly what the UMW officers meant by the phrase "what is best."

A reluctant, but nonetheless compliant, Grand Council of the PWA adopted a resolution dissolving the Association and transferring all its assets to the new organization, but with the stipulation that it must remain "a purely provincial union," and refrain "from entanglement or connection with any union whose officers and headquarters are outside the province."[4] But despite the apparent UMW agreement to accept the new adventure in organization, and despite the PWA stipulation of no foreign entanglements, a number of the elected officers immediately took steps to begin the process of bringing the Nova Scotia miners into the UMW fold.

Among the officers elected were Silbey Barrett, J.B. McLachlan, and Robert Baxter, all of whom were strong supporters of international union connections. They were considerably more aggressive than those officers who favoured a distinctly provincial and independent organization. Outside of the scope of the agreement, and therefore beyond the bounds of the new union, were about 3,000 miners organized under charters issued by the American Federation of Labour. In the spring of 1918, less than a year after the signing of the peace and unity pact, it was reported that a referendum taken among the miners of Nova Scotia favoured affiliation with the UMW.[5]

Subsequent to the referendum, a conference of mine owners and representatives of the Amalgamated and the federal locals, met in New York city to consider the problems involved in the transfer of the union contracts to the custody of the UMW. The owners, having abandoned their reluctance to deal with "foreign agitators," combined with the unionists in addressing a request to the Labour Minister—who just happened to be international unionist Gideon Robertson—to act as intermediary in the calling of a second conference, to be held at Montreal in January 1919.

In Montreal agreement was reached on the replacement of the Amalgamated and the federal locals with the UMW as bargaining agent for the miners.[6] An article in the *Labour Gazette* in February reveals the most probable reason why the owners dropped their opposition to recognition of a union "under foreign control." In the "memo of agreement" between the mine operators and UMW officers, the union assured the owners that their assumption of control over the miners' union "does not arise from any intention to make the wage rates and working conditions of Nova Scotia conform to those obtaining in other Districts," and the UMW further agreed to recognize "the limitations of Nova Scotia in regard to outside competition in the sale of coal." This attitude, while affording the mine owners an assurance that their difficult competitive position would receive favourable consideration, came into conflict with the aspirations of the miners, who hoped to see at least a narrowing of the gap that separated conditions in Nova Scotia from the standards enjoyed elsewhere in the coal mining industry. The miners could hardly be overjoyed by the way in which the initiative in negotiations had been handed over to the operators.

With the benefit of hindsight, J.B. McLachlan, one of the original supporters of the UMW, commented six years later that the AMW "was probably the best union that the miners of the province ever had," that it had united the miners, healed the bitterness caused by division, won improvements in wages and working conditions, and above all "it responded splendidly to the wish and decisions of the rank and file."

That comment was made when a new spirit of bitterness, the bitterness of disappointment in the UMW performance, and the new divisions arising therefrom, created more problems when the union was confronted with owner intransigence and consequent struggle in the 1920s.

In November 1920, both parties rejected a compromise proposal put forward by a Royal Commission, but a strike was narrowly averted when the union signed the "Montreal Agreement" that conceded only half the wage increase demanded by the miners. This agreement expired in November 1921, and the operators entered negotiations claiming that there had been a decline in living costs and, in addition, they were experiencing some difficulty in raising needed capital because of low earnings. The owners proposed a wage cut, but the miners argued that the Montreal Agreement was an unsatisfactory compromise anyway, and if living costs had declined in the interim, the drop only compensated in part for what had been sacrificed in 1920 in order to reach agreement without resorting to strike action.

Union representatives suggested that if the operators wanted to claim inability to pay and difficulty in competing with a foreign product, then they must be prepared to submit their records to public examination, a proposition which the owners firmly resisted.[7] The life of the Montreal Agreement was extended to the end of December 1921, but two rounds of negotiations, plus intervention by a Board of Conciliation in January 1922, failed to bridge the differences between company and union. The miners had resigned themselves to the inevitability of a wage cut but, as the Sydney *Post* reported on December 21, the men were both surprised and thoroughly resentful of the size of the reduction proposed by the company negotiators: "All along they had been expecting a wage reduction," said the *Post*, "but not such a slash as the company has now imposed. A cut of 10 or 15 per cent might have been accepted but the 37.5 per cent reduction has left the UMW staggering."

The union got a Board of Conciliation, but the company refused to cooperate and, in complete defiance of the labour law, immediately implemented the new reduced wage scale. The union won an injunction from one judge, but another, Judge Mellish, who had acted as attorney for the company before being elevated to the bench, overturned the decision on the basis that since no agreement was in force the corporation had the right to alter conditions of employment from day to day.

The company fueled the resentment of the miners by refusing to collect dues from several categories of surface workers. This represented a flagrant attack on the long-standing industrial structure of the union, which not even Gompers had been able to dismantle. The Mechanics' Local, whose very existence was threatened by the unilateral decision of the employers, invited the OBU in to discuss terms of affiliation, thus bringing the western-based organization into the Maritimes for the first time. This was probably done more to frighten the employers with the OBU bogey than with any serious intention to affiliate with the besieged radicals. In any event, the company beat a hasty retreat, but the Mechanics' Local went on to play a large part in the radical agitation in Nova Scotia throughout 1922.[8]

Under the pressure of starvation conditions in the area, the miners carried out raids for food supplies in company-owned stores and a warehouse. An attempt at a fourth raid was halted by international union Board member Silbey Barrett, in company with the Mayor of Glace Bay and a squad of armed police.[9]

The Conciliation Board that had been appointed finally handed down a majority decision that was based entirely on unverified testimony given by company lawyers, and came very close to the standard unilaterally imposed on the men by the corporation. In a February vote the award was rejected by a majority of 10,305 to 468, but confidence in the UMW was rudely shattered when President Lewis recommended reopening negotiations, telling the members that they were on their own, and not to expect any financial help from international headquarters.[10]

New discussions were opened in Montreal from which the miners representatives, on a split decision and in violation of a resolution not to agree to anything below the 1921 wage standard, returned to the mining District with a wage offer no better than the one that had been overwhelmingly rejected.[11] One member of the negotiating team, in a statement that could be interpreted as a criticism of lack of support from international headquarters, argued, "If we get any more it will have to be through direct action and you know direct action is impossible because we cannot finance a strike, and without funds failure is the ultimate end, and without a successful end, disorganization is the result. We cannot afford to allow that situation to occur even at a greater reduction."

Secretary-Treasurer J.B. McLachlan and his supporters argued that the proposed reduction was impossible of acceptance, and that the corporation having modified its position once, would do so again if the miners would only offer them resistance. "Four times have the coal companies crawled. There is great hope that with a few more crawls they will arrive at a living award."[12]

On March 14 the proposed settlement was rejected by a margin of seven to one. With nothing in the way of financial support, and certainly no bank account to fall back on, the miners decided to resort to the old syndicalist tactic of "striking on the job," i.e., by slowing down production to a level approximately equal to the reduced pay scale. According to McLachlan in an article printed in the May 1, 1922 edition of the *Worker*, the tactic was proving highly successful:

> For months on end the production of that mine [Dominion No. 2] was pulled down to a point between 800 and 1,000 tons per day. On special days when all the bosses from other mines were gathered there for the purpose of "chasing the drivers" the output would tumble to as low as 280 tons.
>
> At Caledonia Mine, 750 men are employed; from 1,800 tons per day, the output was pulled down to around 600 tons. Here at this mine the boss gave the men the credit of having "striking on the job down to a perfect science."

Whatever may be said for the extent of its success as a tactic in the Nova Scotia strike, "striking on the job" became a popular topic of discussion throughout the mining District, and it brought forth a very interesting argument on the right of the miners to resort to the tactic. The controversial decision handed down by Judge Mellish in favour of the corporation was now cited as a defence of the slow down. This was the central theme of an article published in the February 11, 1922 edition of the *Maritime Herald*, which argued the double-edged consequences of the Mellish decision: "The employer may, if he so desires," reported the *Herald*, "vary the wage rate from day to day and never be guilty of breaking the law . . . Since January 1, 1922 the employer has, without the consent and against the wishes of his employees, given just so much money in wages. Since January 1, 1922 the employee may give in return for this one-sided wage agreement just so much work and of such and such a quality as he wishes to give without in the least taking his employer into consideration."

On February 27, the Halifax *Herald* testified to the success of the "on the job" tactic. The paper published a report that said, "[striking on the job] had spontaneous growth, arising with the men themselves as their method of expressing dissatisfaction with the wages now in force, and with the same wages in force it is likely that the practice will continue. Beyond question it has operated to cut down production, in some mines something like 50 per cent."

While the tactic was winning public support in the coal area, and promising some success in the struggle, it was being frowned upon by international officers of the UMW as an immoral measure. John White, a former international president, had been sent into the province to bring the situation under control. He informed the delegates to the 1924 international Convention of the union that he had tried to coerce a Truro delegate meeting into discarding "the contemptible practice of striking on the job."

But McLachlan responded to all such cringing "moderation" with an open call to class war, and for an assault on corporation profits. The *Maritime Labour Herald* of March 18, 1922 published McLachlan's ringing call to arms, which declared:

> War is on, and it is up to the workers in the mines of the British Empire Steel Corporation to carry that war into the "country" of the enemy. There is only one way to fight this corporation and that is to cut production to a point where they cannot any longer earn profits. Every contract man who voted against acceptance of the wage agreement last Tuesday should at once cut down his production to a point where he can get about the same wage as the low paid men in the mine, and at the same time see to it that every day paid man takes the full eight hours each day to land his reduced output on the surface.

James Murdock, a Vice-President of the International Brotherhood of Railway Trainmen and a Liberal, replaced Tory Gideon Robertson as Minister of Labour in the Liberal Government that had come to power. Murdock was also one of those who reversed his position on collective bargaining at Winnipeg when Robertson was Minister. Murdock now entered the debate on "striking on the job" on the side of the company. In a 1922 debate in the House of Commons, Murdock charged the miners and their leaders with irresponsible tactics. He claimed that "any strength which organized labour possesses at the present time is the result, not of the underhanded and dishonest methods of undercutting, or, as it is sometimes called, sabotage, but of straight and honest dealings, each worker giving the best that is in him for the wage agreed upon."[13]

Murdock chose to ignore the fact that there had been no "wage agreed upon." He must have known that the wage rates were unilaterally imposed by the corporation and that no contract had been signed. He must also have known of the court decision that the miners were citing as legal support for their position. But, nevertheless, Murdock was at least implying that the company was acting honestly and above board in contrast to the "dishonest" union miners. But McLachlan placed the matter in proper perspective in his reply to the Minister:

> This tactic is a method of retaliation for a highly unjust encroachment on the wages of their workmen and an invasion of an already too slender living. I have proclaimed openly and in the face of day and there is nothing dishonest about it . . . I shall do it again this week knowing that a miner has a perfect right to work with his coat on if

he wants to . . . Our method of fighting this unjust wage imposition is effective and within the law . . . We shall continue to fight the imposition of this iniquitous wage reduction if we have to rock the ramshackle institution known as the British Empire Steel Corporation from its rotten sills to its bending and shaking rafters.

To this defence of the miners' case, the Minister of Labour and international labour man tartly retorted, "In my judgement it is un-British, un-Canadian and cowardly to pretend to be working for a wage rate in effect while declaring to the world that only partial and grudging service will be given. My experience is that men quit like men and walk off the job when unwilling to work for wage rates or conditions offered . . . Two wrongs . . . do not make one right, and red-blooded Canadian citizens will not, in my judgement, follow your advice in the pretense of loyally staying on the job for the purpose of penalizing the employer."

The mind of the international union representative seems to lack the capacity to absorb any ideas other than those that are solidly based on "moderation" and "responsibility." A tactic, even if it is successful in winning a struggle, must not be employed if it "penalizes" the employer. And that is the crux of the Murdock stand. Penalize the worker with a crushing wage reduction on wages already at starvation level, but do not damage the profit position of the corporation.

In the end Murdock's invective was too much for even the notorious Senator Robertson to swallow. Under a wave of protest the Minister beat a hasty retreat, claiming that he held "no brief for or personal sympathy with certain methods adopted by the British Empire Steel Corporation." McLachlan sought to seize advantage of what he thought to be a small opening for dialogue and proceeded to press his case for the appointment of a Commission of investigation "to tear wide open the rotten heart of this corrupter of public life and starver of the workers of Nova Scotia . . . If you and your young government have the courage of your convictions, you shall appoint a Commission now and give it this man's job of cleaning up this corrupt tragedy."

The request for a Commission of investigation was rejected because, it was alleged, to act otherwise would mean "placing a premium on the advocacy of methods most prejudicial to the public interest." A labour Member, William Irvine, pressed the debate on the proposition, and Murdock defended the Government position by repeating his former charge that the miners were being un-Canadian. No Royal Commission, he said, "will be appointed at the behest and at the dictation of these gentlemen in Nova Scotia . . . who are advocating such an un-Canadian policy."

Despite his earlier burst of criticism of corporation policies, the spokesman for international unions and Minister of Labour ends up giving aid and comfort to the owners. By denying the request for an investigation he is placing a premium on company methods, which involved a unilaterally imposed 37.5 per cent wage reduction. In effect, Murdock is saying the action of the British-controlled corporation in this regard is "good Canadianism."

The experience of "striking on the job" and the discussions accompanying the use of the tactic called attention to ideas for a more radical solution to the problems of the coal District. It was suggested that the coal seams did not belong to the company at all but to the people of Nova Scotia, and should be exploited for their benefit. The local at Dominion No. 2 mine summed up this position, growing in popularity, when its members asserted, "The rank and file, after due deliberation, are of the opinion that the possession of the coal leases by the British Empire Steel Corporation is a detriment to the public, as the coal areas have been overcapitalized by that corporation for the purpose of trying to persuade simple persons to invest their money in securities of doubtful value."[14]

A Convention of the Nova Scotia District, held at Truro in June, passed a resolution censuring the negotiating team, which precipitated the resignation of the entire Executive Committee and the ordering of a new election of officers to take place in August. The Convention also passed a policy declaration, very similar to the one passed by the Calgary Conference. It read: " . . . we proclaim openly to all the world that we are out for the complete overthrow of the capitalist system and capitalist state, peaceably if we may, forcibly if we must, and we call on all workers, soldiers, and minor law officers to join us in liberating labour."

At this point, factors making for "normal" strike action began to assert themselves: 1. There was a protracted and continuing strike in the United States, which caused an increase in demand for Nova Scotia coal; 2. It was now summertime, and striking seemed a relatively easier proposition than it was in mid-winter; 3. International Executive Board member Silbey Barrett returned from a visit to the United States enthused over the solidarity of the strike there, and bringing with him a message that President Lewis wanted District 26 out on strike.

In fact, it was suggested that Lewis was prepared to lift the District charter if the response was not favourable. Mid-August was set as the deadline for restoration of the 1921 rates or, alternatively, for strike action.[15] On August 2, union officers announced that the membership had voted 96 per cent in favour of strike action. The Executive Committee reached yet another compromise with the company, but it was overwhelmingly rejected by the men, and the strike began at midnight on August 14.

The contest in the election for new Executive officers was a straight contest between radicals and moderates. Held on August 15, the first day of the strike, the outcome was a foregone conclusion—the slate of radicals won by a wide margin, headed by Secretary-Treasurer J.B. McLachlan, who was re-elected. A.M. Stewart, a McLachlan supporter, was elected to replace Barrett as international Executive Board member, but the international Board refused to accept the decision, contending that Barrett's June resignation was in violation of the constitution.

Under radical leadership the call went out for a "100 per cent" strike, i.e., pumpmen, fanmen, engineers and special maintenance workers who were normally left on the job to keep water and gas accumulation under control were, in this instance, ordered out. The tactic, which arose automatically out of eight months of bitter confrontation with the company, was very effective in the prevention of strikebreaking.

Naturally the 100 per cent tactic was denounced by the owners, who described it as a revolutionary "move by men who have overridden law and order." They forecast total destruction of the mining properties, but the miners insisted that no permanent damage would be done, and two weeks of work would restore any of the properties to prime condition. Company officials and office staff, though worked beyond the point of endurance, were able only to slow, but not halt, the accumulations of water and gas in the mines.[16]

John L. Lewis came out in support of the operators' charges when he warned the strikers that refusing to allow maintenance crews to remain at work "to protect property in every necessary way" was in violation of the policy of the international. Lewis neglected to mention that a necessary condition to the carrying out of this policy was the payment of rates existing under the expired agreement. But this was contravened by the owners, who had imposed a wage reduction. In any event, it ill-behooved Lewis to offer criticism of the Nova Scotia miners after refusing financial assistance and telling the miners that they were "on their own." Lewis also informed Labour Minister and international union colleague Murdock of his disapproval of the tactics employed in the Nova Scotia dispute.[17] McLachlan on the other hand, seized the opportunity for a telling and final rejoinder to the Murdock charge of "un-Canadian." "When we were striking on the job in order to secure a living you said it was un-British and un-Canadian and that red-blooded Canadians did not practise such, but quit like men and walked off the job. Today we have a real red-blooded Canadian strike in strict accordance with your definition and walked off the job 100 per cent."[18]

The Great War Veterans Association in Nova Scotia, in a letter on August 18, supported the strikers and denounced King for his service to American financiers. One paragraph of a very caustic letter read: " . . . this meeting of the returned men . . . inform King that he is not carrying out the purpose for which the War was fought, but, (just) as in war time he was helping Rockefeller to make millions out of the sweated labour of Colorado miners, now he is helping Wolvin make a fortune out of starving miners and their families."

When the new Executive took office on August 17, they effected a compromise with the company through the intervention of the office of the Premier of Nova Scotia. The compromise involved a considerable retreat on the part of the corporation, and put the maintenance men back to work. On August 31, 1922, following eight months of militant confrontation with the company, supported by the state, the miners voted by a margin of nearly three to one in favour of a new agreement submitted for their approval.

On August 18, the Halifax *Citizen* described the eight months of confrontation as "a solid strike, with leaders ordered to take orders from the rank and file or get off the job." But the embattled miners received none of the promised support and solidarity from the international union office. On the contrary, the international officers opposed effective strike tactics on the grounds that "owner rights" should be respected and protected by the workers as a top priority.

There was momentary, but only momentary, peace in the coal fields of Nova Scotia. Before the new agreement was a year old the miners were fated to become involved in a new engagement with the corporation in solidarity with striking steel workers. As in the former contest, the officers of international unions, on the pretext of honouring legal and contract obligations, would be ranged on the side of the employers against the workers.

At the steel plant in Sydney men worked eleven and thirteen-hour shifts, seven days a week, with a 24-hour swing-shift from 7 a.m. Sunday to 7 a.m. Monday. Where the corporation had been repulsed in the attempt to impose a 37.5 per cent wage cut on the miners, it was successful in imposing a 45 per cent reduction on the workers in the steel plant. The steelworker received a grand total of $2.85 for each long and arduous day of backbreaking work. It was a life of toil and hunger, bereft of any form of recreation or real family life, and without apparent hope of betterment in the future, at least so far as voluntary action by the company was concerned. Profits were the sole priority of a soulless corporation whose only concern was its bondholders.

Influenced by miner militancy, the workers in the steel complex began organizing an industrial union in opposition to the company union setup proposed by the corporation. In February 1923, the firing of a union militant sparked a mass walkout which forced the company to retreat. But the retreat was only temporary, and the corporation officials began immediate preparations for a showdown with the militant workers.

Instructed to prepare for a battle against "Bolshevism" at the steel plant, Provincial Government authorities recruited a special armed force which they shipped to Sydney. Simultaneously the company organized its own private police force. With a sense of security derived from the presence of provincial police, special armed squads, and company police, the corporation began a systematic campaign of blacklisting militant workers and the hiring of scabs, with the aim of breaking the union and the resistance of the steelworkers.

Refusing to be intimidated by the terror tactics of the company, some of the steelworkers walked off the job at 3 a.m. on June 28 while others of their number seized control of the furnaces so that they could not be operated by scabs. This was not just a strike—it constituted an invasion of private property which must be repulsed at all costs. The Mayor of Sydney read the Riot Act and the men were forcibly driven from the plant by the available armed squads of goons. On June 30 a troop of 250 infantrymen arrived from Halifax prepared to protect company rights in a situation of deepening crisis. The 1923 edition of *Labour Organization in Canada* described the opening days of the strike:

> On June 28, 1923, the steel workers in the employ of the British Empire Steel Corporation in Sydney went on strike for a 20 per cent increase in wages and the unionizing of the plant . . . On the first day of the strike . . . the local magistrate read the Riot Act . . . On being informed that the local police were unable to cope with the situation, one of the county judges . . . made a requisition for troops . . . and on June 30 a detachment of troops arrived in Sydney. The sheriff of Cape Breton County, the chief of police of Sydney, and the magistrate made representations . . . that even with the troops . . . the local police were inadequate to cope with the situation . . . a detachment of provincial police was also sent to Sydney . . .

Incensed by the preponderant show of brutal force in defence of a foreign-owned corporation as well as by rumors of exceptional acts of police brutality against the protesting citizens, the mine workers began walking off the job. On July 6, Secretary-Treasurer McLachlan circulated the miners' locals with a letter of infomation on current developments:

> Brothers; This office has been informed that all the Waterford, Sydney Mines and Glace Bay sub-districts are out on strike this morning as a protest against the importation of provincial police and federal troops into Sydney to intimidate the steel workers into continuing to work at 32 cents per hour.
>
> On Sunday night last these provincial police, in the most brutal manner, rode down the people at Whitney Pier who were on the street, most of whom were coming from church. Neither age, sex nor physical disability were proof against these brutes. One old woman, over 70 years of age, was beaten into insensibility and may die. A boy

nine years old was trampled under the horses' feet and had his
breastbone crushed in. One woman, beaten over the head with a
police club, gave premature birth to a child. The child is dead and the
woman's life is despaired of. Men and women were beaten up inside
their own homes.

Against these brutes the miners are on strike. The government of
Nova Scotia is the guilty and responsible party for this crime. No
miner or mine worker can remain at work while this government turns
Sydney into a jungle. To do so is to sink your manhood and allow
Armstrong and his miserable bunch of grafting politicians to trample
your last shred of freedom in the sand. Call a meeting of your local at
once and decide to spread the fight against Armstrong to every mine
in Nova Scotia. Act at once—to-morrow may be too late.[19]

The edition of *Labour Organization in Canada* that carried the
McLachlan communique also reported that 8,000 miners walked off the job
to protest the presence of troops and armed police. Further, it was reported
that McLachlan and District President Dan Livingstone were arrested on
the evening of July 6 on a charge of circulating false information, contrary
to Section 136 of the Criminal Code, the Commissioner of Police having
emphatically denied the charge of police brutality. On July 9, additional
charges of misdemeanour and seditious libel and conspiracy to publish
seditious libel were laid. Both men were held without bail until July 11.

On the very evening of the arrests, John L. Lewis entered the
controversy with a telegram to the arrested Livingstone and the District 26
Executive ordering them to get the miners back to work. The text of the
telegram was as follows:

I am in receipt of your telegram sent in reply to my previous query
stating strike of members of United Mine Workers has been in
progress in District Twenty-six since Tuesday midnight in protest
against presence of provincial police and troops who are in the district
in connection with matters outside the mining industry. Such a strike
is unquestionably a violation of the existing agreement between
District Twenty-six and the coal companies parties thereto. It is also a
violation of the principles and policies of the United Mine Workers
which has a record of fulfilling its contract and discharging its
honourable obligations. The action of the district in also permitting
the withdrawal of engineers, pumpmen and other maintenance men
from the mines is most indefensible and constitutes a wanton
destruction of property.

The existing agreement in District Twenty-six was negotiated by
the officers of that District and ratified by a referendum vote of the
majority of the mine workers affected. I previously advised you that

formal complaint and protests had been lodged with the international union by coal companies affected who asked that they be accorded good faith in compliance with agreement. In consideration of this complaint, and in consideration of your admissions of the present astounding state of affairs prevailing within the District, I request that you as President of District Twenty-six, together with your associate Executive officers, take immediate steps to have the men return to work so as to permit of full protection of property interests affected and an early resumption of mining operations. I will be glad to receive early advice from you indicating your full compliance with these directions.

While on a visit to Nova Scotia some fourteen years earlier, when the UMW was engaged in a campaign to take over miner representation from the PWA, Lewis had told the miners: "The principle of the UMW's methods of doing business is that this District 26 of the UMW has absolute autonomy . . . without any dictation whatsoever from headquarters."[20]

When it suited his purposes, in the early stages of a tough battle with the company, Lewis stuck to this rule, informing the striking miners that they were on their own against the corporation. But in the "striking on the job" and in this incident, when he considered property rights were being invaded, Lewis entered the fray on the side of the company. Mr. Lewis was much concerned for the "wanton destruction of property" and the honouring of contract obligations. He appeared to have little concern for the wanton destruction of workers' lives.

On July 11, the Executive Board, in the absence of their jailed officers, met to discuss the contents of the communication from the international President. The following reply was sent to Lewis over the signature of the Vice-President of District 26:

District Board considered your telegram and state that this strike has no connection whatever with contract with corporation or wage demands. The only issue is to prevent use of armed force against workers in every industrial dispute in this province, and for release of our President and Secretary.

The membership unanimously pledged itself not to return to work until troops are removed and our officers released. For any District officers to advocate return to work would be quite useless in face of the determination to stay on strike. We have repeatedly guaranteed immediate resumption of work if troops are withdrawn and officers released.

This struggle is supported by trade unions *of Canada* and is a political struggle of *Canadian* workers against an evil from which we have suffered for years. Our international union must understand that its jurisdiction does not give it authority to prohibit workers *in Canada* waging a political struggle against use of armed forces which are being used to smash *our labour movement*.[21] (emphasis added)

Unimpressed with the assertion of autonomous rights in the sphere of political action, Lewis notified the District officers of his determination to take steps to enforce compliance with the back to work order issued by the international. On July 17, Lewis notified the District President of the revocation of the international charter and the automatic removal of all District officials from union office and the establishment of a provisional District under direct supervision of international headquarters. The Lewis "war communique," which accorded uncritical support to the corporation and the state authorities and repeated the "anti-Bolshevist" refrain of the reactionaries, was printed in the 1923 edition of *Labour Organization in Canada,* and read as follows:

Since early in July some 8,000 or more of the members of the United Mine Workers in District 26 have been in a sympathetic strike. Not only did this strike interfere with the production of coal in mines working under agreement with the UMW, but it resulted in the withdrawal of engineers, pumpmen, and other maintenance men with resulting jeopardy to property interests. This strike was admittedly incited, encouraged, and conducted by you and your official associates who are members of the Board of District 26. On July 6, after the situation had been officially drawn to my attention by the formal protest of the British Empire Steel Corporation, Limited, who are parties to the agreement with the UMW, in that section, I wired you asking for a statement in connection therewith.

On July 6 you wired a reply admitting that 9,000 men were on strike, attempting to justify the unwarranted abrogation of contract provisions by specious argument. On the same date I telegraphed you in behalf of the international union a request that the men on strike be immediately directed to return to work and provisions be made at once for the full protection of the mining properties.

On July 8, you replied saying that my instructions would be considered at a meeting of the Executive Board of District 26 on July 10. On July 11, Alexander McIntyre, Vice-President of the District, telegraphed me that the Executive Board had declined to accede to my request, and that the illegal strike would be continued until its objects were attained. Notwithstanding the lapse of time, I am informed today that there is still no indication upon your part as President of District 26, nor on the part of your associates in office, to terminate the strike and discharge your honourable obligations under the agreement, or to heed the instructions of the international union, in pursuance of its laws and policies.

I am not unmindful that it is probably a fruitless task to attempt to reason with you in the midst of your mad adventure, yet in your sane moments you must recognize that the course you have been and are pursing violates every tenet of your organization. It ruthlessly tramples upon every rule of conduct of our union and consitutes a departure from its every tradition. This deliberate breach of the existing contract between the operators and miners of Nova Scotia is indefensible and morally reprehensible. Your assault upon these laws and institutions of your Provincial and Dominion Government cannot be countenanced by the United Mine Workers of America. The official statement of the District Executive Board that the strike was for political purposes is illuminating, and gives additional proof, if such were needed, of your true intent.

I have in mind that you are a self-proclaimed revolutionist. I am familiar with the constant intrigue between yourself and your evil genius McLachlan and your revolutionary masters in Moscow. I can recall the sentiments which you enunciated at a comparatively small meeting of the international Executive Board at Indianapolis when, with the cold ferocity of a five-year-old defying its mother, you announced you were a believer in revolution by force.

No doubt the present strike in Nova Scotia corresponds with the idea of a revolution against the British Government and is in pursuance thereof.

In consideration of these strange facts, the international union feels warranted in intervening for the protection of its membership and to permit the discharge of its properly assumed obligations. You may as well know now as at any time in the future that United Mine Workers is not a political fanatic who seeks to strike down the established institutions of his Government. Neither can it be used to sustain officers of perverted business morals or individuals suffering from mental aberration such as yourself and the aggregation of papier-mache revolutionists who are associated with you.

By virtue of the authority invested in me by the constitution of the UMWA, of which I am President, and in consideration of the further authority granted in the premises by the international Executive Board, I herewith advise that the charter of District 26, United Mine Workers of America, stands revoked effective this date. Under this action District 26 ceases to be an entity and you are automatically deprived of your office as President thereof. Alexander McIntyre, Vice-President, and J.B. McLachlan, as Secretary-Treasurer, likewise have their offices vacated through the same precise action. All members of the Executive Board of District 26, including any and all other officers of said District, are in like manner automatically removed from office and can no longer undertake to represent in any capacity the UMW of America. This applies with equal force to Andrew Stewart, member of the international Executive Board. Under separate order I am today creating a provisional District to function within the jurisdiction of former District 26 under the direct authority and control of the international union.

International representative Silbey Barrett of Glace Bay, N.S. has been designated as provisional President thereof, with sweeping authority to function in every proper capacity. In compliance with the laws of the international union governing such matters you will, together with each of your associate retiring officers, turn over to Mr. Barrett, President of provisional District 26, all moneys, official records, and documents, together with the District office and furniture and any other property or things of value belonging to former District 26. President Barrett will hold such property in trust for the future use of the members of our union in that District. Instructions will be issued to all local unions whose members are now on strike in Nova Scotia to immediately return to work under the existing agreement.

Local unions continuing in defiance of such orders will be summarily dealt with in conformity with the laws of the UMWA. This office is today notifying Mr. R.M. Wolvin, President of the British Empire Steel Corporation, Limited, that the international union, through its provisional District 26, is assuming the equity and obligations of the existing joint wage agreement in that territory as represented by the subsidiary coal companies of the British Empire Steel Corporation.

The monarch speaks, and the subjects must come to attention. Lewis went far beyond any simple act of class collaboration. He intervened in the internal affairs of a foreign country and in the rights of its citizens—and that in collaboration with a corporation foreign-owned. In the first place, the international President supplied the employers with "anti-communist" propaganda for use against the striking miners and their arrested officers. But beyond that, Lewis interfered in the political rights of Canadians. Even if the allegations of revolutionary aims were correct, that was properly the business of the people of Canada to deal with, without interference from an American union official. But strange indeed was it that the alleged "revolutionary conspiracy" should have remained unrevealed until it became useful to Lewis and the company as a propaganda ornament.

It is not surprising that District 18, which was no better than a company union, set up by the UMW in cooperation with the employers and the

Government to defeat the OBU, should come out in defence of Lewis. The *Alberta Labour News* of August 4, 1923, attacked the deposed District 26 Executive, and lauded the international union for what it had accomplished in the coal fields in the west.

There was an exchange of correspondence between the Trades and Labour Congress and Prime Minister King, from July 10 to July 12, focussing mainly on the use of troops in a strike situation and on a Congress petition for the appointment of a Royal Commission to investigate the conditions of labour and company policies in Cape Breton. At one point in the letter of July 10, Tom Moore for the Congress almost seems to be expressing support for the strikers, when he says: "The apparent intimidation of men on strike against almost inhuman conditions of labour has aroused the indignation and resentment of all workers throughout Canada, and has resulted in a stoppage of work by the miners employed by the same company, with a grave possibility of similar action by workers in other parts of Canada."[22]

If it was Moore's original intention to express sympathy for the Nova Scotia miners, he quickly recovered from his illusions of independence and adopted his normal role of servility to the American union dictators of Trades Congress policy. On the Lewis appointment of the provisional District 26 Board, Moore issued a public statement approving of the move, advised the miners to dutifully bow their necks to the yoke of slavery, and joined the anti-communist witch hunt:

> The miners of Nova Scotia will do well to remain loyal to their international union by giving their full support to the new provisional President, Silbey Barrett, and thus frustrate the efforts of J.B. McLachlan and his colleagues to destroy the solidarity of their organization.
>
> Their ill-advised strike has been of no value to the steelworkers in their struggle for the establishment of proper conditions. On the contrary it has helped to confuse the minds of the public as to the real issue and has retarded the efforts being made by organized labour to have the militia removed from the Nova Scotia strike area.
>
> J.B. McLachlan's only objects are publicity and power. While continually "mouthing" the doctrine of a "United Front," his past record has been one of continually seeking disruption. Upon the formation of the One Big Union . . . he became one of its strongest advocates and frittered away thousands of dollars from the treasury of District 26 in the futile attempt to make the miners part of that organization . . .
>
> He circulated the labour organizations of the Dominion, asking them to form a dual organization . . . under the guise of a "council of action" . . .

McLachlan turned for support to Moscow, and . . . has carried on a continuous campaign to have the policy of Communism, as advocated through the Workers' Party and the Trade Union Educational League, replace the policies of international trade unions.

The acceptance by the miners of his advice to reject the awards of several Boards and Commissions established to deal with their requests has robbed them of hundreds of thousands of dollars that otherwise would have been in their pay envelopes, but instead went into the coffers of the British Empire Steel Corporation.[23]

The lies and servility contained in this statement are scarcely in need of reply. But if such should be deemed necessary, it may be found in an independent and personal investigation carried out by the Rev. Canon Scott, who said:

As regards wages, if employment is continuous the maximum earnings of the large number of the miners would be about $3.35 a day, which would amount to $80 a month, but owing to various conditions employment is far from continuous with the result that the men frequently fail to obtain a living wage. The steelworkers are in a much similar position as regards pay.

The general atmosphere is one of gloom, and a spirit of depression pervades the whole region. The men do not trust the company and the company does not trust the men.

The "red" element is of very little importance beyond the fact that it is used to blind the eyes of the public to the real issue and bad conditions under which the people live.[24]

Labour Organization in Canada (1923) reported that a mass meeting of miners was held in Glace Bay on July 18, at which Lewis was denounced and the miners refused to return to work, against the direction of the provisional officers. A second meeting at Dominion followed the Glace Bay example, and at both meetings the following resolution was adopted:

Whereas, President John L. Lewis of the United Mine Workers of America has lined up with the Provincial and Federal Governments and the British Empire Steel Corporation in an attempt to smash the miners' union in Nova Scotia and has deposed the officers of the District and instructed the local unions to return to work under threat of expulsion from the international union, and

Whereas, John L. Lewis in his foul attack on the miners of Nova Scotia has appointed one Silbey Barrett as so-called President of the organization and demands that the miners take orders from this man who has forfeited the confidence of the rank and file as was demonstrated when he was removed from office in the last District election, and

Whereas, this attack of Lewis is for the purpose of handing the miners of this province over, bound hand and foot, to the corporation, therefore

Be it resolved, that this mass meeting of miners held in Glace Bay on Wednesday July 18th, 1923 condemns the action of Lewis and declares that his action is a violation of the autonomy of this District, and instructs the District officers to carry on the work of the District until such time as they are removed from office by vote of the membership of this District, and be it further

Resolved, that we will not return to work on the instruction of the men appointed by John L. Lewis, but will only return when that decision is arrived at by all the men involved in this strike of protest against the use of armed forces against the workers, and be it further

Resolved, that copies of this resolution be sent to John L. Lewis, the British Empire Steel Corporation, to every local union in the District, and to the labour press of this country.

In order to cripple the strike by preventing the miners from having access to their union funds and records, Silbey Barrett, acting for the UMW, applied to the court for an injunction restraining anyone from interfering with his operation of union affairs. Counsel for the union members held that the action was based on the appointment of a provisional President by Lewis, who had no status in the court in which the case was being tried or among the miners, and that Lewis was incapable of suspending the District or setting up another. Nevertheless, the court handed down a ruling in favour of the international.

Barrett, who had been defeated in an election a short time before, was not finding much favour among the miners in the District, and was under considerable pressure. According to a report in *Labour Organization in Canada,* Barrett resigned his office while the case was being continued in court, and he was replaced by an imported American by the name of W. Hueston.

A number of striking miners faced a variety of charges, and were given sentences of up to two years in penitentiary. The miners' strike was broken and soon afterwards the steelworkers went back to work with only a company union—Mackenzie King's favourite remedy for social ills—to show for their hard battle. And so far as the "victory" for the "responsible business unionism" of John L. Lewis and his UMW was concerned, it brought to the coal fields of Nova Scotia in 1925 possibly the bloodiest and most costly strike ever fought by the miners, who had to carry on in near starvation without any meaningful support from their international union.

The Emergence of the CIO

From 1917 to 1926, the Trades Congress and the internationals seemed to be swamped in a sea of troubles. The region west of Ontario was out of their control most of the time, and insistently demanding new approaches to organization. Since 1902, the internationals had enjoyed something less than a tenuous existence in Quebec, and a variety of independent union groups flourished there. The Maritimes, led by Nova Scotia, was a less than secure bastion for American business unionism. And the CBRE, expelled from the Trades Congress because it failed to pass the test of internationalism, was scanning the horizon for evidences of a sentiment in support of an independent Canadian labour movement.

Only southern Ontario appeared to be a secure stronghold for the AFL, and even here one could hear rumblings of discontent and demands for new initiatives in organization. At the 1923 Convention of the Trades Congress the Toronto local of the International Machinists submitted a resolution calling for a wider autonomy, and the Pattern Makers in the city urged Congress to take the lead in bringing about the amalgamation of the various craft unions "so that there will remain only one union for each industry."

In brief, throughout nearly a decade of militant labour battles it seemed that only a lack of united effort around a common cause—the founding of an independent Canadian industrial union movement—stood in the way of the birth of a new movement, and an end to American domination of labour in Canada. Given the undoubted potential, a dedicated and determined leadership might have drawn all of the pieces together and radically altered the course of Canadian labour. As it was, those who might have filled the need for leadership played a vastly different role, and the AFL drew assistance for its cause in Canada from an unexpected source.

Nearly all of the most able and dedicated radical union leaders in Canada into the 1920s responded to a call for the formation of a revolutionary party affiliated with the Communist International headed by Lenin. Following a preliminary conference at Toronto in 1921, the Workers' (Communist) Party of Canada held its founding Convention in February 1922.

The first question to provoke sharp debate, and ultimately a split, at the Convention occured at the introduction of the resolution on work in the trade unions. Earl Browder of the American Communist Party was present as a fraternal delegate to press the line of W.Z. Foster and the American Trade Union Educational League (TUEL), which advocated the formation of left blocs within the established unions—i.e., inside the AFL—to encourage the amalgamation of the crafts and transform the leadership from right oriented to revolutionary.

Perhaps in ignorance of the fact that the Federation and the international unions were acting as transmission belts for the realization of United States imperialist objectives, and not fully appreciating the extent to which the American monopolies were pressing the economic conquest of Canada, the majority of the delegates accepted the application of the Foster line for Canada and the call for unity within the American unions. Clause two of the resolution on trade unions read: "Not only must the policy pursued by some groups in the past of seeking to revolutionize the labour movement by splitting away to form new ideal unions be completely abandoned; not only must dual unionism be vigorously combatted; but positively all tendencies to consolidate the trade unions by amalgamating the related crafts on the basis of one union for each industry must be fostered within the existing trades."[25]

Approval of the resolution brought the Party into conflict with the radical OBU and IWW, and with other anti-AFL but less revolutionary union groups. Delegates from Toronto, Montreal, Guelph, and Winnipeg, attended the TUEL conference at Chicago in 1922, and Canada was constituted the Fourth District of the organization, with Tim Buck as leader.

At the 1924 Congress of the Red International of Labour Unions (RILU), Buck stressed the factor of unity under the Trades Congress banner which, if the policy was to be successful, could only mean submission to American domination. In his report Buck said: "Bring the Canadian Federation of Labour members back under TLC unions and work against dual movements like that exhibited by the 'IWW rebels' in the coal mines of District 26.

"Educate the Catholic Union membership through the preparation of special leaflets to weaken the demoralizing influence of the clergy and draw the best clergymen into the trade union movement."[26]

The policy of "unity" within the international craft unions brought the Communist trade unionists into conflict with the most militant and advanced workers. In the case of Catholic (Quebecois) Unions, it involved inviting the workers of French Canada to accept the racism of the AFL leaders—for the sake of unity.

In 1924, 143,000 of the approximately 260,000 organized workers in Canada—a clear majority—were in organizations *outside* of the international unions. In addition, thousands of dissident members of American unions were prepared to rally to any viable alternative. In other words, the vast majority of the organized workers were ready to respond to a call for the formation of an independent centre. But rather than making the effort to provide an alternative to American unionism (by drawing together in a single centre the diverse elements in the non-AFL unions), the Party chose to adopt a policy entailing submission to the dictates of American union leaders.

The March 15, 1923, edition of the *Worker* reported that delegates to the second Convention reaffirmed the trade union policy of the Party, and went on to outline the policy in some detail:

> Experience of the past year has definitely proved the soundness of this policy, particularly in combating the disruptive influence of dual unionism and secession, setting up in their place a policy of unity through amalgamation of the craft unions into industrial unions . . . The policy of fighting for militant leadership, as against the passive and reformist bureaucracy, has yielded great results and has proved that the workers of Canada are ready for a forward step in labour unionism. They are preparing to take this step in conjunction with the militant unionists of the United States under the leadership of the Workers' Party of Canada, which has been the outstanding exponent of unity in the labour movement. The slogans of amalgamation, the Labour Party, and the Red International have taken firm root in the Canadian unions.
>
> United action of Workers' Party members with all other sincere and progressive workers for our trade union program has been brought about through the medium of the Trade Union Educational League. We call upon all our members to participate in the activity of the League and whole-heartedly support its work; to identify themselves with the international industrial Committees being established, such as the International Committee for the Amalgamation of the sixteen standard railway unions; and to keep the Canadian movement firmly united in one uniform movement covering the North American continent—with one common program of amalgamation, militant leadership and the rest of the League program. The fate of the Canadian left wing is entirely bound up with that of the United States. National autonomy is an illusion; international unity the need.

To put it mildly, Buck overstated his case. His report was steeped in generalities for the simple reason that no real advances had been registered. The favourite defence in explaining this inability to make any substantial gains was to blame the "secessionists" for every problem, which was in harmony with the line of the international union and Trades Congress officials.

Loudly preaching their doctrine of "unity," the communist trade unionists came into open conflict with a growing body of workers who favoured independence for Canadian unions. In the end the communists found themselves isolated because in promoting the RILU and TUEL, they themselves were rejected as secessionists and dual unionists.

Beginning in 1927 and continuing into 1929, TUEL members were on the defensive. The Ladies' Garment Workers in Montreal and Toronto expelled nine members of the TUEL as part of a general continental clean-out of communists in the organization. Jack McDonald, the Party Secretary, had his credentials rejected by TLC Convention delegates because of his alleged support for "other movements calculated to supersede the Congress." Buck was expelled from his local in the Machinists' Union in May 1928 on a charge of having aided in the organization of dual unions in competition with the established international bodies. Officers of the Amalgamated Clothing Workers in Toronto arbitrarily expelled six members for refusing to condemn an unsigned article published in a left-wing journal. Labour Councils in both Toronto and Windsor, Ontario expelled delegates who were known or suspected communists. The International Brotherhood of Railway Carmen authorized the President to expel any member of the organization suspected of holding communist sympathies. Shortly thereafter the international President revoked the charter of the Edmonton local of the Brotherhood for having protected one of its officers who was a known communist.

Many of those expelled by the conservative majorities in their international locals, and deprived of employment under closed shop conditions, found work in unorganized sweat shops and, most of them being able organizers, built unions around themselves. The Needle Trades National Industrial Union of Canada, for example, was organized in that way. Such unions later became the base for a left-wing federation affiliated with the RILU.

In July 1929, the Communist International completed a "left turn" begun a year earlier at the World Congress. The Executive Committee, in line with the Congress decision, decreed the end of the "united front" tactic and the implementation of the policy "class against class," with the complementary classification of social-democrats as "social-fascists." To implement the policy in the trade union sphere, the RILU called for the formation of "revolutionary" trade union centres in all countries.

Responding to the call of "class against class," the TUEL transformed itself into the Workers' Unity League (WUL), the Canadian section of the Red International of Labour Unions. The unions established by the communists expelled from the internationals provided the base upon which the WUL was founded. The Party was now definitely and openly committed to a policy of dual unionism.

Due to many problems, not all of them internal, the new "revolutionary" centre did not hold its first national Convention until August 1932. In 1935 there was a return to the united front tactic, and in April of that year the international Executive addressed an appeal to those formerly labeled "social-fascists" for joint demonstrations against fascism and war. The Executive proposed to the Labour and Socialist International "to organize in all capitalist countries joint May Day demonstrations against the capitalist offensive, against fascism, to safeguard peace, against imperialist war, and for the defense of the Soviet Union."[27]

In August the Seventh World Congress called upon all of its affiliates "to strive in the future by every means to establish a united front on a national as well as international scale." Of course it was not possible to carry out the decision and, at the same time, fight for dual unions. Logically enough, the RILU ordered the dissolution of the "revolutionary" trade union centres and a return to the "main stream" of the labour movement. In Canada that entailed the dissolution of the WUL and a return to the international unions—a decision which was carried out in 1935.

Just when the WUL was arranging its own burial a new movement for industrial organization emerged within the AFL. Organized under the name of the Committee for Industrial Organization (CIO) in 1935, the group, composed of representatives of a number of international unions, was first scoffed at, then suspended, and finally, after refusing to disband, expelled by the Federation.

In March 1937, John Noble, President of the Toronto and District Labour Council and AFL organizer in Ontario, ordered the Hamilton Labour Council to expel all CIO delegates. The Council rejected the ultimatum by a vote of 51 to 22, and Noble lifted its charter, thus suspending the Council from the TLC. But the Congress Executive was clinging to the hope that they could avoid the split that had occurred in the United States, and President Draper intervened to heal the breach.

A bitter fight over credentials broke out at the 1937 Convention of the Trades Congress, but again a split was averted when the Executive appealed to all groups to refrain from harmful activity pending the outcome of negotiations between the AFL and the CIO. The Executive also offered to mediate the dispute between the two hostile camps.

Just before the Congress Convention in 1938, Green wrote to the TLC Executive advising them that "the CIO and the organizations associated with it are dual to organizations affiliated with the AFL" but the Convention reaffirmed its unity policy.

Later in 1938, the American Federation Convention ordered the Congress to suspend all CIO affiliates, or the AFL would sever its relationship with the Canadian organization. That meant that all TLC affiliates would lose their Federation charters. In January 1939 the Congress Executive complied with the demand, ordering the suspension of the CIO affiliates. Explaining their decision to the Convention in 1939, the Executive Council reported: "One large organization temporarily withdrew its support of the Congress, and the Executive bodies of a number of others authorized their officers to take similar action if CIO unions were continuing membership in the Trades and Labour Congress of Canada."

One result of the sharpening of the quarrel was a heated exchange between Federation President William Green and John Buckley of Toronto, who was a staunch craft unionist but a leader in the fight to keep the CIO unions in the Trades Congress. In the exchange of letters which took place during March and April 1939, Green charged Buckley with deception and with always supporting the CIO. Green also accused him of harbouring an antagonistic attitude towards the Federation, and of sailing under false colours. In conclusion, he added: "I am suffering under no illusions, I have watched the recorded action of you and others in Toronto, in which you have reflected your hostility, yes, your antagonism towards the American Federation of Labour. I resent your action. No sophistry in which you indulge and no reference to 'unbecoming dignity' as you have indulged in your letter can offset the facts. I know what you are, and have placed you where you belong for that reason."

This resembled more the tone of an emperor addressing his colonial subjects than that of a communication from the head of a sovereign labour movement in one country to the representative of a supposedly autonomous movement in another. Buckley closed the correspondence with a blistering retort:

> As reason, truth and logic seem to have no place in your mental make-up, and as I do not deal in sophistry, our mentalities are as far apart as the poles. In the past, I have remained tolerably passive, under the accusation you have made upon myself, and my associate trade unionists, in which you indulge on every possible occasion . . . but I for one do not recognize in you any such vast immeasureable superiority to myself, as to entitle you to pronounce, dictatorially, upon my moral tendencies, my principals or my mentality . . . In the past it has been considered a mark of wisdom to deride all progressive schemes or ideas of human progress as visionary. Yet in the majority of cases posterity has been wiser than the generation that preceded them. To call an individual Communist or pro-CIO is not proof of wisdom or even infantile intelligence . . .

The suspension of the CIO affiliates by the Executive Council came up for discussion and decision at the TLC Convention in 1939. Almost a full year before, in November 1938, the Committee for Industrial Organization had severed its remaining tenuous links with the AFL and established an independent identity as the Congress of Industrial Organizations. Pressure was immediately put upon the Trades Congress to take appropriate action against the rebels. The AFL met in Washington in December and informed Trades Congress representatives in attendance that "further delay in taking action respecting CIO organizations would lead to the almost complete disorganization of the Congress as it had been constituted since 1902."[28]

At the Convention in 1939, Congress officers sought to cover their humiliation with the plea that the CIO had altered the situation by changing its name, and had thus "become a dual organization." It was a weak defense and Buckley took aim at it. The Toronto trades unionist argued strongly that now more than ever, with Canada at war, trade union unity was essential to the well-being of the Canadian worker. But the presiding officer revealed where the real power lay when he countered Buckley's opposition with the argument that the TLC had been warned by most international unions that they would cease paying per capita tax on their Canadian membership if the CIO unions were allowed to remain in the Congress. The report of the Executive reminded the delegates that "there is one fixed principle common to all AF of L organizations, which is that they will not continue membership in any federated body or central council where organizations of a dual character are also seated."[29]

As always, the American Federation and its international union enclave in Canada had their way. The resolution for expulsion was approved by 231 votes to 98. That was a sizeable margin of 133 votes, but approximately 160 delegates from CIO unions were barred from the Convention by reason of being under suspension. A new schism, unwanted by workers in Canada, had been foisted on the Canadian union movement at the behest of the international unions.

CIO unions in Canada were established as a result of the dedicated efforts of Canadian organizers, and without financial support of any kind from the movement in the United States. Because of this, and because of preoccupation with problems at home, American officials of the organization were inclined, if not compelled, to leave the Canadians to their own resources. In the early years of the movement's existence this resulted in its enjoying a wide degree of autonomy in Canada.

One would have thought that the manner of its origin would have guaranteed permanent autonomy and close fraternal relations as the basis of international contact. But this was not to be so. American unionists in the CIO, aided by the personal ambitions of some of the Canadian organizers, were soon to demonstrate a strong tendency towards domination over the Canadian section.

One of the first acts of interference occurred in 1940 when discussions with the All Canadian Congress of Labour (ACCL), a national movement, were begun on terms for affiliation of CIO unions to the Canadian centre. American officers demanded assurances that the merger would not result in the severing of international connections in favour of a national movement. Supporters of affiliation to the ACCL were also warned that before the CIO would approve, there must be an agreement that all "dual unions" would be transferred to the appropriate jurisdictions.

Agreement was finally arrived at and the Canadian Congress of Labour (CCL) was born of the merged units. But friction soon developed between those in the Congress who were nationally oriented and those who considered their future lay with the American connection. Pat Conroy of the UMW was brought into the CCL as Secretary in an attempt to heal the breach that was developing.

As in the AFL, control of finances was a source of dispute. The American organization was collecting a per capita tax of five cents per month from all CIO members in Canada. Just two cents of this was being returned to the Canadian centre. Conroy wanted to have the entire five cents paid directly to the CCL by the Canadian affiliates. After a great amount of debate the American centre agreed that the five cents would be returned to Canada, but three cents of the amount would be controlled by the Canadian director of the CIO. This, and many other contentious issues, finally led to Conroy's dramatic and questionable resignation in the midst of a stormy Convention session in 1942.[30] Before he resigned Conroy expressed his dissatisfaction with the role of the Congress and its American affiliates:

> My personal opinion is that I should resign from office, and let the Congress of Industrial Organizations and its International Unions take over the Congress. I am quite sincere in this, as I have been mulling the thought over for some time. The Congress is supposed to be an autonomous body, but in matters of jurisdiction the Congress is left without any authority, thereby reducing it to the status of a satellite organization at the mercy of its affiliated unions. These organizations choose to do whatever they want regardless of Congress desires, and in accordance with what their individual benefit may dictate they should do. My own reaction is that I am completely fed up with this situation and within a few weeks it may be that I shall submit my resignation. In short, the Congress is either going to be the authority in its field, or it is not. If it is not to exercise authority, then the more quickly the Executive Council appoints someone to hold a satellite position, the sooner the Congress will know that it is a purely subject instrument, with no authority and a servant of the headquarters of International Unions in the United States. This thought has been running through my mind for the last three or four years, and I have not arrived at it overnight. It is just that as the chief executive officer of the Congress, I am in the untenable position, and I am not going to work in that capacity.[31]

While a vast amount of political in-fighting was carried on between the CCF and the CP in Canada for the next several years, wartime conditions and appeals for unity during the War helped to mute some of the conflict surrounding the question of independence or American domination. But as the War drew to a close the issue once again gained prominence under changed conditions.

11

THE AFL AND THE POLITICS OF
ANTI-COMMUNISM

In February 1949, the Executive Council of the AFL expressed alarm concerning "evidence" which "discloses a shocking picture of the influence wielded by the communists in Canada in the affairs of the Trades and Labour Congress," and demanded that Congress officers take "vigorous action to eliminate completely every vestige of communist influence and control." The urgent overtones in the Federation's cry of shock and alarm might very well lead one to believe that Canada was in the process of being overrun by "red hordes," and no one giving a damn. The fact is, though, that some of the most devout anti-communists in the Americas had anticipated by several years the Federation's call to arms.

Dedicated as they are to the preservation of capitalism and United States domination of the world, the international unions have consistently opposed the radical economic and political programs advanced by socialists. And since the victory of the Bolshevik Revolution in 1917, they have given expression to a hatred of communism that is even more paranoid than that reserved for the milder socialists of old. The final outcome of the War did nothing to mitigate the fear and hatred of a phenomenon which represented a terminal social disease, or so it was viewed by American unionists. American capitalists, of course, shared their view.

War's end saw America economically and politically more powerful than ever—more powerful than any single state hitherto known to history, not excluding Britain at the peak of her imperial glory. American imperialism seemed well on the way to world domination. There was just one fly—rather big and menacing—in the ointment.

The fortunes of war had placed the Soviet Union on the Elbe, in the very heart of Europe and in control of a territorial expanse more vast than anything the Czars had ever dreamed of. Even Prussia, that solid and reliable bastion of European reaction for more than a century, had passed under Soviet control. More than that, Russia's prestige was at an all time high, and some of her most devoted disciples seemed to be in a position to capture the Governments of several highly industrialized countries in western Europe. The capitalists of America were scared, and when the capitalists are scared the American unionists are terrified.

There is one point here that should be brought into proper focus before proceeding further. Within half a decade after the end of the War all sorts and sizes of St. Georges were laying claim to the honour of having slain the communist dragon (which incidentally, seems to have a particularly irritating and nasty habit of forever emerging from the grave to which it has so often, and so unceremoniously, been consigned). For example, in October 1950, the Journal of the Trades and Labour Congress trumpeted, "65th CONVENTION LIQUIDATES COMMUNISM." And yet, a quarter of a century after their "liquidation" communists were still being unearthed in the Canadian unions. (It is dubious that the anti-communist braggadocios should be so proud. In fact, the leaders of the Communist Party of Canada could, and did, do far more to liquidate themselves than could ever be accomplished by anyone external to the movement.)

At its outset the Party declared that the world conflict was a clash between imperialist powers in which the working class had nothing to gain. When Russia was dragged into the war as the result of a German invasion of Soviet territory, the Party leaders executed a 180 degree turn and declared that man had no nobler objective than the extermination of the nasty Nazis. The working class was called upon to make every sacrifice in the interest of total victory. Even the right to strike in defense of their class interests was to be surrendered by the workers, while the capitalists gave up nothing of substance. The fact that the means of production and the power of the state still reposed safely in the care of the capitalists no longer seemed to have any significance. Prosperity and class collaboration would go on for ever.

Of course the Party scored gains in both numbers and influence. But the gains were the result of the reflected glory of Russian valour on the battlefield, and not by reason of any outstanding accomplishments in Canada. The appeal was mainly to middle class professionals and academics. The working class was represented in Party ranks by the bureaucratic functionaries and the relatively well-paid highly-skilled tradesmen. The most exploited sections of the class were a rarity in Party organizations. It was a nearly empty shell. When the first icy blasts of the winter of reaction struck, the wartime "honeymoon" came to an abrupt end. It was nearly game over for the Party.

The leaders of both the Cooperative Commonwealth Federation (CCF) and the Communist Party saw control of the unions as the key to electoral success. For some years a semi-epic struggle had been in progress over the issue of union control. In the conditions of war the CCF was able to take advantage of CP discomfiture in numerous situations, and the inability of the Party, due to its wartime policies, to represent the basic interests of the working class in Canada.

It may be worth digressing here in order to bring out one peculiar point about these wartime union politics. In the quarrel that erupted in 1944 over the policies pursued by the CIO's Political Action Committee in Canada, it was the CP and not the CCF partisan majority that was closest to the traditional American union position of "no partisan politics." PAC policy was in flagrant contradiction with that tradition in its partisan support of the CCF. In November 1944, the *Canadian Unionist*, official organ of the CIO unions, stated, "The official policy of the Congress calls for support of the CCF and the Congress proposes to co-operate with that party to the fullest possible extent."

Politics, as they say, makes strange bedfellows and, as we shall see later, the international officers supported this display of partisan politics. The object, of course, was to combat the "reds," whose position as stated in the *Canadian Tribune* on February 3, 1945 was studiously non-partisan: it "opposed restricting support to one political party and advocated a non-partisan policy similar to that of the CIO . . . for the election of . . . progressive candidates regardless of party, and looking toward a coalition of all progressive forces."

That old, dedicated, and hardened communist-hater David Lewis simply drooled at the sight of the golden opportunity that presented itself in wartime, and he and his colleagues hastened to take advantage of the situation, not even hesitating to conspire with American union leaders to advance the fortunes of a Canadian political party. And the American unionists most directly concerned were pleased to accommodate. Although it is by no means the main thrust of the book, *Canadian Labour in Politics* by Gad Horowitz (U of Toronto Press, 1968) is most revealing in this regard.[1]

When the B.C. District of the International Woodworkers of America, along with several other unions under CP influence, resigned from PAC, Director Eamon Park reported that the international President of the IWA, in response to a complaint, had "instructed Brother Pritchett that the affiliation of the IWA to the CCL is through the international union and that they do not concur in the actions of the District Council."

In order that the record be held in balance it should be noted that the CP element was just as ready to seek American intervention, although with remarkably less success. The CP Presidents of four Steel locals in Vancouver appealed to CIO President Murray to halt the use of Steel funds in support of the CCF. Millard, the Director for Steel in Canada, replied that support of the CCF was the official policy of Steel in Canada and the international knew it.[2]

George Burt, Canadian Director of the United Auto Workers, was not a communist, but the CP wielded considerable influence in his union and he was dependent on the Party for support. When Burt signed an application for membership in the Ontario CCF, Lewis reported, "I discussed George with Walter Reuther in Detroit quite frankly. Walter told me that George still is completely in the camp of Addes and Frankensteen. He always votes with the Communist gang on the international board. Even within the last two months he made quite an antagonistic speech about the CCF at a board meeting . . . In short, I am a little puzzled about George's present actions."

In the Ford-Windsor strike in 1945, there was a sharp disagreement over strategy between the CP leaders of the local on the one hand, and the CCL officials on the other. When the strike was settled on the basis of a compromise, the CCF *News*, on December 27, 1945, sniped at the CP members in an article written by Steel official Murray Cotterill:

> The formula for settlement . . . stems . . . from the realization of men like Burt and Addes that the Communist control of the Windsor locals was dangerous for the future of the union . . . and from the . . . good sense of the Ford workers who . . . rejected the LPP [CP] leadership and reposed their confidence in sound union leadership.

But David Moulton relates how this strike was really settled in Detroit, with Burt at least collaborating with, if not taking leadership from, Ford officials to "win" the strike. Here is how Moulton tells the story as related by George Burt:

> According to George Burt, Campbell [head of Ford, Windsor] initially proposed a ballot that simply read, "Are you in agreement with the company's offer?" No mention of the UAW was of major concern because by this time a majority in the Ford plants had been signed up. Burt went to R.J. Thomas, the international president of the UAW, and R.T. Leonard, Ford UAW director in the U.S., and told them of his problem in Windsor. Unless the Canadian plant was closed down, Burt believed that the union could lose the whole thing by not being on the ballot. Apparently Harry Bennett, the labour-relations head at Ford in Dearborn, heard about this and invited Burt, Thomas and Leonard to dinner. During the occasion at the Rotunda building, Bennett asked Burt what he wanted. Informing him of the problem, Bennett replied, "I never did like that Campbell. He's too proud a man for me. But what do you want Thomas to do? Surely you're not going to ask Thomas to close down the River Rouge to satisfy your demands against the company in Windsor are you? That little tin-can place over there?" Burt said all he wanted was the material going to the Canadian plant from the States to be stopped. This would strangle

production in Windsor and force government involvement because Ford Windsor was a war plant. Bennett then stated, "This is the answer isn't it? We'll show that guy over there, Mr. Burt." He then proceeded to phone the Ford transportation department and ordered the supervisor to stop all shipments destined for Windsor. With Bennett's action, production began to fall off and the government stepped in. It is at this point that the UAW-CIO was included in the ballot . . . Mr. Burt informed the author that he has written confirmation from R.T. Leonard concerning the above incident with Harry Bennett.[3]

A labour-relations Director ordering a stoppage of shipments to a branch plant? Probably the only fairy tale element about it is that Burt really believed what he imagined he was seeing and hearing. Ford was ready for a settlement and carefully set the stage for the best deal available. However, the incident is instructive in demonstrating just how dependent Canadian industry is on decisions made in the United States, and on how the American corporation and the American union work together toward a common goal.

In the wake of the strike the CCF set up a Trade Union Committee for the avowed purpose of overthrowing the now vulnerable CP leadership in the UAW. David Lewis arranged contact with Reuther so that activities in both Detroit and Windsor could be coordinated. The Windsor liaison group reported to Lewis: "Our meeting was held with Walter Reuther last night as planned . . . We all came back with a firm determination to work harder than ever . . . We are determined to keep our group going and to caucus regularly throughout the year and . . . to keep in contact with the Reuther group in Detroit. Thus we will be able to take care of the two main points upon which the Communists had an advantage over us: They were organized, we were not, and they had a pipeline into the International office, we had not . . . If we can keep it up . . . we are in."

Reuther won control of the international Executive Board of the UAW in November 1947 and received congratulations from Lewis, along with suggestions that the Canadians were expecting to benefit from his influence. Lewis wrote, "I cannot tell you how delighted we all are with your decisive victory . . . We all look forward to the influence which the UAW should now be in a position to exert on the policies of the union movement both in the United States and Canada. I am only sorry that our people were unable to deliver a victory in the Canadian region. My impression is that it is only a matter of time now, and that continuing work will ensure a victory at the next convention."

Both the CCF and the CP were weak in the traditionally conservative Trades and Labour Congress and in its craft union affiliates. The guerilla-like campaign raging within the CCL was not duplicated in the

Congress. In fact, there was a hiatus in the strident anti-communism that usually featured TLC affairs, and a climate approximating brotherly love characterized the relationship between CP members and the union leaders.

There happened to be a historical coincidence of views that paved the way for the uncharacteristic bonds of friendship existing between the two. The early war years saw the TLC bitterly opposed to the war policies of the King Government, so far as they affected the labour movement. At the 1942 Convention the Congress President compared King's labour policy to that of Hitler and said, "We want to see this war against the labour people in this country stopped." This coincided with the era when the CP was outlawed and was maintaining the position that the conflict was "an imperialist war" from which the working class had nothing to gain. When King made concessions to organized labour, the TLC patched up its quarrel with the Liberals and established friendly relations with the Government. At the 1944 Convention the President announced that the Congress and the Government had arrived at "a basis of friendly cooperation."

Almost simultaneously with the TLC, the CP had arrived at a basis of "friendly cooperation" with the Liberals, and was vigorously advancing the proposition for a Liberal-labour coalition for victory in the War, thus solidifying friendly relations within the confines of the Trades Congress. This was not so strange a development since the Liberal Party was more than receptive to the CP advances. In a by-election in Ontario the Liberals ran a newspaper ad that featured the photographs of seven CP union leaders across the country as supporters of the Liberal candidate. In Essex County, Ontario, the Liberal Party accepted as an official Party candidate a CP member who was one of three UAW nominees in a provincial election. (He was elected and joined the Liberal caucus while still retaining CP membership.)

The Trades Congress was also fully in accord with the CP "non-partisan" policy in the unions. The report of the TLC Executive Council to the 1944 Convention read like a Party statement on non-partisan political action, and contained a thinly veiled condemnation of the CCF: "We do not agree that any section or group of our society should endeavour to take advantage of the war situation. We cannot agree that now is the time for political parties to utilize this crisis and waste valuable time in advancing their own political prestige . . . We would much prefer to aid and assist the government than devote time protesting undue infringements upon our liberties."

The full significance of the non-partisan declaration was made clear in a Congress statement issued in connection with the Grey North by-election in 1945, a declaration which could only be interpreted as support for the nominee of the Liberal Party. It received official CP approval when it was published in the party organ, the *Pacific Tribune*, on February 3:

Our Congress voted at its last convention to set up a PAC, but refused to attach itself to any political party. It is therefore impossible for our Congress ... to join in any partisan move. Our attitude in this critical stage of the struggle against fascism is best seen in our reaffirmation of the "no strike pledge" at our last convention. We can only hope that the people of Grey North will put victory first and relegate Party politics to a secondary position.

Given the prevailing attitudes, it is not surprising that J.A. "Pat" Sullivan of the Canadian Seamen's Union could become Secretary-Treasurer of the TLC in 1942. Since Sullivan had been recently released from internment as a member of a prohibited organization, the Communist Party, it is hardly credible that anyone would believe his pre-election statement that he was not a member of the Party. This became an embarrassment to Congress officers when Sullivan revealed his membership and denounced the CP in 1947.

Although the American union leaders were deeply involved in anti-communist activities throughout the entire war period, their attention was mainly taken up with the European cockpit, and Canadian affairs were given a minimum of consideration. Since the Communists were actually illegal under the War Measures Act, and Party policies and political activities were not such as to cause undue alarm, it is not strange that the AFL leaders should give so little thought to Canada.

But the temper of the times changed, and Congress officials were slow to change with it. They lagged behind the political needs of the day, and seemed reluctant to sever new-found relationships. Hence the "shock and alarm" belatedly expressed by the American unionists in 1949.

Even then it was a jurisdictional dispute that touched off the storm. The controversy that erupted is most enlightening as regards American union attitudes toward the "colonial" subjects in Canada. Supported by the American Federation, the Seafarers' International Union foisted a criminal on Canada in the guise of a union leader, and defied the Government of Canada.

Destruction of the CSU—First Stage

Focal point of the storm in Canada was the TLC-affiliated Canadian Seamen's Union, which Sullivan, a former President of the union, had publicly denounced as "communist controlled."

If this was true then the union could be used as a strategic base in sabotaging the Marshall Plan, which was vigorously opposed by Moscow and the Party. Judiciously organized strikes and protests around "immediate issues" could serve to interrupt shipment of American goods to Europe, hence American imperialism's burning desire to smash the Canadian Seamen's Union in the only way possible—by replacing it with a goon squad under the charter of an international union, and led by a petty American criminal. The AFL, other international unions and the Government of Canada had their roles to play in the drama—and played them to the hilt. Only the officials of the Trades Congress stumbled along, seemingly unable to comprehend what was taking place around them. Their incomprehension led to an historic and revealing confrontation with the top American unionists.

Seamen in Canada had once belonged to the International Seafarers' Union, which quit the AFL to cast in its lot with the CIO. Canadian seamen retained their affiliation with the Trades Congress, but the AFL was without a seafaring affiliate for several years. In 1944 the Federation accepted the Sailors Union of the Pacific in affiliation and renamed it the Seafarers' International Union of North America. In a modified version of the script by which the Pope gave half the world to Catholic Spain, the 1944 Convention of the *American* Federation of Labour awarded the SIU "jurisdiction over seamen and fishermen in all waters of North America and Canada." In due course, Congress officers were notified of this momentous decision by letter, and in a letter dated July 18, 1945, the Trades Congress raised the issue of the CSU with the President of the AFL, who admitted he knew nothing about the existence of the Canadian union. Discussing the contents and import of the Federation resolution on seamen's jurisdiction, the Congress said:[4]

> The fact is the organized seamen in Canada desired to stay with our Movement and as there was no International affiliated with the AFL, they retained their affiliation to this Congress and were chartered as a national Union to be known as the Canadian Seamen's Union with all the rights and privileges of chartering local unions . . .
>
> The Seafarers' International Union have some 300 members in two locals in the Province of British Columbia. They have not sought affiliation to this Congress until I received a telegram to that effect this week.
>
> The Canadian Seamen's Union, desiring to stay with our Movement was chartered by the Trades and Labour Congress of Canada in 1936; has over 7,000 members East and West and Great Lakes; is recognized by the Government of Canada as the bona fide union for seamen; is certified as the exclusive bargaining agency for seamen on all government-owned and operated ships, and you seriously ask this Congress to now put this organization out as a dual organization, and take in exchange this "corporal's guard" on the Pacific Coast that has been quite satisfied to stay on the outside of our Movement.
>
> . . . when International Unions allow themselves to be broken up

they cannot expect to find everything and everybody all ready to come back when they so wish. Members of unions cannot be just taken out of one union and put into another like cattle taken out of one stall and moved into the next . . .

It must be recognized that in Canada the Seafarers' Union of North America is the dual organization. The proper thing to do would be to endeavour to get this small group to transfer their membership to the organization that has the vast majority of Canadian seamen and has the agreements with the most shipping companies, namely, the Canadian Seamen's Union . . .[5]

In retrospect it would appear that the fight to smash the Canadian Seamen's Union was well planned in both the United States and Canada, and involved unions, shipowners and Governments in its web of plotting and deceit.

Pat Sullivan demonstratively resigned from his position as Secretary-Treasurer of the Trades Congress and from his post in the seamen's union, publicly denouncing the Communist Party en route to a new career. In a move that undoubtedly represented the first attempt to replace the CSU with what amounted to nothing more than a company union, Sullivan founded the Canadian Lake Seamen's Union, which was immediately recognized and dealt with by the leading shipping companies, despite the fact that the CSU was the official bargaining agency, accredited by the Federal Labour Board. Sullivan's willingness to quit a relatively good position, his well known penchant for the "better things" in life, and his later display of ostentatious wealth, point to the fact that Sullivan was well compensated for his defection.

There was the inevitable harassment and conflict that accompany an employer-induced split of this kind. The Government appointed an Industrial Disputes Inquiry Commission to investigate the situation on the Great Lakes. The report of the Commission, released on July 13, 1948, aimed some telling blows at the company and its home-made union:

It appears to your Commissioners that the Company in its arguments has confused the obligation to make an agreement with the obligation to attempt to take all reasonable steps to make one. In this particular case, the Company, by entering into an agreement with another union has made it impossible to negotiate with the union with whom it has dealt for so many years . . .

. . . it is our opinion that the failure to negotiate, the substitution of a new union for the existing bargaining unit and the assertion of the Company of the right to refuse to negotiate because of its objections to alleged political opinions, are contrary to accepted practices and the law as it has heretofore been followed. We feel too, that in the result injustice has been done to the rank and file of the Canadian Seamen's Union, particularly those to whom seniority rights have accrued.[6]

The Sullivan interlude was a complete dud and there was no possibility that the AFL could undertake to bail out the CLSU. A new solution had to be worked out, and with that in mind a number of shipowners, together with some representatives of international unions in Canada, approached the American head of the SIU with an appeal to take over the job of smashing the allegedly "Communist dominated" CSU. Hal Banks was dispatched to handle the situation. The 1948 issue of *Labour Organization in Canada* reported the developments as follows:

The inter-union strife on the Great Lakes which has been waged during the past year between the Canadian Seamen's Union and the Canadian Lake Seamen's Union—formed by J.A. (Pat) Sullivan who had bolted the former because he charged it was Communist-led—took another turn on September 1, when the CLSU, regarded by its rival as a "company union," was absorbed into the Seafarers' International Union of North America, an affiliate of the American Federation of Labour.

The merger was announced by Mr. Frank Hall, vice-president of the Brotherhood of Railway and Steamship Clerks, who conducted the negotiations.

In his announcement, Mr. Hall stated that agreement was reached whereby the CLSU becomes a part of the Canadian District of the Seafarers' International union embracing deep sea as well as Great Lakes operations.

The announcement also said: "Pat Sullivan, erstwhile president of CLSU has been retired from the scene. The Seafarers' approach to the discussion which led up to the agreement was conditioned upon the elimination of Sullivan, and this was achieved by the CLSU before entering into the negotiations."

The merger was followed a day later by a meeting of executive officers of 23 international unions who established a committee which, according to press reports, endorsed this action and, in the words of its chairman will "work for the maintenance of the TLC's integrity."

The Canadian Seamen's Union is an affiliate of the Trades and Labour Congress which, in turn, has close ties with the American Federaton of Labour.

After Mr. Hall's announcement, Mr. Percy Bengough, president of the Trades and Labour Congress, stated that the merger had been effected without consultation with the TLC and that it would be a matter for the Congress membership to decide at the convention in Victoria early in October.

The position of the Trades and Labour Congress executive, as indicated to its membership, was that the Hamilton convention of 1947 instructed it "to continue to recognize and assist the Canadian Seamen's Union as the only bona fide union of seamen in Canada" and ruled that the Seafarers' International Union shall be considered as a dual union.

Alleging that the "question of Communism has been brought into the issue by the employers" and asserting that "the present issue is not one of Communism" the executive declared:

"If this Congress ever submits that the employers have a right to say who shall represent a union, then all unions will soon become company unions."

Hall was the Canadian head of the very same Railway Brotherhood that laid claim to the jurisdiction of a Canadian union—the CBRE—in 1919. Now he, in turn, was helping yet another invading American union—one, moreover, often cited for lawlessness in the United States—to seize the jurisdiction of the Canadian Seamen's Union.

The exercise was in complete violation of a Convention decision and represented a flagrant contempt for Congress members and Canadian sovereignty. The Congress Executive could not possibly ignore the violation. Consequently, a meeting was held on September 11, 1948, at which time the Executive Committee resolved to suspend the Brotherhood of Railway and Steamship Clerks:

Whereas the 62nd Annual Convention of the Trades and Labour Congress of Canada went on record that the Canadian Seamen's Union is the only bona fide union of Seamen in Canada and that the Seafarers' International Union be considered as a dual organization;

And whereas such Convention decisions, once arrived at, become the laws governing all Officers of the Congress and affiliated organizations;

And whereas Frank Hall, Vice-President of the Brotherhood of Railway and Steamship Clerks . . . has taken upon himself to invite the Seafarers' International Union to come into Canada and take over the jurisdiction of the Canadian Seamen's Union, a duly affiliated organization of the Trades and Labour Congress of Canada;

And whereas such actions were taken during a period in which the Canadian Seamen's Union was engaged in a legal strike and without any consultation with the officers or consideration of the membership of the Canadian Seamen's Union or with the Trades and Labour Congress of Canada;

And whereas the actions of Mr. Frank Hall, together with the boastful publicity given to such actions, are a direct and flagrant

violation of the Constitution of the Trades and Labour Congress of
Canada;

Therefore be it resolved—That this Executive Council, in
accordance with the provisions contained in Article III, Section 8, of
the Constitution of the Trades and Labour Congress of Canada,
suspend the Brotherhood of Railway and Steamship Clerks . . . from
membership in the Trades and Labour Congress of Canada in that
. . . [they] have violated both the letter and the spirit of the Constitution . . . and have rendered assistance to a dual organization to the
detriment of a duly and accredited affiliated union.[7]

Also in September, the Congress Executive called a conference of union
representatives in support of the CSU strikers, and to protest the violence
of the anti-CSU element. Lipton describes the conference setting as
follows:

More serious than the shipowners' violence was the SIU's role. Such
was the opposition of trade unionists to this organization, that
normally its entry into the situation would have been impossible. But
its way was paved by the "Roadmen"—full-time Canadian
vice-presidents of international unions. When the TLC called a mass
trade union conference at Ottawa in support of the CSU, many
Roadmen opposed the conference, and set up a "picket line" at the
entrance to the hall, to scrutinize delegates as they came in. Later, the
Roadmen told the press that this conference—with delegates
carrying credentials from trade union locals grouping half a million
members—was composed of 98% communists and 2% fellow
travellers.[8]

The issue of the Congress *Journal* for November 1948 took editorial note
of statements in the New York press attributed to the American head of the
BR & SC. According to one such report, the American unionist proposed
"to take away from all local unions, including the locals of the Railway
and Steamship Clerks, a right they have had since this Congress was
organized sixty-five years ago, namely the right to elect delegates from
local unions to the conventions of the Congress and substitute delegates
appointed by the General Officers."

Suspension of the BR & SC, and the status of the CSU, were the main
items on the agenda of the Trades Congress Convention when it met at
Victoria, B.C. in October 1948. The Committee on Officers' Reports
introduced the controversial subjects on the morning of the second day,
recommending that the matters be dealt with under two separate headings:

1. The matter of the dispute between the shipping companies and the
Canadian Seamen's Union;

2. The amalgamation of the Canadian Lake Seamen's Union with the Seafarers' International Union and the ultimate action of the Congress Executive Council in this connection.

On the first point, the Committee reported that they had examined the evidence and were of the opinion that "the position of the Executive Council has been entirely in accord with decisions of last year's Convention . . ."

In their report the Committee went on to elaborate on a charge that the Department of Labour must accept full responsibility for the situation on the Lakes. It was pointed out that the Department had failed to "implement the unquestionable authority it had at the outset of the dispute," and in this connection the Report concurred with the findings of the Commission of Investigation appointed by the Government, the Commission having reported:

> We are unanimous in stating our belief that the defiance of the existing law, the breach of the existing agreement, and the failure to fulfill the promise made by these companies to the Government are a serious threat to the recognized practice of labour conciliation, and are, moreover, the worst possible weapons any employer could use in a dispute with the legally constituted bargaining representative of his employees.

> We have reason to believe also that this conduct, which goes to the root of labour relations in this country, raises far wider issues than the isolated dispute with the Canadian Seamen's Union, and that there is grave danger that the discord will not be restricted merely to relations between the union and these companies.

The CSU was currently in a confrontation with some shipping companies on the Great Lakes, and the Government-appointed Commission judged the Seamen's struggle justified and the owners culpable in the dispute. There was little, therefore, that any delegate in a body of unionists could say in opposition to the stand recommended by the Committee. The proposition was given a unanimous vote of approval.

Having thus unanimously approved of the seamen's strike, it seemed logical that the same body of delegates should, without hesitation and without dallying too long on debate, condemn the Seafarers' and Frank Hall for their divisive role in the strike. Such, however, was not to be the case.

The Committee on Officers' Reports recognized the inter-relationship between the Lakes strike and the Hall-Seafarers' intervention, and they met it head on:

> It is most regrettable that an affiliate of this Congress was involved in

a desperate struggle for union recognition on the Great Lakes, and the negotiation of new agreements for deep sea shipping, they should also become involved in a struggle for their very existence as a trade union. It is also to be regretted that a senior officer of another affiliate of this Congress, without consulting the Executive Council of this Congress, was a medium through which an effort was made to substitute a union dual to this Congress for a properly accredited organization of this Congress . . .

Your Committee must concur in the decision of the Executive Council that an officer of an affiliate of this Congress rendered assistance to a dual organization to the detriment of a duly and accredited affiliated union. Their only recourse therefore was the suspension of the affiliated organization to which the responsible officer belongs.

Your Committee . . . recommends endorsation of the action taken by the Executive Council and that their action in this matter be sustained.

A.R. Johnstone of the Hotel and Restaurant Workers Union argued that the resolution passed at the previous Convention of the Trades Congress was in violation of the Congress constitution. In support of his point, Johnstone said:

In support of my thought along those lines I wish to read Section 2, Article III . . . "Any International Union holding a charter from the American Federation of Labour shall be entitled to affiliate its entire Canadian membership, and any local unit in Canada of an International Union chartered by the American Federation of Labour which is not so affiliated shall be entitled to direct membership in this Congress." Therefore any action of this Congress in Convention that would abridge this section of the Constitution will of necessity be illegal, and I contend to the delegates that any group chartered by the American Federation of Labour has a right to affiliation in this Trades and Labour Congress of Canada. That is beyond doubt and beyond peradventure. If this Convention of the Trades and Labour Congress of Canada desires to change this section of our Constitution it can only be done by Constitutional amendment, and that was not done.

Hall cited the example of his own union's displacement of the CBRE under the provisions of the constitution nearly thirty years before, and he rested his case on the same constitutional grounds advanced by Johnstone, arguing that "the law, therefore, is plain. American Federation of Labour Unions have unqualified right to affiliation. Other International Unions and National Unions can only be admitted by a two-thirds vote of a

Convention and then only provided their jurisdiction does not conflict with an affiliated union."

In essence, both Johnstone and Hall were arguing that the Trades Congress was merely a depository for charters issued by the American Federation of Labour. Rejection of any such charters, duly issued, did not fall within the scope of Trades Congress rights. Furthermore, the AFL could issue a charter at any time, to any group, and the group so chartered automatically possesses the right to claim jurisdiction over related groups of workers organized by Canadians in Canada. That was seen to be done in four particularly outstanding cases: the Amalgamated Society of Carpenters and Joiners; the Amalgamated Society of Engineers; the Canadian Brotherhood of Railway Employees; and the Canadian Seamen's Union.

In effect, unanimous endorsation of the Committee recommendation concerning the first part of the report was equivalent to outright naming of the SIU as an organization of scabs. Furthermore, under its former title of Sailors' Union of the Pacific, the SIU was notorious for its goon squad tactics and lawbreaking activities in the United States. One of Hal Banks' more respectable addresses before migrating to Canada was San Quentin Prison, California. But in spite of its scabbery and its infamous outlawry, the SIU was not to be impeded by the Trades Congress in taking control of the CSU. In fact, the Congress was expected to facilitate the process because the SIU was in possession of a charter issued by the American Federation.

A delegate from Winnipeg, representing a Railway Brotherhood local, brought in the question of finances. The Trades Congress could not initiate any meaningful action because the international unions had control of the funds. He contended that it was only Hall's own union that had the power to discipline him, and it did not lie within the capacity of Congress to take any action. "Now, I contend, as others have," said the Winnipeg delegate, "if there was any discipline coming to Brother Hall . . . that his organization was the proper party to discipline Brother Hall. The Trades and Labour Congress doesn't get its per capita tax from the 12,000 railway clerks in Canada. They get it from the international organization, which is the proper organization for them to communicate with."

It seems that on the issues in dispute many of the delegates were suffering from tunnel vision. This Winnipeg delegate, for example, could only see the per capita tax coming *from* the international union, he was unable to see it going *to* the Americans from the Canadian railway workers in the first place, or that only *part* of the money collected in Canada was being returned to the Trades Congress.

It was Hall who introduced the issue of "Communism" into the debate, and this was the issue that was to plague Congress affairs down to the present time. If it is against "Communism," real or suspected, then any tactic was justified. Hall contended that since there were some known Communists in the leadership of the Seamen's Union, then the organization must be destroyed no matter what the effect on the working seamen, and even if the job had to be done by gangsters in the guise of international unionists. Addressing himself to this point, Hall stated, ". . . fundamentally what is involved is the question of Communism, because you cannot separate Communism from the Canadian Seamen's Union. I suggest that the question here today is not one of recalcitrant and reactionary employers, the question here is one of revolutionary trade unionism and whether that's the kind of thing we are going to tolerate or whether we are going to continue as an Industrial organization . . ."

The Committee on Officers' Reports made a four-part recommendation as a conclusion to the discussion. The first three parts proposed: 1. That the suspension of the BR &SC be lifted; 2. That Hall be censured; 3. That Hall's union be notified of the action taken by the Convention. The fourth point in the recommendation read: "That since the Seafarers' International Union, brought into the dispute, is an affiliate of the American Federation of Labour and not of this Congress, and the Canadian Seamen's Union is a duly chartered affiliate of this Congress, the Co-ordinating Committee of the AFL and the Congress be asked to discuss the matter with a view to arriving at an understanding whereby the sovereignty and prestige of this Trades and Labour Congress of Canada will continue unchanged."

The Co-ordinating Committee referred to in the recommendation was composed of equal parts of AFL and TLC representation. It was established for the precise purpose of circumventing the sort of dispute revolving around the CSU-SIU affair, but it had never functioned and was certainly not activated as a means of settling the jurisdictional dispute regarding union representation for the seamen. The Convention delegates were proposing that this ephemeral Co-ordinating Committee be put into service as mediator.

Immediately following the Convention, and in pursuance of the instructions from the delegates, the two top officers of the Congress requested a meeting of the Committee, and duly received a call to attend a meeting in Miami in February 1949. The President and the Secretary-Treasurer of Congress responded to the invitation and arrived in Miami on the set date. The Congress *Journal* for March 1949 carried a lengthy report of the Miami experience. The story is best told by the officers themselves, as published in the *Journal*:

During the past year our Congress has been faced with a serious attempt by the American Federation of Labour to completely ignore our sovereign rights. This is not the first occasion by any means. As early as 1910 the American Federation of Labour suddenly decided to consider whether The Trades and Labour Congress of Canada had the right to charter Trades and Labour Councils. The strong protests of our Congress administration of that year resulted in the American Federation of Labour backing down and graciously agreeing to give the Congress such rights. Prior to this we had already held and exercised that right for over a quarter of a century. Furthermore we will see by the following events taken from the annals of our history that our present difficulties with the American Federation of Labour only differ in degree with the many liberties taken by the American Federation of Labour at our Congress expense during past years.

In 1937 the American Federation of Labour Executive Council decided that our Congress was not authorized to issue Trades and Labour Council charters despite their uncalled for decision in 1910. Again in 1939 the American Federation of Labour Executive Council redecided that we did have this right but placed certain restrictions without substantiating their authority to impose these conditions. Once again in 1940 President William Green advised the late President Moore that more restrictions should be adopted if the Congress was to continue chartering Trades Councils. Finally in 1945 the American Federation of Labour Executive Council in effect rescinded all four above mentioned directives, which they had never had the authority to make in the first place, by recognizing that the Trades and Labour Congress of Canada had full rights to issue such charters to Trades and Labour Councils.

The matter of Trades Council charters was only one of the many issues where the American Federation of Labour, situated in another country, attempted to dictate and impose itself on our Congress concerning purely Canadian affairs. A flagrant example of muddling, if not impudence, was the question of the United Mine Workers in the year 1939. We had no differences with the thousands of Canadian miners or their organization. Nevertheless we were expected to participate in every American quarrel and to follow blindly American Federation of Labour decisions whether or not they were practical or feasible in Canada. Therefore because the miners left the American Federation of Labour we were called upon to expel their organization (as well as others). We put the miners out, but it is significant and appalling that several years later when the United Mine Workers rejoined the American Federation of Labour in the United States their Canadian membership continued affiliation with a rival trade union centre in Canada.

We later learned that while we had practically severed our Congress in two on the entire 1939 issue, President William Green, who had taken it upon himself to issue instructions that we throw out the miners, had his own membership card kept in good standing with the

United Mine Workers.

Then came the machinist issue. Since they were no longer in the American Federation of Labour we were pressured to expel their Canadian membership through instructions issued to international representatives by the American Federation of Labour. A ridiculous parallel was created. While we were expected to expel machinists in Canada the miners were still in a rival Congress in this country and on this the American Federation of Labour seemed quite unperturbed. Only the united efforts and determination of the Canadian membership saved the day.

At one point this Congress received a copy of a most amazing letter sent by President William Green to District 50 of the United Mine Workers in Canada. How little this man knows of trade union affairs in Canada! His letter to this rival organization states that he disagrees with Canadian organized workers being divided into two Congresses and from the tone of his communication our Congress seems to share some of the responsibility, and he is even surprised that there should be two trade union centres in Canada. He had already seemingly forgotten that the split was precipitated in his own Executive Council and relegated to this country on his own instructions.

That is the way it has gone for years: jurisdictional fights, "break-aways," and "make-ups." No consultation or consideration deemed necessary. Just issue orders with a total disregard of how the Canadian membership and the Trades and Labour Congress of Canada was affected.

By the year 1946 the situation had rapidly deteriorated. Our Congress therefore welcomed the setting up of a Cooperation Committee . . . While seeking to remove and forestall any possible domination we strove for a strengthening of real ties of brotherhood between the American Federation of Labour and the Trades and Labour Congress of Canada.

. . . The officers of your Congress, acting as members of the Cooperation Committee, arrived in Miami on the set date. They were kept waiting an entire week. The American Federation of Labour had changed its mind. There would not only be no meeting, but it seems that the Cooperation Committee is dissolved.

Instead the American Federation of Labour Executive Committee, by a flagrant usurpation of authority, sets itself up as a tribunal to try the elected officers of a trade union centre representing workers from another country. Still desiring harmony between the American Federation of Labour and the Trades and Labour Congress of Canada your Congress officers appeared before the Executive Committee. Also present for this occasion was Frank Hall and several of his supporters.

The "Halls" were invited to present their case, which proved to be made up of some truths, half truths, and many outright erroneous assertions. Their garbled surmises and inferences, both written and oral, were expounded for over an hour and a half. The Congress representatives were given less than a half hour to reply, following which the session came to an end. A further session was held where the American Federation of Labour Executive Committee proceeded to render their sentence:

1. Expel all Communists.

2. Scrap the present constitution by changing delegate represent- ation at Conventions.

. . . The second point is nothing less than an audacious attempt to disfranchise Canadian members and to make the Trades and Labour Congress of Canada a stifled appendage of the American Federation of Labour.

For many years the American Federation of Labour has attempted to control Congress Conventions by issuing orders and directives to organizers and international union representatives on their payroll who are stationed in or sent into Canada.

The Victoria, B.C. Convention reached an all time high in interference with a Canadian Convention deliberating on Canadian affairs. The American Federation of Labour and many, though not all international unions issued specific instructions to their paid representatives to fight the elected officers of the Congress. Recently the American Federation of Labour hired two former organizers of the CIO. For years these men had travelled far and wide denouncing and slandering all our affiliated organizations as well as the American Federation of Labour. These two as well were sent to Victoria to oppose the Congress administration. Credentials were procured for them from defunct local unions that neither had bargaining rights nor represented the membership. At this point the Congress wishes to say that those organizers and officers who refused to take orders and simply voted on the facts are to be congratulated. But what price will they pay for having the courage of their convictions? One organizer has already been dismissed for refusing to vote against the officers of the Congress. How many will follow? What measures will be taken against local union officers who attended the Convention as delegates and did not vote the American Federation of Labour way?

It is an abominable situation when a trade union centre in a foreign country attempts to influence delegates attending a Convention in this country. That is what we mean by "mimicking totalitarian methods." Having rejected such methods from Moscow, Canadian members will reject them from any foreign source. The American Federation of Labour therefore raises a question for all members in Canada to face and answer. Can we permit a situation where Canadians attending a Convention in Canada and voting on national affairs may suffer reprisals from abroad?

Who are the men gathered around Hall? In the main they are international representatives discredited by the Convention delegates from their own organizations. Here is a worthwhile example. One "Hall" follower represents an international union which had sixty-seven delegates at the Convention. On the crucial vote, only five including himself voted his way and most of the five are paid organizers of the international union. These are the men who went to Miami to plead with the American Federation of Labour Executive Council to force our Congress to disfranchise the very members they are supposed to represent.

It is these men who have drifted away from their membership in their anxiety to follow instructions from "pay headquarters" that must now be rescued. That is why the American Federation of Labour demands that henceforth each international union be permitted to deliver a block vote by one hog-tied paid official on behalf of all their members in Canada.

The American Federation of Labour bases its demands for changes in the constitution of this Congress on the claim that the per capita tax is paid by the head office of the international union. Therefore their chosen delegate should have a voting strength in direct proportion to the number of tax paid members in the union in Canada. The fact remains that the per capita is collected from the Canadian membership in the first place and then remitted back by the respective international unions to the Congress. In some instances the "brokerage fees" run as high as 50 per cent of the amount collected, by only paying the Congress on half the actual Canadian membership . . .

Threats are being advanced that if the Congress does not accept the American Federation of Labour Executive Committee ultimatum, certain international unions will withdraw. The Congress would sincerely regret such a move. We will continue to lend all our efforts to heal the breach with reason and with justice. All that can be done will be done to avoid precipitating such an unfortunate situation. Nevertheless the Congress will not be domineered by threats.

This document, most but not all of which has been quoted, constitutes a devastating indictment of the crude interference and arrogant and domineering attitude that has featured Canadian-American trade union relations for more than eight decades. But despite the sharpness with which interference by the AFL was condemned (regardless of the resounding note of defiance that ended the article: "Cooperation yes—Domination no!") the Executive of Congress capitulated to American threats and the CSU was suspended from membership on June 3, 1949.

Destruction of the CSU—Final Stage

True enough, the questionable tactics of the CSU leadership, and a Government statement condemning the union, provided the Congress officers with a blanket to cover their humiliation. The calling of a strike by the CSU leaders in the face of a unanimous award from a Board of Conciliation, and in the circumstances prevailing at the time, seems at best to have been a foolhardy act. But the first public reaction by Trades Congress spokesmen which appeared in the Congress *Journal* in May was comparatively mild in tone, and was still suggestive of support for the union:

> A joint statement was issued on May 3rd, 1949 by the Hon. Humphrey Mitchell, Minister of Labour, and the Hon. Lionel Chevrier, Minister of Transport, on the Canadian Seamen's Strike, calling to the attention of the public, and the Seamen concerned, the fact that strikes at sea or in ports abroad, in disobeying the lawful orders of the Master, are in violation of the Canada Shipping Act. The Trades and Labour Congress of Canada is in full agreement with the statement of the Ministers of the Government respecting the need of obeying laws. No good purpose can ever be achieved by violation of established laws. We clearly state that this must be the policy of organized labour at all times and this applies equally to laws that are good laws as well as to laws which we believe are unfair and discriminatory and are desirous of changing. It even applies to the Hon. Lionel Chevrier's company act, known as the Canada Shipping Act, designated by one learned judge as a monstrous law and disapproved of by other judges when cases under it have been brought before them. However, much as we dislike it, as long as it remains on the Statute Books we cannot advocate or condone its violation. This goes for the seamen, the shipping moguls, and the Ministers of the Crown.
>
> The Ministers' joint statement states: "Under the Canada Shipping Act, Seamen must obey the orders of the Master until the voyage is completed. Everyone who has knowledge of the ways of the sea accepts and supports this principle. The Canadian Merchant Marine cannot be built up or maintained unless this principle is followed. The law provides that the voyage must be completed and the ship and cargo placed in security at her terminal port in Canada before the members of her crew can engage in a lawful strike."

Let us agree that this is the way it should be. However, while the law says that workers cannot go on strike in foreign ports, the shipowners can fire the whole crew, including the officers. They not only can but they have done so on more than one occasion and got away with it in spite of the fact that there was no labour dispute in effect at the time but an agreement was in effect for the completion of the voyage to Canada. Why was this done? The Company wanted foreign labour at low wages. There were and we think there are yet about twenty-four ships under Canadian registry sailing with foreign crews. Canadian seamen were all fired. In total this represented a wage loss to Canadians of about four million dollars per year.

Isn't it sufficient that while all these merchant seamen, both officers and men, were being displaced with foreign crews, that the so-called Canadian companies concerned were not condemned by the Government and no joint statements were issued by the Ministers? The Minister of Transport contented himself by giving a statement to the press that as long as the men were returned to Canada by the shipping companies everything was quite alright, or words to that effect.

During the present Seamen's strike errors may have been committed by the Seamen but what about the Canadian National Steamships and their gun-toting strikebreakers? Isn't it true that many, not sailors, were put in boats contrary to the requirements of the same Canada Shipping Act? Are the Ministers only concerned with the delinquencies of the working people? These are paramount questions at this time. They are questions that are in the minds of many thousands of Canadians from one end of Canada to the other. Efforts to dispel wholesale strike-breaking with Government assistance by parroting that it is a jurisdictional dispute is not satisfying to most people.

Before the end of May the CSU had spread the strike to Canadian ships in ports abroad. By then someone must have pointed out to the Congress Executive Committee that they had been presented with a glorious opportunity to abandon their commitment to the CSU and get into line with the instructions of the American Federation. In any event the tone of CSU criticism had altered and the union was suspended from membership. By July, the suggestion of a possible Communist conspiracy that had crept into the June editorial statement had been strengthened and became more obvious. By then the Congress officers came to the decision to announce the severing of all ties with the CSU, which was tantamount to expulsion from the organization and an open invitation to the SIU to move into the jurisdiction. The June editorial statement on the suspension of the CSU reads in part:

While the Executive of this Congress has fully recognized its responsibilities to the Canadian Seamen's Union, and has rendered all reasonable assistance within the limits of its ability and authority, the Canadian Seamen's Union on the other hand has failed in many respects to recognize and accept its responsibilities to the Congress and its affiliated unions.

The Executive Council takes the position that any organization, having once received the endorsation of the Convention of the Congress, has not necessarily thereby received a mandate of endorsation of future decisions and actions, particularly when such decisions are taken contrary to Congress policies and such actions create unnecessary and embarrassing difficulties for other affiliated organizations . . .

While the Executive has been greatly concerned about many of the leaders of the Canadian Seamen's Union, it has been convinced that the bulk of the membership of the union is a body of Canadians fully loyal to the ideals and institutions of this country. The Executive has always held the view, and finds no reason for changing it now, that the successful development of a sound and effective merchant marine requires that those employed in it should be Canadians with unquestioned loyalty to Canadian ideals.

. . . the situation has steadily deteriorated . . . it has interfered with the welfare of workers in other affiliated unions. Picket lines that were ostensibly established to deter the filling of the jobs of Seamen on strike soon were extended with the effect of preventing members of other affiliated unions from the performance of their usual work.

. . . fourteen affiliated international unions have taken the stand that they will not continue in affiliation as long as the Canadian Seamen's Union remains affiliated. This has had the very careful consideration of the Executive Council.

The Executive Council also considered the scurrilous literature being issued by the Canadian Seamen's Union vilifying tried and trusted trade union members who had supported them and their cause, but who had been unable to agree with unwarranted acts of violence committed in their own cities and Districts. This is exemplified in a news sheet issued by Branch 6, Canadian Seamen's Union . . . in which four affiliated members were designated as dirty scabs. . .

After rendering all possible assistance to the Canadian Seamen's Union both prior to and since the beginning of the east coast shipping strike, the Executive Council of the Trades and Labour Congress of Canada, following full and careful consideration of all the issues involved, are unanimously of the opinion that the continuation of the present strike can result only in the placing of this Congress and its

affiliated unions in further untenable positions unquestionably not in
the best interests of this or any other bona fide trade union
movement.The Executive Council has decided that the name of the
Congress shall no longer be associated with that of the Canadian
Seamen's Union while the Union has its present leadership.

... the Canadian Seamen's Union therefore stands suspended from
the Trades and Labour Congress of Canada as from this third day of
June 1949.

The July issue of the Congress *Journal* reiterated the findings of the June
Executive meeting, expanded the charges of disruption which had by then
expanded to ports abroad, and for the first time from the Congress
Executive level introduced the issue of Communism:

... when the very freedoms valued and enjoyed in a democratic
institution become skillfully used to advance the cause of communism,
some protective measures must be taken.

It cannot be contradicted that those in charge of the CSU strike did
not accept the unanimous findings of a properly constituted Board on
which they had their representative. ... one would have expected the
CSU to accept the unanimous recommendation of the Board which
recognized the union as the bargaining agency and while not all that
could have been desired, the findings of the Board were not by any
means bad. Many unions have accepted worse awards and have lived
to continue building and improving their conditions. The CSU
decided differently. Whether the officers of the CSU or somebody else
decided for them makes little or no difference. The time had arrived
when the Canadian Seamen's Union had become expendable. The
strike presented too good an opportunity to pass up to embarrass the
British Labour Government. It presented a medium of effectively
hindering the Marshall Plan and a counter move to the Atlantic Pact.

The World Federation of Trade Unions, comprised of the
organizations entirely controlled and operated by Communist
Governments, has now taken over the direction of the strike. What
started out as a bona fide industrial dispute is far removed from the
aims and aspirations of free trade unions and this fact has to be
recognized and faced. It is a world wide campaign to advance the
cause of communism by decreasing as much as possible the
effectiveness of the Marshall Plan.

There are solid grounds for suspecting skullduggery on the part of the
leadership of the CSU. But the officers of the Trades Congress were not
combatting this in order to advance the cause of the striking Seamen. They
used it to get themselves off the hook with the AFL and as a reason for

taking up their battle stations in the war on communism. The Canadian working Seamen were pawns in a game of high level politics in which they were expendable. But far from protecting the basic interests of the Seamen, the Congress officers entered the fray as partisans aligned with the AFL and, in the ultimate, prepared to use the gangster-ridden SIU as an ally in the struggle.

Immediately following the Executive announcement of the suspension of the CSU, the *Canadian Forum* editorialized:

> . . . In Canada the Trades and Labour Congress suspended the CSU on June 3, under pressure from the AFL, which had threatened to withdraw its international unions from the TLC. Deprived of Congress support, the CSU leaders offered to call off the strike if the Government would guarantee the strikers' back wages and supervise a union vote, but the Government refused.
>
> That is what has happened in brief. The various forces at work are tangled, but they have all been shaped by the fact that the CSU is Communist-dominated. Otherwise the SIU would hardly have entered the picture, or, if it had, it would not have been so heartily welcomed by the Government and employers. But if the CSU had a sound case (as it had last summer when the Great Lakes companies refused to accept the decision of the Government arbitrators), it would be the duty of labour and progressive groups to support the Seamen in spite of their leadership. However this time the situation is different. It is the CSU leadership who refused to accept the recommendations of the Conciliation Board, even though the union nominee on the Board concurred and the TLC leaders advised acceptance. Certainly it is hard to see what the CSU expected to gain by a strike when the SIU was waiting to step in. Indeed, shortly after the strike started, the CSU appeared ready to settle on terms no better than those which the employers had accepted in February. It seems clear that as far as the welfare of the union members is concerned the strike was a bad tactical blunder—a blunder that no experienced union leaders could have made unwittingly. Nor would union leaders acting in good faith have deliberately confused the issues by misrepresenting the terms recommended by the arbitration Board. Perhaps such misrepresentation was necessary to secure strike solidarity, but it throws suspicion on the motives of the leaders.
>
> Culpable as the CSU leadership is, it could not have wrought such widespread damage by itself. It has had the cooperation of the Canadian Government and the shipowners, of the SIU, and of the employers of the British dockworkers. The Communist leadership of the CSU does not justify the strikebreaking and racketeering tactics of the SIU, nor does it justify the Government and employers making use

of the SIU to dislodge the Seamen's established bargaining agent. The Government may justify its acts legally on the ground that the CSU has been certified as the bargaining agent on less than 10 per cent of the ships involved, but the Labour Code should prevent companies who have signed agreements with one union from signing with any other until it has proved that the employees concerned wish to change their affiliation.

The Trades Congress Convention of 1949 endorsed the Executive decision suspending the CSU, and on a roll-call vote carried a recommendation to expel the union from membership in the Congress. Reporting on the expulsion, *Labour Organization in Canada* referred to the case as a "jurisdictional dispute," which was certainly an important element but not the whole reason for expelling the Seamen. *Labour Organization* stated: "Expulsion of the Canadian Seamen's Union from the TLC represented the climax of a lengthy period of labour troubles in the shipping industry. Events in 1949 which gave immediate effect to the expulsion grew out of a jurisdictional dispute between the CSU and the Seafarers' International Union on the east coast. This dispute prompted the CSU to take strike action although the Executive of the TLC had formally advised against it, as did many other unions. Suspension of the CSU from the TLC followed a series of unsuccessful efforts by the TLC Executive to settle the strike and in September the general Convention of the Congress passed an expulsion order."

It was obvious that not all of the CSU's constituent organizations wanted to fall under the control of the Seafarers' International, and some of them took immediate steps to avoid that undesirable fate. In the same issue of *Labour Organization* we find that: "Following these events, 700 west coast Seamen ended their membership with the CSU, formed a union known as the West Coast Seamen's Union (Canada) and signed contracts with eighteen freighters. At the same time the Fish Handlers Union locals of the CSU in Halifax, Lunenburg, North Sydney, and Glace Bay voted to end their affiliation with the CSU and to seek affiliation with the TLC as a national union."

The Congress *Journal* for October 1949 reported that there were two important questions that came before the Convention: the Canadian Seamen's Union and Communism. On the question of controlling Communists in the unions the Congress Convention adopted a practice that was common in the AFL and most of the international unions. In a lengthy resolution on Communism the delegates resolved: "That no known Communist shall be permitted to hold office in the Trades and Labour Congress of Canada, its Provincial Federations and Central Bodies, nor be permitted to sit on any Committee of the Convention."

This resolution was fortified with a constitutional amendment requiring all candidates for office to take an oath of allegiance and to swear that they were not members of a Communist organization. Far-reaching as it was, the Convention delegates must have viewed this as no more than an additional safety valve, for if another resolution was carried out to the letter, no Communist would ever succeed in getting to a Trades Congress Convention. It was resolved that the TLC "Condemns the Communist doctrines" and "severely censures the activities of Communists and fellow travellers and recommends to all affiliated organizations to remove them from any key positions or offices they may hold and to expel them from their ranks."

There were several accusations of capitulation before AFL and international union pressure which the officers vigorously denied. The first time the question was introduced the President ruled the speaker out of order, but when it was raised again later, he refuted the suggestion that there had been interference from any centre outside of Canada. "That was a question that had arisen and had been amicably settled," he declared. "There was a public statement by President Green that the Trades and Labour Congress had full autonomy. That was recognized and is still recognized."

In the normal course of events one might logically conclude that the supporters of the CSU were merely raking up old quarrels in an attempt to embarrass the Congress officers. But this was no normal situation. The President of the Trades Congress knew very well that autonomy had *not* been recognized. He had joined with the Secretary-Treasurer in a thundering denunciation of the AFL Executive for their failure to accept the autonomous character of the TLC, and for having accorded the top Congress officials the sort of treatment meted out to subservient colonials.

Was it to be believed that President Green had casually apologized for his cavalier attitude and conceded autonomy to those whom only a short time before he had treated like lowly serfs? What were the terms of the amicable settlement arranged between the Trades Congress and the American Federation? It is not that the question was left entirely in limbo. It was dealt with by the Committee on Officers' Reports who told the delegates they had best not enquire into the details of settlement. A most curious and deeply suspicious performance on a matter of such paramount importance to the Congress. The Committee disposed of this embarrassing subject with the following report and recommendation:

> The Committee also believes that the Executive Council endeavoured to the best of its ability to settle the dispute involving the Canadian Seamen's Union through discussions in the Joint Cooperative Committee of the American Federation of Labour and the Trades and Labour Congress of Canada—always endeavouring to maintain the sovereignty and prestige of the Trades and Labour Congress of

Canada unchanged.

Your Committee notes . . . that the Executive Council made constructive efforts to settle the dispute within the scope of the Joint Cooperative Committee without success in the first instance.

The Committee, however, further notes that the differences between the Trades and Labour Congress of Canada and the American Federation of Labour have since been harmonized satisfactorily and that the best interests of the parties will not be served by going into details in matters involving the final settlement.

Your Committee strongly concurs in this opinion and it urges the delegates at this Convention to respect what is, in the Committee's opinion, excellent advice. Your Committee concurs in the opinion that no good purpose can be served by re-opening wounds that are now nicely healed.[9]

In view of the fact that the SIU was not immediately admitted to the membership of the Congress, it can be safely assumed that the Congress officers were granted a "face saving" arrangement by not having to take in the Seafarers until a "decent waiting period" had elapsed. A second significant indicator of settlement details is found in the fact that the constitution was completely overhauled. As the *Journal* report on Convention proceedings states: "There is hardly a section of the constitution which was not amended, if not completely rewritten." And most significantly, as the report says, "one of the most important changes in the constitution was that cutting down representation." As was seen earlier, one of the ultimatums handed down at Miami was for a sweeping change in Convention representation. While the amendment no doubt did not give the Americans all that they had demanded, the trend was in the direction of satisfying their demands. Within the limits of the information available to us it seems safe to assume that, on balance, the Trades Congress gave up far more than was received.

1949 was a vintage year for expulsions. In addition to the Trades Congress expulsion of the CSU, the CCL expelled the United Electrical Workers and the Mine, Mill and Smelter Workers. The 1949 issue of *Labour Organization in Canada* reported:

During 1949, a dispute arose between the CCL and the United Electrical, Radio and Machine Workers of America which resulted in the suspension of the latter from the Congress.

Differences also occurred during the year between the Congress of Industrial Organizations and the UEW in the United States which resulted in the expulsion of the latter from the American Congress. Thereupon, the CIO sponsored the organization of a new electrical workers union to be known as the International Union of Electrical,

Radio and Machine Workers. Its activities were also extended to Canada.

Early in November, the CCL suspended the UEW for non-payment of dues and invited the new union of electrical workers to affiliate. The year closed with both unions vying for membership among Canadian electrical workers. While these were the immediate reasons for the expulsion of the UEW from the CCL it is to be noted that divergent political ideologies have been a continuing problem between the executives of the UEW and CCL.

On March 24, 1949, the International Union of Mine Mill and Smelter workers was suspended from the CCL . . . At the fall convention of the CCL the executive . . . called for a vote to expel the union . . . The vote was in favour of expulsion. Since that time the CCL and the United Steelworkers of America have been active in organizing workers in the mining and refining industry.

The war in Korea which erupted in 1950 lent added impetus to the anti-Communist hysteria that had become the most outstanding feature of the international union movement. Like the Seamen a short time before, the whole of the working class was caught between the social democrat-liberal anti-Communist coalition and the CP contenders for hegemony over the trade union movement. Either way the working class had nothing to gain. Both camps posed as staunch defenders of democratic rights, while each in their separate spheres of influence practised outrageously bureaucratic methods of operation. The Congress *Journal* for October 1950 accused CP members of hollering "the loudest for their democratic rights while looking forward to the day when they can eliminate the whole of them."

But in the very same article the Congress leaders brazenly suggested a limitation on democratic rights as a means of advancing their own interests. "It must be understood," they claimed, "that the workers of Canada, as represented by the Trades and Labour Congress of Canada, are loyal to Canada and Canadian institutions. They value their established freedoms and democratic way of life. They value them to the extent that they will even accept more discipline if in that way they can better protect our way of life from those who seek its destruction."

Of course the institution that was being so forcefully protected from the threat posed by its own membership was not Canadian at all, but very specially American in its origins and style of operation. But the particular reason for the exercise in soul-baring at this point in time was because delegates who had been properly elected by their locals as Convention delegates were being barred from attendance. Since the CP was already a minority so small that they could not get even a moderately "left" resolution past Congress, the tactic was so outrageous as to demand some kind of official recognition.

A similar tactic by the internationals in the United States, which was supported by the power and authority of the American State Department, was even more ridiculous. Even at the best of times Canadian unionists could never muster more than five or six per cent of the total delegates at any AFL or international union Convention, and only a small proportion of them would be members of the Canadian CP. Under the circumstances, any suggestion that CP members posed a threat to either the United States or the international union movement is simply hilariously funny. Nevertheless, the State Department came to the aid of the American bureaucracy by denying admission to members or suspected members of the CP, or just plain left wingers in the union movement.[10]

The same October edition of the *Journal*, in an article that proudly boasted about the "liquidation of communism" at the 65th Convention, confessed that it was necessary to hold actual membership in the CP in order to qualify for disbarment. The point is unequivocally stated in a paragraph that reads: "The main highlight of the opening day of the Convention was President Percy R. Bengough's address and a statement which he later read into the records on foreign policy, in which the Communists, Communist aggression in Korea, and Communist tactics in the Labour Movement were roundly condemned by the Executive Council. The latter followed action on the part of the Credentials Committee in refusing to accept the credentials of a number of delegates, some of whom were suspected Communists or Communist sympathizers."

How does one decide who is or who is not a "suspected communist" or "communist sympathizer" if not on the basis of opposition to official policy? The true test of the democratic process is in the right to dissent from the majority, and the tactics pursued by the Congress could end only in the elimination of all opposition and the consolidation of a dictatorial bureaucracy. In short, the TLC leaders were adopting the very tactics they condemned their opponents for using.

The Government was fully prepared to aid the Congress' anti-Communist crusade, and there is evidence of that in the operations of the Canada Labour Relations Board. The CSU had managed to retain one certification as bargaining agent for employees at Branch Lines Ltd., at Sorel, Quebec. In January 1951 the company applied for decertification on two grounds: firstly, on the ground that the union no longer represented the majority of the workers in the bargaining unit; and secondly, on the ground that the union was a Communist-dominated organization, and not a trade union entitled to certification under the Act in view of its purposes and activities. On the ground of failure to represent the majority of the employees the Board ruled: "As the applicant has not submitted evidence to support its contention that the Respondent no longer represents the majority of employees in the bargaining unit, the application for revocation, insofar as it is based upon this ground, fails.''

The first point thus disposed of, the Board proceeded to an examination of the second ground cited as reason for decertification, stating authority and precedent for their procedure as follows:

> [where] it is necessary for the Board to determine whether an organization is a trade union for the purpose of the Act, the Board ordinarily accepts the purposes set forth in the constitution of the organization as the purposes of the organization where it is satisfied that the organization has not engaged in activities and operations which establish beyond reasonable doubt that the primary and real purposes of the organization are other than those set forth in its constitution, or are other than those alleged by the organization to be its purposes.

The ruling of the Board on the first reason given in support of decertification can only be taken as de facto recognition that the union still represented the majority of the employees of Branch Lines Ltd. It appears from the proceedings of the Board that the company was equally delinquent in the provision of evidence that would sustain the application under the second ground.

But then affairs took a strange turn; the Board, in effect, took up the prosecution of the case as though it were its own, turning the proceedings into something like an inquisition in open pursuit of the pre-determined aim to decertify the union.

We have seen that the Board admitted their procedure in this case was not one ordinarily followed in such applications for decertification. Did this admittedly extraordinary procedure produce results that were also out of the ordinary? This is answered in the findings and decision of the Board, stated as follows:

> It is common knowledge in Canada that the Respondent is a Communist-directed organization. The political affiliation of an organization does not affect its status as a trade union . . .
>
> The Respondent was expelled from membership in the International Transport Workers' Federation . . . The . . . record of expulsion cites that the Respondent "gave out instructions which conflict with all tradition of maritime trade union action and also Canadian law . . . [and action] contrary to all rules of trade union strategy [which] harmed the interests of its own members and those of other affiliated unions.''
>
> The Respondent was also expelled from membership in the Trades and Labour Congress of Canada . . .
>
> Expulsion from a trade union Congress cannot in itself deprive a

union of its status under the Act. The Board wishes it to be clearly understood that it does not base its decision on the action taken by the trade union Congresses. The Board does, however, give weight to the reason given by the trade union Congresses in the expulsion of the Respondent from membership as lending weight to the conclusion that the primary purposes of the Respondent are no longer the purposes of a trade union as set forth in the Act.

In their desire to finish off the CSU and replace it with a gangster-ridden American-based organization, the Board indulges in sheer jabberwocky that would have touched Lewis Carroll's sense of humour. Political affiliation is not cause for decertification; expulsion from trade union Congresses is not grounds for decertification; but the findings of those Congresses—which were based on the questionable conclusion that the CSU had a particular political affiliation—are cited as cause for decertification. On the basis of this rather contrived "logic" the Board handed down its decision:

> For the reasons given above, the Board finds that the Respondent is not a trade union within the meaning of the Act, and therefore is not entitled to certification as a bargaining agent under the provisions of the Act.
> The Board accordingly revokes the order of November 20, 1947, certifying the Respondent as the bargaining agent of the employees of the applicant consisting of unlicensed personnel upon the ships of the applicant.[11]

The Communist Party, in its own way, could always survive in a minority role, but could never seriously challenge the power and influence of the American Federation and the international unions. The international base of the Party was too far removed from the scene and too remote from Canadian traditions to become a really serious contender for leadership. Had the Party chosen to champion the cause of trade union independence in Canada it might have become, at the very least, an opposition to reckon with.

But striving for the building of an independent movement was far from the thoughts of the Party leaders. Continentalism has always been the foundation of Party policy in the unions. Together the parties of the United States and Canada would capture the entire continental movement for "communism." That explains why, in the beginning, the Trade Union Educational League was constituted as District Four of the American organization, rather than being established as an independent Canadian organization. Changing conditions and attitudes have forced some alteration in tactics, but basically the CP position has remained constant, and this is evident in the way in which the Party opposes any attempt to build an independent Canadian trade union movement.

A common interest in advancing the crusade against Communism at last began to heal the split of twenty years duration that existed between the AFL and CIO. Following several years of negotiations on the technicalities of uniting, a merger agreement was reached in 1956. In Canada, the result of the merger of the two bodies was the creation of the Canadian Labour Congress (CLC). The SIU constituted one of the most virulent anti-Communist organizations within the new Congress.

With the aid of the Congress and the international union representatives, and the way having been cleared for them by the questionable decisions of the Canada Labour Relations Board, the SIU became comfortably lodged in Canada. Once his position amongst the seamen was consolidated, Banks turned his attention to raiding other unions as the quickest way to build his own little labour kingdom. Among his early victims were the Canadian Brotherhood of Transport and General Workers (CBRT—formerly the CBRE), the National Association of Marine Engineers (NAME), the Canadian Merchant Service Guild (CMSG), the United Steel Workers of America (bargaining agent for employees on some ore carriers) and one of his former Brotherhood buddies, the Brotherhood of Maintenance of Way Employees.

In his raiding activities, Banks followed the same tactics that had served him in the CSU takeover: sign a "sweetheart" agreement with the companies on behalf of workers who belonged to other unions, without consulting the affected workers as to their needs and desires. Banks also guaranteed to underwrite the legal costs should the companies be sued for breach of contract.

The SIU raiding tactics finally resulted in charges being laid with the Congress Executive against the raiders. The outcome of Congress investigations was the suspension of the SIU, which was changed to outright expulsion when Banks refused to appear before the Congress Convention in 1960.

Undaunted by the disciplinary action taken by Congress, and able to gain the cooperation of shipowners, Banks signed contracts that covered licensed personnel on the Great Lakes who were members of another union. An application for certification was rejected by the Canada Labour Relations Board on the grounds of fraud. But this did not slow down the Czar of the Great Lakes, who went ahead with the signing of agreements on the same lines with other shipping companies.

By the beginning of 1961 only one company, Upper Lakes Shipping, remained outside the Banks orbit. Upper Lakes concluded agreements with the CBRT and the Canadian Maritime Union—the latter set up with the backing of the CLC in opposition to the SIU. Banks responded by withdrawing SIU members from the company's ships and organizing a campaign of terror and harassment that eventually led to the Norris Commission and the establishment of a Government trusteeship over the SIU.[12]

During the harassment campaign, members of the crew of an Upper Lakes Vessel, the Northern Venture, were attacked and brutally beaten by SIU goons at Marquette, Michigan. President Jodoin of the CLC communicated with AFL-CIO President Meany on the subject on several occasions, appealing for intervention to halt the violence. The only visible response to all such appeals was a Maritime Trades Department resolution fully supporting the SIU raids on Canadian Unions. The resolution also condemned the CBRT, a Canadian union, for "conspiring with the owners of the Northern Venture to undermine the rights of Canadian Seamen to man Canadian-owned ships."[13]

Jodoin again corresponded with Meany, protesting the Maritimes Trades Department resolution and warning the AFL-CIO against intervening in Canadian affairs. The Jodoin letter concluded: "Any action by the Maritime Trades Department, as outlined in the 'resolved' portion of the resolution adopted, will be vigorously protested by this Congress to the AFL-CIO, if necessary by retaliatory action in Canada, and by protest through the Canadian government to the U.S. government."[14]

Failure by Meany to act in the matter caused Jodoin to write Prime Minister Diefenbaker, listing fourteen instances of violence against Canadian seamen during the preceding forty-two days. Jodoin also requested a full investigation into SIU affairs, and he later informed the CLC's legal department: "Through External Affairs, the United States government has received a note on the subject matter. I am recommending to some connections I have that the president of the AFL-CIO, Mr. George Meany, be approached by a high ranking official to the U.S. government, no less than Dean Rusk, Arthur Goldberg, or President Kennedy himself, to call a stop to this illogical attitude."[15]

This extraordinary decision to seek action through the United States Department of State is clear and irrefutable evidence of just how powerless the Canadian union movement is in dealings with American union headquarters. The director of U.S. District Four of the United Steel Workers (whose union was threatened with SIU raids in Canada) informed Jodoin that Meany, responding to a Duluth request for advice on working ships manned by the Canadian Maritime Union, bluntly replied, "I see no reason why a national policy decision is necessary to point out the simple fact that the Seafarers' International Union is an affiliate in good standing with the AFL-CIO while the Canadian Maritime Union is not."[16]

Confronted on all fronts with the failure to obtain guarantees for the safety of Canadian seamen in American ports the CLC decided on a policy of direct action. A call was issued by the Congress Executive for a boycott of all SIU-manned ships to be undertaken in Great Lakes and St. Lawrence River ports. This move forced the appointment of a Government Commission (the Norris Commission) to investigate the disruption of shipping. The response of the AFL-CIO Maritime Trades Department was a condemnation of the appointment, and along with it a condemnation of the CLC and the CBRT, and a characterization of the Commission as "a union-busting program instigated by the Conservative government of Canada for the purpose of destroying the Seafarers' International Union of North America, Canadian District, at the behest of the Canadian ship owners unwilling to pay decent wages."[17] The heads of all international unions were unanimous in their support of the SIU.

There was a fruitless attempt by Jodoin to have the American Secretary of Labour intervene, and protests over the dynamiting of a Canadian ship in Chicago elicited from Meany an inquiry for "information" on the incident.

Out of the proceedings of the Norris Commission came a recommendation for a Government-administered trusteeship over all union operations in Great Lakes and St. Lawrence River Shipping. Despite the humiliating treatment they had received from the American unionists, the Congress Executive tried to negotiate a private trusteeship to be administered jointly by the Congress and the AFL-CIO which would have guaranteed the Americans a major say in what happened to the SIU in Canada. This proposal was not acceptable to the Government, so Jodoin cooperated with the Labour Department in drawing up rules for the guidance of the trustees. Now came an extraordinary turn of events that could only be compared to the action of Gideon Robertson in calling on Gompers for aid in breaking the Winnipeg strike. It was a turn of events that could occur only within the context of the unique status of Canadian unions, having their headquarters in a foreign country.

Before the trusteeship was imposed, and in order to discuss final arrangements with the Americans, a meeting was held in Boston, attended by both the Minister and Deputy Minister of Labour of Canada, the United States Secretary and Assistant Secretary of Labour, Donald MacDonald for the CLC, and Lain Kirkland, Executive Assistant to George Meany, for the AFL-CIO. Given the draft plans for the trusteeship the Americans withdrew for a private discussion. On their return to the conference the U.S. Secretary of Labour, Willard Wirtz, emphasized that if the memorandum of understanding "raised the question of government versus private trusteeship of the SIU in Canada, that they favoured the latter, private trusteeship, and regarded the former with complete disfavour," and he went on to say that the sections dealing with the Canadian Government involvement in the affair were unacceptable to the Americans. The fact that the trusteeship was to be imposed by the Canadian Government on a union representing Canadian seamen employed by Canadian companies on ships of Canadian registry did not cause any hesitation on the part of the American Government officials and American union representatives.

Furthermore, Kirkland insisted on the SIU's right to veto any type of trusteeship, which meant that both the American Government and trade union officials were determined on dictating policies concerning the labour movement in Canada. Supported by Kirkland, the head of the SIU demanded that two of the three trustees should be appointed by the AFL-CIO. Kwavnick summarizes these negotiations as follows:

> . . . the United States government and the AFL-CIO had been made parties to the settlement of a Canadian problem in order to obtain freedom from harassment for Canadian ships in American ports. As a result of their involvement, the U.S. government and the AFL-CIO had been able to obtain concessions which implied acceptance of their major objective—that the trusteeship be non-governmental and, with respect to the SIU, voluntary. This meant that the success of the trusteeship would be dependent upon the cooperation of Paul Hall.[18]

But the humiliating experience was not only the result of a desire to end the harassment of Canadian seamen. It was rooted in United States economic domination of Canada, and the parallel domination of Canadian unions by American business unionists. But imposing a Government trusteeship did not overawe the SIU goons. Canadian seamen continued to be harassed in United States ports. As Kwavnick describes it, "In the end the policy of violence paid off for the SIU of North America. While the United States government, at the behest of the AFL-CIO, condoned the violence of the SIU, the SIU leadership was able to use this violence as a bargaining counter to protect their interest in negotiations with the Canadian authorities."

The trusteeship changed nothing of a fundamental nature in the operations of the SIU. Banks was arrested and jumped bail after conviction of conspiracy in the beating of an officer of another union. When Canadian authorities conveniently failed to locate him, a Toronto *Star* reporter experienced no difficulty in finding Banks living on a luxury yacht in New York harbour. A New York court ruled in favour of Banks' extradition to face charges in Canada, but highly placed Government officials in Washington intervened to void the court ruling. The rest of the SIU officers in Canada did not change and the SIU was back in favour, and back in the CCL by 1966, and coming under more Government investigation in 1975.

The Limits of "Autonomy"

There were numerous other less spectacular incidents related to the "house cleaning" of Communist influence in the American unions in Canada. There was the case of the Lumber and Sawmill Workers' Union, consisting of 10,000 workers in northern Ontario who had been handed over to the International Carpenters as second class citizens by the WUL in 1935. Mostly Finns with radical traditions, these workers were a source of constant opposition in the carpenters union. In 1951 the international officers took direct control of the union and went to court to secure an order for seizure of the funds, while the members denounced "inquisition by aliens."

Dissident officers of the large Consumers Gas Local of the International Chemical Workers' Union in Toronto were put on trial by the international President who journeyed to Toronto specially for purposes of the trial. A number of the local's elected officers were expelled from the union and dismissed from employment under closed shop provisions of the union contract.

On April 1, 1952, following eight months of frustrating and fruitless negotiations and arbitration, 5,500 workers, members of the Canadian District of the United Textile Workers of America, struck the mills of the Dominion Textile company at Montreal and Valleyfield. The company flatly refused to deal with Canadian leaders of the union, an attitude which received support from Claude Jodoin, then President of the Montreal Labour Council.

On May 25, after weeks of strike action, Lloyd Klenert, Secretary-Treasurer of the union, arrived on the scene from Washington, D.C. and put in an appearance at a Montreal-Valleyfield joint strike Committee meeting in progress in Montreal. He was evasive in his responses to queries concerning the financial assistance and rumoured changes in local union leadership to be imposed by the international office.

On the morning of May 26, the union office was forcibly entered and the records seized. Later in the same day came a Washington announcement that the entire Canadian staff of twelve was dismissed and replaced by a "safe, clean" leadership appointed by the international officers. Within a couple of days the collusive aspect contained in the headquarters intervention was emphasized when the company President expressed pleasure over the fact that the union now had leaders who "understand that the well-being of the workers depends largely on the well-being of the industry." After a further seven weeks on the picket line the workers' resistance was broken and the strike called off. Many of the workers lost their jobs.[19]

At the 1957 Convention of the AFL-CIO it was revealed that Klenert and other international associates, starting in April 1952 and continuing through the period when they were bringing "safe, clean" leadership to Canada, were engaged in a conspiracy to embezzle union funds to the tune of hundreds of thousands of dollars. Klenert is reported to have pocketed a quarter of a million dollars and then retired on a $100.00 a week pension.[20]

The United Auto Workers leaders boast of the wide autonomy granted to and practiced by the Canadian District. In view of this claim the experience of 4,000 members of one Canadian local of the UAW can surely be taken as a lesson in the limitations of autonomy when it comes into conflict with the interests of American business and American unionists.

In 1971 the workers in Douglas Aircraft at Malton, near Toronto, rejected a company offer and went out on strike. Meanwhile Douglas employees in the U.S. had accepted the offer, which was within the economic guidelines set by President Nixon. The workers in the Canadian plant saw no good reason why they should let an American President set their wage standards.

The plant at Malton produced wing assemblies for the U.S. plants, and it was clear that a long strike would halt production, putting out of work thousands of production workers who had already accepted what the workers in Canada had rejected. The company sought to put pressure on the strikers with announcements of contemplated plans for a removal to the United States, but to no avail. Then the international officers entered the picture.

On November 15 the international Executive Board met at Detroit and ordered the local strike Committee to submit the company offer to a secret ballot of the members. The telegram to the local conveying this instruction, which was signed by President Leonard Woodcock, Vice-President Kenneth Bannon, and Canadian Director Dennis McDermott, also instructed the local officers to ensure the representatives of the international headquarters "their constitutional right to share in the reporting to the membership."[21]

A stormy Toronto meeting greeted McDermott and Bannon with a chorus of jeers as they urged acceptance of the company offer. The proposition was rejected by a vote of two to one, and plant Chairman Archie Wilson, who opposed the settlement offer, placed the role of the international officers in proper perspective when he wired Detroit headquarters: ". . . the membership rejected the company and international union offer." In an interview with a reporter for the *Globe and Mail* on November 20, Wilson said, "Unionism has lost all concept of its purpose. It's like big business. You have to bargain with the company as well as with the union."

Another strike meeting was held on December 10, and again a battery of high priced union help was on hand to argue in favour of the company offer, which was again rejected by a large majority. Within a few hours of adjournment of the meeting, the strike leaders were in receipt of a wire ordering them to appear before the international Executive Board on the following day. At the Detroit meeting the Canadian strike leaders were informed that strike pay was forthwith terminated and they were to get their members back to work.

Without funds of any sort, and with about one-third of the members already favouring a return to work, the position of the Toronto local was rendered untenable. Reluctantly, the strike leaders advised a return to work on the Monday morning following.

In defense of their stand the international officers claimed to have been defending democracy and the interests of the workers because, they contended, Wilson and a minority of radicals were obstructing the will of the majority. This was contradicted in three successive plant elections that saw the defeat of the "back to work" element, and the re-election of Wilson and his alleged "radical" colleagues. But in the two years following the defeat of the strike, five members of the union Bargaining Committee had been fired and dozens of activists suspended.

In October 1973 the company suspended three workers for reporting late to work. The following day several hundred workers protested by reporting sick. In mid-afternoon, company officers used the PA system to announce the firing of the entire five-man Bargaining Committee, and to threaten that the company would move to the United States if they did not receive cooperation from the employees.

International headquarters had little to offer in the way of support for the fired workers. Where it had taken only a couple of hours to assemble the Executive Board for the purpose of issuing an order to call off the strike in 1971, it now took three telegrams and a period of three weeks to get the information that there were no plans for a meeting of the Executive therefore the appeal from Local 1967 could not be heard. After eighteen months of waiting an arbitrator ruled in favour of the company in four of the five cases of fired members of the Bargaining Committee.

Many scores of examples of such interventions, both major and minor could be cited. But whether major or minor in character, each one represents a bureaucratic invasion of the rights of Canadian workers by a union headquarters based in another country and placed beyond the reach of the workers directly involved.

While it is true that not all, indeed not nearly all, of the American-based unions in Canada have experienced intervention so flagrant and so devastating in its consequences as the examples cited above, nevertheless all American international union leaders have the "right" and the capacity to intervene in the affairs of Canadian locals when they consider the situation calls for it. When any conflict of interests develops, the American bias dominates, so that the real limits of Canadian autonomy are determined by American union and business interests. In the final analysis these American interests determine the direction of Congress policies and actions.

It has long been established that Congress Conventions exercise no real control over the union movement in Canada. Whatever the Congress may decide, what happens in practice rests with the separate unions, and in 70 per cent of the cases that means with the American unionists. Policy decisions arrived at by the internationals will strongly influence Congress deliberations, but seldom indeed is the contrary the case. While distinctively Canadian unions such as CUPE and CBRT are undoubtedly growing, the internationals are still the main power in Congress Conventions. Occasionally a Convention debate arises that can be most enlightening in this respect. At the second Convention following the merger, the President's report commented on Canadian autonomy as follows:

> We are not ashamed of our close and friendly association with the workers of the United States. We regard it in many ways as a model of international relationships between the peoples of two countries. We are also aware and highly appreciative of the tremendous assistance which organized Labour in the United States has given to organized Labour in Canada.
>
> At the same time, we are proud that the Canadian Labour Congress is an autonomous Labour centre. I cannot do more to prove this assertion than to quote the distinguished President of the American Federation of Labour and Congress of Industrial Organizations, Brother George Meany, who spoke at our First Constitutional Convention in Toronto, as follows: "So far as the AFL-CIO is concerned, we wish this trade union centre every success. Let there be no misunderstanding as to the relationship between the AFL-CIO and the newly-formed Canadian Labour Congress. This organization that you are founding is a free, independent trade union centre for Canada, just as the AFL-CIO is a free, independent trade union centre for the United States."
>
> May I say that, in the two years that have passed since Brother Meany spoke these words, there has not been the slightest effort in any way by the AFL-CIO to influence the Canadian Labour Congress. This is in no way surprising; it is no less than we expected.[22]

In view of the known and ascertainable circumstances, it is difficult to comprehend how any one in his right mind—if he was in his right mind—could deliver that kind of an address to a Congress Convention. The SIU debacle was building up to a climax that would soon take the joy out of Jodoin's high regard for the Canadian-American relationship. But it would not be necessary to wait the year or two for that disastrous experience to impress upon him the true nature of the relationship. His romantic nonsense was to be challenged within a day or two—at the very Convention where he spoke. There were resolutions before the delegates recommending the suspension of two unions guilty of raiding the jurisdictions of other affiliates. Both of these decisions were being subjected to challenges, mostly on the question of Congress authority to carry them out—in other words, the autonomy of the Congress was being challenged. In reply to such a challenge from plumbers union representative John Bruce of Toronto, Executive Vice-President Cushing, who was in the chair, stated, "This Congress is a completely autonomous body." To which remark Bruce replied:

> I deny that.
> I raised the point at the founding convention, and you will remember then that, while President Meany had said we were an autonomous body, we were going into that convention with the same conditions that prevailed in the Trades and Labour Congress which had jurisdiction only over legislative and some small matters, so that we have no trade jurisdiction, whatever . . .
> . . . you have no right to disaffiliate an organization without the consent of the parent organization.

Amongst the many resolutions submitted to this Convention were three that seemed to warrant instant and unanimous endorsation without the formality of debate. The three in question read as follows:

> 1. Be it resolved this Congress in co-operation with its affiliates, embark on a vigorous and extensive program of organizing; and
> Be it further resolved that, in instances of conflicting jurisdiction where agreement cannot be reached by affiliates, this Congress take the initiative in organizing in such fields, with a view to transferring such groups to the appropriate national or international union, at a later date.
> 2. Be it resolved the Canadian Labour Congress take the necessary steps to immediately organize unorganized workers of Canada.
> 3. Be it resolved that the Constitution of the Canadian Labour Congress be amended to give workers in Canada their democractic rights to belong to their chosen union, by majority vote of the workers concerned, without high-sounding denials meaning nothing to the lay members involved.

The Resolutions Committee recommended non-concurrence in all three propositions and the Convention majority voted accordingly. The fact is that it was beyond the existing authority of the Congress and its Executive officers to put any, or all, of these resolutions into effect. The organizational proposals contained in all three resolutions were the sole prerogative of the international unions, and outside of the limited jurisdiction of the Convention.

Autonomy and its close relation, jurisdiction, were questions that never failed to arise at every Canadian union Convention since 1897, always giving rise to heated debate. In 1964, at the fifth Convention after the merger, autonomy was again the subject of a number of resolutions, and the Chairman of the Resolutions Committee, replying to debate, put the problem in proper perspective and, at the same time, underlined the limited sovereignty of the Congress and the dominant power of the international unions in the settlement of all such contentious matters. Defending the Committee's recommendation of non-concurrence in all the resolutions on autonomy, the Chairman stated:

> . . . after much deliberation on these resolutions here, the Committee feels as a whole that the only way that this can be done is by changing the Constitution of the Affiliates of the different unions. It is not the right of the Congress to act upon this; it would have to be done by changing the Constitution of the International Unions. This has been our thinking on the matter.[23]

Put in its briefest and simplest form: within the context of the international union movement, the Canadians had just that amount of autonomy that the American unionists wanted to give them. This has to be so since Canadian unionists do not possess the authority to change the constitution of any international union. Pleas for understanding and greater autonomy are nothing more than appeals to the Americans to let their Canadian subjects out on a longer leash, so long as they don't annoy anybody.

The delegates to the 1974 Convention at Vancouver had the voting strength to set independent policies for a Canadian union movement, but they recoiled from battle. In the event they settled for a reiteration of the rather mild "guidelines" passed at the 1970 Convention, which were voluntary and unheeded by most internationals. The 1974 Convention did suggest taking a series of steps to make the guidelines compulsory, and this enraged the particularly conservative building trades unions. The *Globe and Mail* on November 4, 1974 quoted Ronald Taylor of the Sheet Metal Workers as saying in response to proposals for enforcement: "There is no way that bunch of garbage collectors is going to tell us what to do." A redneck statement, and for an international representative, fully in character.

The whole history of the Canadian union movement in its Canadian-American relations proves that the fight for "autonomy" leads nowhere. Only independence, the full and free right to set our own policies, will suffice.

12

SUMMARY AND CONCLUSIONS

While the record is by no means complete in every detail, sufficient documentary evidence has been set before the reader so as to clearly define the international role of the United States unions in the service of American imperialism. In concluding this examination of many years of intrigue and conspiracy, there remains only the task of making some final comments and presenting some of the facts regarding current relations between Canadian and American unions, particularly with respect to efforts to build an independent Canadian union movement.

It has been argued that trade unions are an integral part of capitalist society whose function is inherent in the regime of capitalist property. Viewed in this light trade unions are seen as being dialectically both in opposition to capitalism and a component part of it. Therefore it is correct to say that trade unions do not pose any fundamental challenge to the survival of a society based on class divisions—they merely express those divisions. In *Ordine Nueovo* the noted Italian theorist Gramsci wrote:

> Trade unionism is evidently nothing but a reflection of capitalist society, not a potential means of transcending capitalist society. It organizes workers, not as producers, but as wage earners, that is as creations of the capitalist system of private property, as sellers of their labour power. Unionism unites workers according to the tools of their trade or the nature of their product, that is according to the contours imposed on them by the capitalist system.

The nature of the economic system is, ultimately, a political question. Strike action alone does not seriously threaten the survival of capitalism as a social system. Even militant action such as occupation of the factory, while it might be considered symbolic of the fact that the means of production rightly belong to the producers, does not constitute a

215

fundamental challenge to the social order. Failing to take hold of the levers of state power, militancy stops short of affording reality to the symbolic claims of ownership.

As capitalists arrived at the realization that unionists in general were not averse to a policy of cooperation with the social system, abroad as well as at home, when they were at last convinced the cooperating unions could serve in ways not possible of duplication by any other agency, there were concessions available that made the proposition of collusion appear attractive and economically worthwhile, especially when measured against the only alternative possible—a policy of unrelenting class struggle.

It seemed that the benefits accruing from collaboration with the employers could be fairly considerable when shared amongst a limited number of workers organized in the union movement. So from the very beginning of its history the AFL set out with the purpose of restricting trade unionism to the highly skilled workers. The drive for industrial unionism that began in the latter half of the thirties brought little improvement to the situation. The industrial organizations that emerged are dominated by the skilled workers who reap most of the benefits. In North America, as compared to other industrialized regions, a much smaller proportion of the work force is organized and the income differential is much wider, which makes for greater stratification and consequent divisions in the working class.

There could never be any serious thought of this type of movement challenging capitalism *as a social system*. When confrontation does take place—and it often does—it takes place between the union and the individual corporation, not with the system *as a whole*. Despite occasional struggles over relatively minor economic issues and legislative measures, the emphasis of business unionism in North America is on the institutionalization of class collaboration. This is especially so in the aftermath of World War II and in the beginning of a struggle for world hegemony between two superpowers. Viewing this new world relationship of forces and the special role of the union movement, United States historian Thomas R. Brooks said:

> Few historians would dispute the assertion of War Labour Board Chairman Davis that the maintenance compromise was "the greatest piece of industrial statesmenship that I know of." The foundation of collective bargaining as a permanent institution in the United States was firmly laid.
>
> Maintenance of membership, as a device, helped to dovetail the "New Unionism" into the new corporatism. What unions envisaged as "industrial democracy," sophisticated management came to view as a practical means for the handling of personnel problems within a company structure that had become too unwieldy for the old-fashioned

face-to-face relationship to work with equity or satisfaction. Collective bargaining, in this light, became a system of drawing up the rules for employment; and the unions became agencies for enforcing these rules. The usefulness of the unions in this new role was driven home by the wartime experience of management confronted with an influx of new and, in many instances, unruly workers.[1]

In the early years of the twentieth century IWW leader Vincent St. John warned of precisely such dangers arising from fraternization with employers. "The capitalists cannot exterminate a real labour organization by fighting it, " he said. "They are only dangerous when they fraternize with it."

At the highest levels of trade union bureaucracy, fraternization takes on the form of a virtual merging of union leader with corporation Director, in what approximates a form of private enterprise in the field of labour relations. The top-flight union Executive and negotiator becomes essentially a purveyor of labour, interested only in supplying industry's needs in this regard—for an agreed price and conditions. This is a type of unionism in which "job control" is crucial to the interests of both partners to the deal. Consideration of the position of the worker as an individual is of little or no concern, while cooperation with the employer is of paramount importance. This ultimate purpose of business unionism is best expressed by AFL-CIO President George Meany. Commenting on the organizing policy of the plumbers' union, Meany remarked: "We didn't want the people that were on the job, we merely wanted the work. So far as the people that were on the job were concerned, for our part they could drop dead."[2]

But much to Meany's dismay, industry requires workers to operate the machines, and the union leader must contend with the "human element" however distasteful the contact might be. The individual worker (unfortunately for men of the Meany stripe) cannot be switched on and off like the machine, although attempts to do so are often made. Workers are demonstrating an increasing tendency to rebel against the worst consequences of collaboration in ways such as the "wildcat strike" which is a form of struggle directed more against the practical consequences of business unionism than against the employer, even if the unionists are not fully conscious of the fact that they are rebelling against the policies of class collaboration posing as union representation.

But whether Meany realizes it or not, if this rebellious attitude was not present, the union agent would be rendered redundant, for he cannot eliminate rebellion entirely and forever without causing himself and his organization to become obsolete. The American sociologist C. Wright Mills characterized the modern union Executive as a "manager of discontent," who must address his efforts to sustaining a delicate balance between activism and passivism, which Mills regards as a "highly precarious exercise":

> During mass organization drives, the labour leader whips up the opinion and activity of the rank and file and focuses them against the business corporation as a pedestal of the system and against the state as the crown of the system. At such a time he is voicing loudly the discontent and the aspirations of the people next to the bottom, and he is seen and recognized as a rebel and an agitator. Yet, in fact, all the time that he is the leader of a live and ongoing union, the labour leader is in conflict with the powers of property; he is a rebel against the individual business unit and their unmolested exercise of the powers which property conveys. In his timidity and fear and eagerness to stay alive in a hostile environment he does not admit this, and he often believes that he is not a rebel in the senses named, but the fact remains that he is. He is serving the function of a modern rebel by virtue of what his organization must do to live; modern rebels need not be romantic figures. Yet even as the rebel leader rebels, he holds back rebellion. He organizes discontent and then he sits on it, exploiting it in order to maintain a continuous organization; the labour leader is a manager of discontent. He makes regular what would otherwise be disruptive, both within the industrial routine and within the union which he seeks to establish and maintain.[3]

A classic Canadian example of this "management of discontent" was staged in the so-called general strike against wage controls (October 14, 1976), a skillfully handled one-day protest demonstration, carefully controlled and manipulated by the union officials who were never in any danger of losing control despite the loud harangues and rhetoric of an assortment of "left-wing" groups. True, some employers reacted with bitterness and punitive measures against participants, but most accepted the limited protest as a necessary cathartic to prevent more extensive, more lasting and expensive infection at the rank and file level. With the workers returning to the job following the one-day "holiday," the exercise in "management" could be counted a resounding success.

In these often stormy seas of union-employer relations, the state plays a crucial role as regulator and stabilizer. While invariably acting to the advantage of the employer class, official state agencies will not shrink from disciplining unruly individual employers who, seeking to advance their own private interests, threaten to upset the delicate balance in the relationship. In the final analysis it is the intervention of the state that contributes most to the institutionalization of class collaboration in union-employer relations. In the particular Canadian situation this intervention, the enforcement of the regulations laid down by the state through federal and provincial Labour Boards, in the main serves to perpetuate United States domination of the union movement in Canada.

Regulations governing jurisdiction, maintenance of membership and closed shop provisions produce a situation wherein a worker is "locked into" a union chosen by a simple majority vote of the employees and installed by the Labour Board as official bargaining agent in the jurisdiction. Except under highly restrictive conditions which favour the established agent, neither the individual worker nor any substantial minority of a bargaining unit can choose to opt out or to join another union. In view of the fact that the international (American) unions are solidly entrenched in the industries that constitute the commanding heights of the economy, i.e., in the manufacturing and resources sectors, the end result is to inhibit and impede the fight for an independent Canadian union movement.

These inhibiting regulations are reinforced by independent action on the part of international union officers, who invoke available constitutional authority which provides for disciplinary action against members guilty of "dual unionism"—in other words the worker is prohibited from holding membership in any union other than the one holding jurisdiction in a given plant or industry. Punitive action against the offender may include anything from a heavy fine up to and including expulsion from the union, consequent loss of employment, and blacklisting wherever the union holds bargaining rights. Controlling the jobs through the support of state agencies (Labour Boards and courts in Canada generally confirm the union in such matters) and by virtue of their cooperation with the employers, the ever-present threat posed by the power in the hands of union officers who can impose economic hardship is sufficient to cause many workers to hesitate before deciding to change union loyalties, and renders the possibility for change to a Canadian union the more difficult.[4]

Trades Departments, which bring together international unions in a given industry, are singularly effective with efforts directed towards American union control, and the Building Trades Councils are possibly the most outstanding of the directly chartered Trades Departments' affiliates in this respect. For example, building trades unions will refuse to handle materials delivered on vehicles driven by other than members of the International Teamsters Union, who retain membership in the Council despite being outside the AFL-CIO and the CLC. Of course the Teamsters reciprocate by refusing to deliver goods to construction projects manned by non-members of international unions.

In British Columbia in 1978 this type of concerted action was successful in banning a so-called Christian trade union from a construction site where their employer had won a contract in an open bid. Called to make a ruling on the case, the B.C. Labour Board handed down a decision in favour of the international unions on the grounds that only members of international unions be employed on construction in the interests of harmony and stability in the industry.[5]

This means that the quasi-judicial decision made by the Board not only effectively shuts out the so-called Christian unionists, it also sets up an effective barrier to independent Canadian unions. In this instance a state agency, with support of the Provincial Government that created it, assists in maintaining U.S. domination over the Canadian union movement.[6]

A majority of B.C. representatives of construction unions have regularly advanced resolutions supporting a policy of autonomy for Canadian members of international unions. The usual fate awaiting all such resolutions has been stony silence and quick rejection. But nowhere was this dream of Canadian autonomy more rudely shattered than at a two-day meeting of representatives of building trades unions held at Toronto in mid-July. Nowhere have Canadian union representatives been treated with more contempt by officers of international unions.

The representatives' bitter complaints were occasioned by events at a two-day Convention, which had come about after years of agitation for Canadian autonomy. But a number of the delegates concluded that proceedings at the Convention indicated that the Americans were not prepared to relinquish any control to Canadian unionists. The bitterness expressed over events occurring at this first ever "Canadian" Convention of construction unions, arose from happenings such as:

1. The self-appointed Chairman of this "Canadian" Convention was American Robert Georgine, President of the AFL-CIO Building Trades Department.

2. Georgine appropriated the right to *appoint* the seventeen-member national Executive Board of the new "Canadian" building trades organization, and the members of all Convention Committees.

3. Only thirty of the 161 delegates present were elected—all of them from the ten provincial Building Trades Councils. The rest were appointed by the international officers of the participating unions.

4. The international Presidents of the fifteen construction unions involved attended. The Presidents sat at the same tables as their union delegates, an obvious and crude attempt to stifle dissent in view of the disciplinary measures which could be invoked.

5. B.C. delegates presented twenty-two of the thirty-three resolutions that came before the Convention, but not one of them appeared in its original form. One of the B.C. resolutions calling for Executive representation from all provincial Trades Councils on the Executive Board was rejected.

According to the Vancouver *Sun* for July 19, 1978, one delegate referred to the gathering as "goddamned unbelievable," and the elected President of the B.C. Council, commenting on the organization of the Convention, said, "When we came here, it was already a fait accompli. It was signed, sealed and delivered," and he went on to add that he knew the handwriting was on the wall when he discovered that members of the new Executive Board were already listed in delegate kits.

Apologists for American unionism, such as John Crispo of the University of Toronto,[7] contend that the presence of international unions in Canada does not represent any desire on the part of American unionists to rule, nor does it indicate any association with "a grand design to dominate the continent." According to Crispo the infiltration by American unions was merely "a natural by-product of the North American environment" and could not be considered as forming "a conspiratorial part of the American manifest destiny school."

But these unfounded assertions founder on the rock of documentary evidence. This is nowhere more obvious than in the report of the construction union Convention cited above. Indeed, if the American unionists have no more in mind than a brotherly interest and concern for our welfare, why do they engage in such exercises in bureaucracy as the Toronto Convention? Why not just go away and leave us to our own alleged meagre resources when repeatedly requested to do so? Why must they use their job control to maintain their authority over the strenuous objections of a large and increasing number of Canadian workers?

Perhaps part of the reason is to be found in the profits accruing from the operation in Canada. In *International Unionism*, Crispo essayed a protracted but unsuccessful attempt to prove that the American unions spend more in Canada than they take out of the country. Finn quotes the university don to the effect that the internationals "could not be accused of engaging in a kind of profiteering. At least, an economist would not take that view." Finn goes on to say that "[by] his reasoning, international unions would have a right to a fair return on their past investment, and that return would have to be relatively large to compensate for the risks involved."[8]

So the labour saints stand stripped of their halo. What we have is nothing more than a sordid but legitimate business operation, which should draw no complaints since the profits are only a "fair return" on investment. Don't the American "multinationals" do it? So why not the American international unions? Are the two not merged in a long-established, if unequal, partnership seeking hegemony over the whole world?

The latest returns under the Corporations and Labour Unions Returns Act (CALURA) demonstrates that the profit position of the international unions in Canada, which realized a neat $80,000,000 in the seven years from 1962 to 1968, far from diminshing has rather expanded in size. The CALURA Report covering the year 1976 shows that workers in Canada during that year paid $84,000,000 in dues and assessments to United

States-based unions while receiving back only $34,000,000 in salaries to Canadian officers, strike pay, and pension and welfare benefits. That represents a $50,000,000 return in a single year.

Emulating Crispo, union spokesmen engage in vague generalities to prove that the excess is not really there at all. They neglect to say that the CALURA Report is compiled from figures released by the unions themselves. In an editorial reply to claims that CALURA omitted certain pertinent facts regarding finances, the Vancouver *Sun* editor contended that "it is hard to imagine that such omissions could make up all the $50 million gap." In fact, the complaining unionists do not present one iota of hard evidence regarding any substantial amount left out of the CALURA calculations. But no doubt the 1978 report will show expenses for the Toronto Convention of the construction unions as a legitimate expenditure in the exclusive interests of Canadian workers. One of the embarrassments that cause so much vagueness on the part of the protesting officials is the undoubted fact that a part of the salaries of the arrogant and domineering bureaucrats who rode roughshod over the protests of the elected delegates representing building trades workers is counted as an expense in the interests of Canadian unionists.

Beyond the established fact of profit-taking lies the crucial question concerning the control of Canadian local funds, which rests securely in the hands of the international officers. It is this financial control that effectively strips the locals of any opportunity to organize resistance, makes possible the establishment of trusteeships over dissident organizations, and makes a mockery of the dream of autonomy. In the article previously cited, Ed Finn provides an excellent summary of the situation regarding ultimate control of finances:

> A handy yardstick by which Canadian autonomy may be measured is the accessibility to union funds in Canada. That portion of the union dues that is retained by, or remitted to, the locals is, of course, theirs to be used as they see fit. By far the largest share of the per capita dues, however, goes to the internationals' U.S. headquarters. Some boast that they invest or bank all their Canadian revenues in Canada, and indeed their assets in this country total nearly $100 million. But this money might as well be in Switzerland for all the control the Canadian branches have over it. With very few exceptions, these funds are administered and dispensed from the U.S. head offices. If the top Canadian officers require cash for any purpose other than their routine expenses, they must petition their international secretary-treasurers.

> The hand that holds the purse-strings also controls to a great extent the ability of the Canadian branches to implement new ideas or programs, or to give assistance to other unions in trouble. Chronic

financial malnutrition is a characteristic of most sections of American unions in Canada. The latest illustration was provided by the appeal of the postal unions for monetary support in their battle to breach the federal Government's 6 per cent wage guideline. Some of the national unions with direct access to their funds promptly made generous donations . . . In comparison, the internationals' response was a bare trickle. Their Canadian directors and vice-presidents could only relay the postal unions' appeal to their locals, and begin the laborious process of trying to wheedle a more substantial contribution from their U.S. head offices.

If genuine autonomy is to be won for Canadian international unionists, the provision of adequate funds for Canadian purposes— along with the other minimum standards of self-government—must be clearly specified in international union constitutions. It should be understood that the rights of Canadian locals derive solely from these constitutions, which are primarily American documents drafted to suit American needs . . .

An important point to remember in all this discussion about finances is that not only are Canadian unionists being deprived of access to their own funds, but a proportion of those sequestered funds are being used to advance American foreign policy, which is directly opposed to the interests of tens of millions of workers around the world—including the working people of Canada. We ourselves are paying the purchase price of the chains that bind us in slavery.

But Finn is very mistaken when he talks of *autonomy* as though it was akin to some form of true freedom. Autonomy means only setting out the specific limits beyond which our rights cannot trespass—limits that can be restricted at any time by those that have the power to grant autonomy. Freedom is not given or placed within the limits set for the convenience of a bureaucracy. Through autonomy we will have just as much liberty as the American international unionists want to give us. But in struggle for *independence*, we will ultimately attain a freedom which has true significance.

Canada alone among the industrialized nations of the western world has surrendered a major and strategic part of its labour movement into foreign bondage. Even if autonomy allowed us to speak out freely in the world Councils of Labour—which it does not and will not—we will be regarded by all others as only an American satellite, a puppet on an American string. If we are to regain our dignity as working people we must assert our independence. Nothing less will do.

It is absurd to think that we are incapable of surviving as an independent Canadian movement. Only the colonial-minded will swallow the lie that our continued existence depends upon support coming from the powerful American unions. There are all too many who believe that it was the American unions that organized Canadian workers. But if it is true that the American union leaders are contributing so much to the organization of workers abroad, why is it that they are able to accomplish so little at home? The United States unions in 1977 declined by well over half a million members while the labour force was showing a large increase. (More than half the loss was represented by women workers). Less than 20 per cent of the United States labour force is presently organized into unions, contrasted with more than 30 per cent in Canada, and even higher percentages for western Europe and the Scandinavian countries. The AFL-CIO obviously has lots of work to do at home without going abroad to find it.

The relatively tiny Service, Office and Retail Workers Union of Canada (SORWUC) exposed the allegedly mighty CLC and the internationals as nothing but a sawdust Caesar. For years the mighty internationals had made empty threats to organize bank workers, office employees, and other low-paying occupations mainly staffed with women employees. For years there was a repetition of defeats and admissions of dismal failure on the part of these experts at organization. Then in 1977 little SORWUC appeared on the scene, made up mainly of women and staffed by part time, voluntary organizers. The CLC just laughed at the mouse that proposed to tackle the lion, refused to give any assistance, and instructed affiliates to follow suit, contending that the jurisdiction, although long unoccupied, belonged to international union affiliates.

But the mouse, not to be deterred, went ahead with the challenge and proceeded with the effort to organize bank branches in western Canada. This supposedly insignificant union organized a number of bank branches in British Columbia and secured a historic breakthrough when it won a federal Labour Board decision that each bank branch could organize and negotiate as a separate unit. The only recognition that SORWUC got for its historic victory was a Johnny-come-lately CLC instruction to its affiliates to take advantage of the breakthrough by going ahead with the organization of bank branches, which would be later handed over to an international. Certainly SORWUC proved that the job can be done without the "big American unions" horning in.

There already exists enough of an organizational base for a Canadian union movement which, united in a single endeavour, could present a formidable challenge to American-based unionism in Canada. Unions like the Canadian Union of Public Employees (CUPE), the Canadian Brotherhood of Railway, Transport and General Workers (CBRT&GW), the two unions of postal workers, and others, are Canadian-based organizations with a combined membership numbering in the hundreds of thousands. By taking the lead in the formation of an independent Canadian centre—possibly together with the Confederation of National Trade

Unions (CNTU) in Quebec—they could bring new impetus to the drive against United States domination. But they choose to remain in the international-dominated CLC, thus denying support for the independent Canadian union movement, while strengthening the hold of the American unions.

The main burden in the fight for a Canadian-based independent union centre is now being carried by the Confederation of Canadian Unions (CCU), which counts among its members little more than 1 per cent of the organized workers in the country. Its main strength is in British Columbia, where militancy and anti-bureaucracy are traditional amongst workers.

The influence and impact of the CCU are much greater than its numerical strength. Ultimately, it may not be the only, or even the major, route to Canadian unionism. But the centre and its affiliates have filled a crucial role as catalyst, and they keep to the forefront the burning issues of freedom from Yankee domination and the struggle to limit and finally eliminate the dead weight of bureaucracy.

The success of the CCU as the advance guard in the battle for new directions in Canadian unionism is fully testified to by the intemperate language directed against the organization and its leaders by its enemies. We can look to Trail, British Columbia for an outstanding—one could even say outrageous—example of such intemperance. In the B.C. smelter city, a CCU affiliate undertook to contest the jurisdictional hold of the Steelworkers, and would have won a vote handily had not the Labour Board cited a technicality as reason for voiding a ballot, thus saving the steel union from considerable embarrassment. During the hot campaign, steel local President Bob Kiever said that the "so-called union leaders who preach nationalist slogans are in league with the worst racists in the Ku Klux Klan or the Nazi Party."[9]

But with people like Kiever, paid agents of Yankee unions in Canada, it is not really a matter of waving or not waving a flag. The real question is which flag you choose to wave. And the people with whom Kiever associates are found amongst the greatest flag wavers in the world.

Consciously or unconsciously (it is for him to decide), Kiever has become a partisan in the ranks of the heralds of manifest destiny. He advances the cause of U.S. domination in the name of working class solidarity, thus soiling the proud banner of true internationalism. Kiever and his like put down the flag of their own country, choosing rather to march with those who raise the standard of a foreign imperialist power.

The AFL-CIO, the body to which Kiever owes his allegiance, and an affiliate of which pays his wages, has loyally carried the battle standard of U.S. imperialist interests since 1898, and has toiled assiduously to advance United States hegemony throughout the world. And, for the benefit of those like Kiever, who seemingly lack the information, details of racist

226 CANADIAN WORKERS, AMERICAN UNIONS

attitudes amongst AFL officials would fill a fair-sized volume.

The Alcan smelter at Kitimat, B.C. was the scene of yet another battle between a CCU affiliate and the powerful steel union. The initial attempt to take over this jurisdiction (by the Pulp, Paper and Woodworkers of Canada—PPWC) was foiled by a Labour Board ruling, the reasons for which were kept "confidential." In the aftermath—no doubt in an attempt to head off future challenges—ten members of the steel local were charged with violating the international constitution by aiding and abetting a "dual union." By an overwhelming majority the local membership threw out the charges, but international President I.W. Abel, proceeding through two international representatives sent from Washington as his agents, revived the charges, found the accused guilty, and expelled them from the union. That surely demonstrated where lies the real balance of power and authority in this U.S.-based union, the Canadian officers of which proudly boast of their "autonomy."

The effort at intimidation was a total failure. A new local, the Canadian Association of Smelter and Allied Workers (CASAW), was set up to initiate a new challenge for the bargaining unit. This time the Canadian challenge scored a resounding victory.

During the two contests the steel union responded by sending in a platoon of high-priced organizers, and purchased hours of local television time to combat the "vote Canadian" campaign. But in spite of the massive expenditure of funds, the international went down to a humiliating defeat by a majority of four to one.

Just how much money steel has spent in British Columbia alone in an effort to combat Canadian union sentiment over the past fifteen years is an unknown quantity. But the amount must be considerable. In this regard it is significant to note that steel Director Monty Alston is amongst those who bitterly complain of the alleged inaccuracy of CALURA figures. It may be that Alston is not satisfied that the Government agency is taking fully into account the amount of money being spent to keep Canadian workers locked into American unions.

Almost as soon as the first American unions had acquired branches in Canada, the fight began for the restoration of sovereignty in the union movement. Throughout the more than a century of struggle that has been conducted inside and outside the American-based unions, the proponents of a return to independent Canadian unionism—which would have free and equal association with similar national centres around the world—have suffered defeat from time to time, but have returned to the fray. One can look back and take heart from the experiences of the past in organizations like the Canadian Labour Union, the Provincial Workmen's Association, the One Big Union, the All-Canadian Congress of Labour, and the Workers Unity League. And we can see that historic struggle being carried on in the present by the Confederation of Canadian Unions, whose affiliates are the rightful heirs of those who carried the standard in past times. In the light of history we have no reason to be pessimistic about the future. The forces battling for the independence of the Canadian union movement are daily growing in strength and experience. Time and circumstances are on their side.

However, there is nothing in the past history of the Americanization of Canadian labour that would support the belief that the U.S.-based unions will voluntarily vacate the arena of battle, or yield self-governing rights to their branches in Canada. Victory will be realized for Canadian unionism only through unrelenting struggle against domination and bureaucracy.

The American unions are firmly of the opinion that once a worker joins one of their organizations, whether voluntarily or involuntarily—and in prevailing circumstances it can be either for the individual—the member forever after remains their property. The Canadian member of an international union becomes bound by rules made in America, by Americans, and for the benefit of Americans. Disobedience to these rules, made and enforced by a foreign-based Executive, will result in sanctions that may, and often do, include denial of the right to make a living in one's own country. And the labour laws, decisions made by courts and quasi-judicial Labour Boards, and the collaboration between American corporations and American unions, tend to keep the advocates of independent Canadian unionism at a disadvantage, while perpetuating the authority of the American-based Executives over Canadian workers.

Considering the might of the forces ranged against an as yet numerically weak union army, the fight for a Canadian-based, independent union centre will for some time continue to be a difficult undertaking. But the forces are there, they need only to be mobilized.

When the Canadian labour movement organizes effective struggle against the handful of foreign-based corporate giants that exploit the nation's resources, when it begins to speak and act more decisively for the 80 per cent who produce the wealth of the country but enjoy little of its amenities, it is struggling and speaking out for Canada and her people. To speak out in this way means breaking out of the narrow confines of business unionism. It means rebelling against the dead weight of bureaucracy.

There is a better chance now for the success of Canadian unionism than at any time in the past—especially if we learn the lessons of history. However it must be said and reiterated that an independent union movement that fails to re-examine old and outworn policies and to experiment with new ideas will be of questionable value to the workers and to the country. But the very act of taking up the struggle is in itself a hopeful sign.

NOTES

NOTES: INTRODUCTION

1. C. Brian Williams, "Canadian-American Trade Union Relations," Ph.D. Thesis, Cornell, 1964, attempts to resolve this problem by calling them "binational unions." But this simply adds to the confusion concerning the real relationship because it leaves one with the impression of an equality of association not present in Canadian-American trade union relations. The true characterization of the relationship is that of U.S. unions with Canadian branches, more or less equivalent to the American branch plant in Canadian industry.

2. Ever since the Berlin (Ontario) Convention in 1902 the Congress has had an international union nominee as President. This tradition came close to being upset in 1974 when proposals for the replacement of retiring Congress President Donald MacDonald were being discussed.

   In the months leading up to the Convention two serious contenders for the presidency emerged. The significant difference between them did not lie in their view on policies—both were long-time members of the CLC establishment—but in their union origins. William Dodge, Congress Secretary-Treasurer, was a member of the CBRT&GW, a Canadian union, while Joe Morris, an Executive Vice-President of the CLC, was a member of an international union.

   Most union members expected that Dodge would receive Executive endorsation in his bid for office. However, it appeared that the "internationals" were more than a little disturbed over a growing demand for Canadian "autonomy," which was being aided by the assault from independent unions from the outside. It was thought to be a safer bet to continue with an international union representative as President, and at an Executive meeting shortly before the Convention, Morris' candidature was endorsed by a vote of ten to nine. Dodge and his supporters failed to carry the fight to the floor of the Convention, thus ensuring the election of Morris.

   Much of the reason for international union alarm was due to the "guidelines" laid down by Congress to regulate Canadian operations of international unions. These "guidelines" called for financial control and the election of Canadian Vice-Presidents by the members in Canada.

   So long as these instructions remained voluntary the international unions let them pass and then just ignored them. But leading up to the 1974 Convention there was a growing demand to make the "guidelines" compulsory, non-complying international unions to be subject to expulsion from the Congress. A delegate from the Sheet Metal Workers International Union, referring to CUPE's arguments for compulsion, asserted that "there is no way that a bunch of garbage collectors is going to tell us what to do" (Toronto *Globe and Mail*, November 4, 1974).

   In a pressure tactic, the building trades unions (on a decision taken by the international officers without consulting the Canadian locals) withheld Congress per capita payments amounting to a total of $350,000. In keeping with time-honoured practice in these matters, the Congress President went on the usual pilgrimage to the United States carrying the deed of surrender, which was magnanimously accepted, and per capita payments resumed.

3. Lewis L. Lorwin, *Labour and Internationalism*, New York, 1929.

4. The United Steelworkers of America once paid the sum of $50,000 to acquire the jurisdiction over mining and smelting held by the International Union of Mine, Mill, and Smelter Workers.

Jose Marti, *Inside the Monster*, ed. Philip S. Foner, New York, 1975. Warning the nations of Latin America against too close an association with the United States, Marti said: "Whoever says economic union says political union. The nation that buys, commands, the nation that sells, serves. Commerce must be balanced to assure freedom. The nation eager to die sells to a single nation, and the one eager to save itself sells to more than one. A country's excessive influence over the commerce of another becomes political influence."

NOTES: CHAPTER ONE

1. European influence in the development of the American labour movement was discussed at length in Volume I. Also useful on the subject of British influence: Clifton K. Yearley Jr., *Britons in American Labour: A History of the Influence of the United Kingdom Immigrants on American Labour, 1820-1914*, Johns Hopkins, 1957.
2. There is solid evidence that trade unions existed much earlier than this, but none that lasted beyond a few years. A union of stone cutters made its appearance at Montreal in the same year that the Toronto Typographical Society was founded.
3. Harold A. Logan, *The History of Trade Union Organization in Canada*, Chicago, 1928.
4. *Ibid.*
5. *Ibid.*
6. The British Amalgamateds and the U.S.-based Knights of Labour had much more substantial claims to the title "international" than the later AFL. The Amalgamateds had branches in many parts of the British Commonwealth as well as in the United States. The Knights eventually expanded into England, France, Belgium, New Zealand, as well as Canada. Like the Amalgamateds, the Knights were destroyed by the AFL on the same grounds of "not being international."
7. *Ibid.* Note the parochial element in the reply.
8. *Ibid.*
9. Margaret Mackintosh, *An Outline of Trade Union History in Great Britain, the United States and Canada, With Special Emphasis On the Present Division in the Canadian Labour Movement*, Department of Labour, Ottawa, 1947.
10. Logan, *op. cit.*
11. *Ontario Workman*, August 1873.
12. *International Molders' Journal*, August 31, 1873.
13. *Ibid.*, June 30, 1874.
14. *Finchers' Trades Review*, October 31, 1873.
15. *IMJ*, January 31, and April 30, 1871.

NOTES: CHAPTER TWO

1. Sidney and Beatrice Webb, *The History of Trade Unionism*, London, 1920.
2. *Ibid.*
3. Yearley, *op. cit.* Yearley is overtly favourable to the principles of new unionism. Nevertheless, part four, "The Great Example," pages 153 to 191, are very useful to an understanding of the extent to which British unions influenced the principles of organization adopted and put into practice by the founders of the AFL and the American craft unions, principles that ultimately matured in the form known as business unionism. Yearley also quotes *The Nation*, reporting on how the British Trades Union Congress allayed the misgivings of some anti-union elements:
"To such fears the Congress, which has just brought its sittings to a close, supplies the best antidote. Not that the alarmist will not find a program . . . distasteful to him, but that if he be fair-minded, he will recognize that it is put forward by men who so far from constituting a class apart, form an integral part of the community, share its feelings and common interests and have the same differences of opinion among themselves as any

other class. If he has heard much of the socialists of the continent or of the doctrines of the 'Internationale' and expects to find furious denunciations of religion, marriage, and private property he will be greatly surprised. The program contains nothing so exciting. The Congress is . . . a business meeting where the special trade interests of the workmen are treated in a practical commonsense manner . . . Throughout its proceedings there reigned a spirit . . . absolutely the reverse of anything that can be called revolutionary.'

4. John W. Dafoe, *Journal of the Royal Institute of International Affairs*, London, 1931.
5. John P. Frey, Secretary-Treasurer, AFL Metal Trades Department, *IMJ*, September 1932.
6. TTS, *Minutes,* January 11, 1866.
7. Harold A. Logan, *op. cit.*
8. Jonathan Grossman, *William Sylvis: Pioneer of American Labour*, New York, 1945.
9. *IMJ*, September 1864. Skedaddler was the name given Civil War period draft dodgers. And skedaddlers included capitalists as well as workers, the capitalists removing their plants to safer locations in Canada.
10. Margaret Mackintosh, *op. cit.*

NOTES: CHAPTER THREE

1. Achille Viallate, *Economic Imperialism and International Relations During the Last Fifty Years*, New York, 1923.
2. Brooks Adams, "The New Industrial Revolution," *Atlantic Monthly*, February 1901.
3. Julius W. Pratt, "The Large Policy of 1898," *Mississippi Valley Historical Review*, September 1932.
4. Walter Le Feber, *The New Empire*, Cornell, 1963.
5. Quoted in William A. Williams, *The Contours of American History*, Chicago, 1966.
6. *Ibid.*
7. Fred W. Field, *Capital Investments in Canada*, Toronto, 1911.
8. *Ibid.*
9. TLC, *Convention Proceedings*, 1907.
10. A. K. Weinberg, *Manifest Destiny: A Study of Nationalist Expansionism In American History*, Chicago, 1963.
11. *New York Times*, August 5, 1898.
12. *Ibid.*, September 18, 1904.
13. *The Globe*, Toronto, May 4, 1900.
14. *New York Times*, June 19, 1900.
15. Pratt, *op. cit.*
16. Weinberg, *op. cit.;* Richard Hofstadter, *Social Darwinism In American Thought*, New York, 1959.
17. Ronald Radosh, "American Manufacturers, Canadian Reciprocity, and the Origins of the Branch Factory System," *CAAS Bulletin*, Spring-Summer 1967; E.S. Moore, *American Influence in Canadian Mining*, Toronto, 1941.
18. *Labour Gazette*, October and November 1902.
19. C.E. Bennett, *Employers' Associations In the United States,* New York, 1922.
20. *Labour Gazette*, October 1902.
21. John C. Appel, *The Relationship of American Labour to United States Imperialism 1895-1905*, Ph.D. Thesis, Wisconsin, 1950.

NOTES: CHAPTER FOUR

1. TLC, *Convention Proceedings,* 1894.
2. *Ibid.*
3. E.F. McSweeny, "Immigration," *American Federationist,* December 1895.
4. TLC, *Convention Proceedings,* 1899.

5. *Ibid.*, 1896. Letter dated August 26, 1896.
6. *The Globe*, Toronto, April 13, 1897. In 1898 the Ontario Government adopted the Loughrin proposal in part by levying a tax on undressed timber when exported.

    In the matter of the Alien Labour Law: the Canadian bill—which was never put into operation—was designed to apply to those countries that had passed similar laws. This meant that the Canadian bill was by way of retaliation against the Americans, and the United States unionists were most vociferous in their denunciations, demanding a law similar to the one passed in the United States, with universal application. In this respect at least, Loughrin was yeilding to American demands.
7. Gompers' Letterbooks, May 1, 1897, quoted in R.H. Babcock, *The AFL in Canada, 1896-1908*, Duke University, 1970.
8. *American Federationist*, March 1897; Samuel Gompers, "The Immigration Laws," *Ibid.*, May 1897.
9. *Ibid.*, January 1898; AFL, *Convention Proceedings*, 1897.

NOTES: CHAPTER FIVE

1. AFL, *Convention Proceedings*, 1898.
2. *Ibid.*
3. J.H. Watson, letter in *Daily Colonist*, Victoria, B.C., February 2, 1902.
4. See Victor O. Chan, *The Canadian Knights of Labour*, McGill University, 1949.
5. AFL, *Convention Proceedings*, 1899.
6. *Ibid.*
7. *Ibid.*, 1900.
8. John W. Dafoe, *Laurier: A Study In Canadian Politics*. Toronto. 1963.

NOTES: CHAPTER SIX

1. AFL, *Convention Proceedings*, 1901.
2. *Report of the Royal Commission on Industrial Disputes in the Province of British Columbia*, Department of Labour, Ottawa, 1903.
3. *Ibid.*

NOTES: CHAPTER SEVEN

1. TLC, *Convention Proceedings*, 1902.
2. *Ibid.*
3. *Ibid.*
4. *Ibid.*
5. *The Globe*, Toronto, September 17, 1902.
6. TLC, *Convention Proceedings*, 1902.
7. *Ibid.*
8. *The Globe*, Toronto, September 24, 1902.
9. *American Federationist*, November 1902.
10. AFL, *Convention Proceedings*, 1903.
11. *Labour Gazette*, October 1903.

NOTES: CHAPTER EIGHT

1. Marshall, Southard, and Taylor, *Canadian-American Industry: A Study on International Investment*, Toronto, 1936.
2. TLC, *Convention Proceedings*, 1903.
3. Gompers to Draper, 1903.
4. *Report*, the Royal Commission on Industrial Disputes in the Province of British Columbia,

Department of Labour, Ottawa, 1903.

5. *Ibid.*

6. *Laurier Papers*, National Archives.

7. *Senate Debates*, April 1903. Debate on introduction and second reading is entered in the records of the Senate between April and July 1903. It is conceivable that a strict application of the provisions of the Lougheed measure would have impeded the operation of United States branch plants in Canada, since many of the prohibited acts were essential to their operation and could only be performed by American managers in Canada.

8. AFL, *Convention Proceedings*, 1903.

9. *Globe*, Toronto, May 1, 1903.

10. *Ibid.*

11. *Ibid.*

12. Senate Committee on Banking and Commerce.

13. *Letter to Flett*, September 12, 1903.

14. *Senate Debates*, April 1903.

15. *Eastern Labour News*, April 2, 1910.

16. For a history of the IWW in B.C. and some opinions on the reasons for the rise and decline of the organization in the province, see, Jack Scott, *Plunderbund and Proletariat*, New Star, Vancouver, 1975.

17. *Letters to Flett from Morrison*, April 12 and 19, 1906.

18. *Gompers Correspondence*, August 1906; AFL, *Convention Proceedings*, 1906.

19. TLC, *Convention Proceedings*, 1906; *Western Clarion*, October 6, 1906.

20. Loosemore, *British Columbia Labour Movement and Political Action*, UBC, 1954.

21. *Morrison to Flett*, March 28, 1907.

22. *Minutes*, Toronto District Labour Council, 1907-1908.

23. TLC, *Convention Proceedings*, 1907.

24. AFL, *Convention Proceedings*, 1906.

NOTES: CHAPTER NINE

1. *Labour Gazette*, October 1912.

2. *Report of Labour Organization in Canada*, 1913.

3. These delusions of grandeur extend into other fields of endeavour. In sports, for example, there are the "World Series" and the "World Softball Championship," involving only American teams in competition.

4. W.E. Greening, *It Was Never Easy*, Ottawa, 1961, is the source for the historical material used in this section.

5. *Ibid.*

6. TLC, *Convention Proceedings*, 1918.

7. Greening, *op. cit.*

8. *Ibid.*

9. TLC, *Convention Proceedings*, 1920.

10. *Ibid.*, 1921. It is worth noting that the CBRE, at the 1919 Convention of the union, repealed a racist clause in its constitution through an amendment admitting blacks to "full membership in the union." The BRSC maintained discriminatory practices, and a resolution submitted to the AFL Convention held at Montreal in 1920 calling on the American organization to strike "whites only" from its constitution and admit blacks to membership drew from the Resolutions Committee a recommendation of non-concurrence on the grounds that it constituted interference with the trade autonomy of an affiliate. A most considerate attitude which was never allowed to intrude on Canadian-American trade union relations.

11. *Borden Papers*, Letter to J.C. Watters, James Simpson, and R.A. Rigg, December 27, 1916.

12. *Report on Labour Organization in Canada*, 1916.

13. TLC, *Convention Proceedings*, 1917.
14. *Ibid.*
15. *Ibid.*
16. *Report on Labour Organization in Canada*, 1920.
17. *Western Labour News*, March 21, 1919.
18. *Labour Organization, op. cit.*
19. *Ibid.*
20. *Borden Papers.*
21. *Ibid.*
22. *Labour Gazette*, August 1920.
23. *Labour Organization, op. cit.*
24. *Labour Gazette*, January 1920.
25. OBU, *Proceedings.*
26. *Royal [Mather] Commission on Industrial Relations*, 1919.
27. David J. Bercuson, "The Winnipeg General Strike, Collective Bargaining and the One Big Union Issue," *Canadian Historical Review*, June 1970.
28. In the debate, Heenan commented on his documentary sources as follows: "I notice that the ex-Minister of Labour . . . lamented the fact that he had left the files behind him when he left the Department, but I want to assure him that the files are all right, and to refresh his memory I shall quote several of his own telegrams and communications taken from the files." Further on in his speech, Heenan hinted that there might be even more damaging material in the files than was coming out in his quotes. He told the House: "I have left out a lot of quotations from the files because I think it is in the interest of the country not to use them." Several years ago the author inquired after these files at both the Public Archives and the Department of Labour, but no one seemed to have any knowledge of them, so they must have been removed after Heenan's use of them. Perhaps for reasons of "public security."
29. *Mather Commission, op. cit,;* and *Labour Gazette*, Special Supplement, 1919.
30. *Labour Organization*, 1919.
31. *Western Labour News*, June 13, 1919.
32. *Labour Gazette*, July 1919.
33. *Hansard*, June 2, 1926.
34. *Ibid.*
35. *Borden Papers*, S.C. Mewburn, Minister of Militia and Defence, May 29, 1919.

NOTES: CHAPTER TEN

1. UMW, *Convention Proceedings*, 1912, 1914, 1916, and 1918.
2. *Labour Gazette*, June 1917: "Report of the Royal Commission in Disputes Between the Dominion Coal Co., Ltd. and Employees at Glace Bay and Springhill, and the Nova Scotia Steel and Coal Co., Ltd. and Employees at Sydney Mines."
3. UMW, *Convention Proceedings*, 1917.
4. *Labour Gazette*, July 1917.
5. *Canadian Labour Leader*, January 12 and March 2, 1918.
6. *UMW Journal*, February 11 and March 15, 1919.
7. *Labour Gazette*, February 1922; *Maritime Labour Herald*, October 21, 1921 and January 28, 1922.
8. *Labour Gazette*, February 1922; *Maritime Labour Herald*, January 7 and February 5, 1922.
9. *Sydney Post*, January 23 to 27, 1922; *Maritime Labour Herald*, January 28, 1922.
10. UMW, *Convention Proceedings*, 1924.
11. *Labour Gazette*, March 1922.
12. *Maritime Labour Herald*, March 11 and 25, 1922.

13. *Hansard,* House of Commons Debates, March 1922. The exchanges between McLachlan and Murdock are reported in the debate.
14. *Maritime Labour Herald*, January 21 and 28, 1922.
15. *Sydney Record*, July 22, 1922.
16. *Montreal Star*, August 16, 1922.
17. *UMW Journal*, April 1, 1922; Lewis to Murdock, August 16, 1922; *King Papers*.
18. *Ibid.*, McLachlan to Murdock, August 21, 1922.
19. *Labour Oranization in Canada*, 1923.
20. *Eastern Labour News*, June 26, 1909.
21. *Labour Organization in Canada, op. cit.*
22. *Ibid.*
23. *Ibid.*
24. *Ibid.*
25. *OBU Bulletin*, R.B. Russell Report, February 1922; *Labour Organization in Canada*, 1922.
26. *Ibid.*, 1926.
27. Jane Degras, *The Communist International, 1919-1943, Vol. 3*, London, 1971.
28. TLC, *Convention Proceedings, 1939*.
29. *Ibid.*
30. I.M. Abella, *Nationalism, Communism and Canadian Labour*, Toronto, 1973, especially chapters 9 and 10, for details on the national versus international conflict in the CIO.
31. Quoted: I.M. Abella, *American Unionism, Communism and the Canadian Labour Movement: Some Myths and Realities*, typescript, Glendon College, York University, Toronto.

NOTES: CHAPTER ELEVEN

1. Unless otherwise indicated, the book by Horowitz is the source for material in the section immediately following.
2. Also reported in the Vancouver *Sun*, April 17, 1945.
3. David Moulton, "Ford Windsor 1945," in *On Strike*, Irving Abella, ed., Toronto, 1974.
4. The letter is in TLC, *Convention Proceedings*, 1948.
5. The "Corporals Guard" in British Columbia was led by CCFer and Communist hater Tom Alsbury, who later became Mayor of Vancouver. The SIU office was located in a store front on Abbott St. under a large sign which read: "The anti-Communist Seamen's Union." The windows had been broken so many times that they were eventually permanently boarded up.
6. *Congress Journal*, July 1948, "Lawlessness On the Great Lakes."
7. *Ibid.*, September 1948.
8. Charles Lipton, *The Trade Union Movement in Canada*, Montreal, 1967.
9. *Congress Journal*, October 1949.
10. In 1947 the author was barred from attending the Mine, Mill Convention at San Francisco. Angus MacPhee and the late Orville Bratten (neither of them CP members) were prevented from attending a Pulp, Paperworkers Convention at Detroit.
11. *Congress Journal*, January 1951.
12. For details of SIU activities during this entire period, see: David Kwavnick, *Organized Labour and Pressure Politics*, Montreal, 1972; also, *Report of an Industrial Inquiry Commission Relating to the Disruption of Shipping on the Great Lakes, St. Lawrence River System, and Connecting Waters* (Norris Report), Ottawa, 1963.
13. Kwavnick, *op. cit.*
14. *Ibid.*
15. *Ibid.*
16. *Ibid.*
17. *Ibid.*

18. *Ibid.*
19. *Montreal Star*, issues of May 1952.
20. AFL-CIO, *Convention Proceedings*, 1957.
21. *Globe and Mail*, November 16, 1971.
22. Canadian Labour Congress, *Convention Proceedings*, 1958.
23. *Ibid*, 1964.

NOTES: CHAPTER TWELVE

1. Thomas R. Brooks, *Toil and Trouble: A History of American Labour*, New York, 1965.
2. Joseph C. Goulden, *Meany*, New York, 1972.
3. C. Wright Mills, *The New Men of Power*, New York, 1948.
4. In the late 1950s a Canadian shipyard union began a drive to expand its jurisdiction to include shipwrights who were under carpenters' union control. Just as the effort was on the verge of success an officer of the shipwright local was apprised of what was happening. Arriving at the shipyard one day at lunchtime he called the men together and issued the threat that anyone found in possession of a card in the rival union would be expelled, and would never again work in the carpenter jurisdiction anywhere in North America. Since the shipwrights depended on construction during slack periods in ship building the threat was most effective. It is job control such as this, and the power it bestows on international union bureaucrats, that makes the fight for Canadian unionism such a difficult undertaking. (From the author's personal experience while working in a Vancouver shipyard.)
5. Under the guidance of Paul Weiler, a former Chairman, the B.C. Labour Board achieved a high degree of sophistication, which has been the object of much praise from both employers and unions officials. It is quite significant that Weiler was the lone NDP appointee to survive the Social Credit purge. The ruling on the building trades case was directly related to a Board decision to enforce joint bargaining by all the unions involved, with the combined vote of all determining the outcome of negotiations. The order in favour of exclusive jurisdiction was seen as crucial to the achievement of the desired stability that would end several decades of chaos in the industry.

Another ruling handed down at the same time went against the union concerned. In that case emergency workers instructed to remain on the job during a strike by hospital workers received a union Executive order to hand over to the union almost all of their earnings. Refusal to comply was ruled a breach of the union constitution, bringing a threat of expulsion and loss of employment. Weiler intervened with a Board order that said the union officers were acting outside of their authority and the workers could not be fired.

These two rulings were hailed as a demonstration of the balance being maintained by Weiler and the Board—one for the union and one against. But both orders were really in favour of the discipline and stability required by the employers. In the building trades case, discipline and union cooperation could be maintained only if exclusive jurisdiction over employment was awarded to the internationals. In the case of the hospital strike, the excessive assessment demanded made it problematic if union members would be willing to fill emergency needs in future strikes when they knew that most of their earnings would be taken from them. In this instance employer interests, critical in a time of emergency, necessitated a ruling against the union officers. The vaunted "balance" shown by the Board orders was all to the advantage of the employers.
6. In an article appearing in the November 1970 issue of the *Labour Gazette* under the title, "The Struggle for Canadian Labour Autonomy," Ed Finn, a former officer of the CBRT&GW, writes as follows on the treatment of his union by the Building Trades Councils: "Building Trades Councils chartered by the AFL-CIO confine their membership to American unions and will not admit Canadian-based organizations. They go even further. In many cities in Canada they force contractors to employ only members of the international craft unions, and extend the boycott against national unionists to cover

sub-contractors and trucking firms delivering materials to the building sites. Trucks driven by members of the Canadian Brotherhood of Railway, Transport and General Workers have been continually harassed by the construction unions when they attempt deliveries to building sites. The craft unions insist that all such trucks must be operated by Teamster union members." Finn goes on to point out that the CLC and the provincial Federations—with whom the CBRT is affiliated while the Teamsters are not—ignored appeals for assistance in protecting the jobs of CBRT members. This is a fair indication of the extent of the "autonomy" enjoyed by the CLC.

7. John Crispo, *International Unionism: A Study in Canadian-American Relations*, Toronto, 1967.

8. Ed Finn, *op. cit.*

9. Quoted in Robert Laxer, *Canada's Unions*, Toronto, 1976.

INDEX
for Volume I
Yankee Unions, Go Home!

INDEX
for the present volume

240